WORKING
FOR
CHILDREN

Securing Provision for Children with Special Educational Needs

WORKING
FOR
CHILDREN

Securing Provision for Children with Special Educational Needs

Peter Bibby
and Ingrid Lunt

David Fulton Publishers
London

David Fulton Publishers Ltd
The Chiswick Centre, 414 Chiswick High Road, London W4 5TF
www.fultonpublishers.co.uk

First published in Great Britain in 1996 by David Fulton Publishers

Note: The rights of Peter Bibby and Ingrid Lunt to be identified as the autho
of this work have been asserted by them in accordance with the Copyright,
Designs and Patents Act 1988.

David Fulton Publishers is a division of Granada Learning Limited, part of
Granada plc.

Copyright © Peter Bibby and Ingrid Lunt

British Library Cataloguing in Publication Data
A catalogue record for this book is available from the British Library.

ISBN 1-85346-376-0

Typeset by The Harrington Consultancy
Printed and bound in Great Britain

Contents

Acknowledgements

A great many people have given their assistance to the writing of this book. Appreciation is extended to each of them including:

Anne Clarke	Dave Shipton	Trevor Aldridge
Pat Boyer	Stephen Bishop	Jessica Saraga
Ian Bolton	Ray McConville	Douglas Willing
Paul Robinson	Chris Dee	Winsom Nicholas
Andrew Waters	Mary Pooley	Simon Rhodes
Gary Redhead	John Wright	Rob Rundle

In addition, most local education authorities supplied copies of their budget statements without charge and many took time to explain details of the policies where the author was in doubt.

Peter Bibby
62 Oakhurst Grove
London SE22 9AQ

CHAPTER 1

Special Needs and Provision

Introduction

The last 15 years have seen major changes in the way in which children with special educational needs are considered and taught. This chapter explains the current approach by reference to the developments in the recent past.

Before 1978

The 1944 Education Act established 12 categories of handicap (or 'defects of body or mind'). Educational provision was made, usually in segregated special schools, according to the children's category of handicap, as shown in Table 1.1. Before 1971, one group, the 'severely subnormal', were deemed to be 'ineducable', and therefore the responsibility of the health rather than the education authorities. In 1971 responsibility for their education was transferred from the health authority to the education authority, with significant changes in the way that provision for these pupils was made.

Following arrangements set up in 1975, children deemed to be in need of special education were formally assessed by a medical officer, an educational psychologist and the school and were 'ascertained' as having a certain kind of handicap. After assessment they were almost always placed in the appropriate special school.

The categories of handicap served as labels, and the segregated and very separate provision in special schools meant that these pupils usually had no contact with their mainstream peers. The curriculum in special schools was often so different from that of mainstream schools that pupils rarely returned to mainstream. Prior to the Warnock Report of 1978, the number of pupils ascertained as requiring special education

Blind
Partially sighted
Deaf
Partially hearing
Physically handicapped
Delicate
Maladjusted
Educationally subnormal: medium
Educationally subnormal: severe
Epileptic
Speech defect
Autistic

Table 1.1 1944 Education Act, categories of handicap

was less than 2 per cent of the school population. This corresponds with figures from other Western countries, which suggests that most countries find it difficult to meet the needs of about 1.75 per cent of the school population in mainstream schools.

Observations

Four points may be noted here.

1   Special Schools

Special provision almost always meant segregated special school. Thus, children ascertained as handicapped were placed in a special school according to the category of handicap. For example, 'maladjusted' pupils were placed in schools for maladjusted pupils.

2   Borderline Categories

A significant majority of pupils in special schools fell into the categories of 'maladjusted' and 'moderate or medium educationally subnormal (ESN(M))', as compared with the other categories; see Table 1.2. These groups, the so-called 'borderline' categories, are difficult to identify and

Category of handicap	Number of pupils	%
Blind	1,221	0.7
Partially sighted	2,456	1.4
Deaf	4,267	2.4
Partially hearing	6,006	3.4
Physically handicapped	16,138	9.1
Delicate	6,272	3.5
Maladjusted	20,995	11.6
Educationally subnormal: medium	81,011	45.7
Educationally subnormal: severe	34,137	19.3
Epileptic	1,332	0.8
Speech defect	2,308	1.3
Autistic	947	0.5
Total	177,117	100

(Source DfE)

Table 1.2 Pupils ascertained as handicapped and in special schools or classes or awaiting placement in 1977

define with any objectivity, and consist of pupils whose special needs are very often the result of a range of factors including socio-economic background. Furthermore, the size of these groups increases with pupils' age, indicating a multiplicity of interacting contributory factors; see Figure 1.1.

3   The 2 per cent in Special Schools

There was nothing absolute about the figure of 2 per cent. This represented the availability of special school places in London at the time when the first educational psychologist, Cyril Burt, devised this system. The level of disability which merited placement in special school was agreed to be a level or score of more than 2 standard deviations below the mean of a standardized test, or an IQ score of below 70, according to commonly used IQ tests. This again had no greater significance than that of producing the appropriate number of pupils for the places in special school at that time.

4

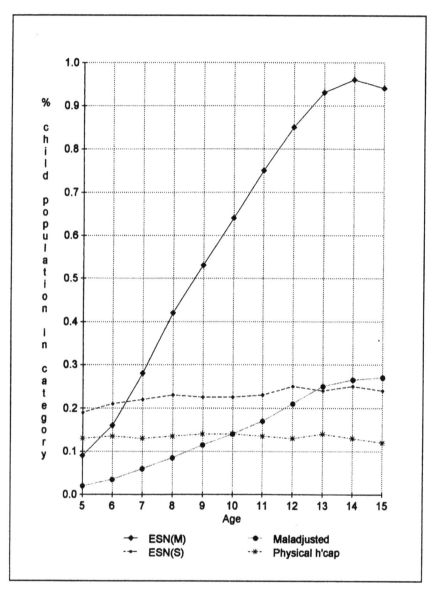

Figure 1.1 Percentage of school population at special school in 1977

4　Costs of Special School

Placement in a special school costs on average around four times as much as placement in an ordinary school and, for some pupils and some schools, considerably more. The national average school budget for each pupil in mainstream primary school is £1,500 and £2,100 for each secondary pupil compared with £7,800 for each pupil in a special school. This is easily understandable, since special schools have much more favourable pupil:teacher ratios, in addition to the use of other professionals and often specialist facilities and equipment. Thus, the decision to place a child in a special school entails the allocation of substantially increased resources to that child.

The Warnock Report of 1978

The Inquiry into Special Educational Needs, set up by the government in 1973 and chaired by Mary Warnock, reported in 1978. The Report (DES, 1978) came at a time when most Western countries were considering greater integration of pupils with handicaps into mainstream schools, and at a time of general concern for equal opportunities and human rights. The Warnock Report proposed several changes to the way in which special provision was made in the United Kingdom.

The Warnock Report suggested that it was not helpful to refer to pupils as 'handicapped', and that it was neither possible nor appropriate to draw a clear dividing line between pupils who were handicapped and those who were not. Since, the Committee asserted, handicap arises as a result of an interaction between factors within the child and factors within the child's environment, it recommended the abolition of categories of handicap and their replacement by the term 'learning difficulties' or 'special educational needs' (SEN). The Warnock Report asserted that children and young people's special educational needs occurred in a continuum of degree: thus the term 'the continuum of special needs'.

Clearly, for some pupils, assessment of disability is more straightforward than for others. Many children with special needs may be identified early on at pre-school age, and have a number of professionals already involved with them. However, there are also a large number of pupils whose difficulties emerge later and as a result of a number of difficult experiences and factors in their lives. For this reason, it was no longer considered appropriate or possible to distinguish between children who were 'handicapped' and those who were not.

The concept of SEN was introduced to include a wider range of children with difficulties than only those who were in special school, thus removing the distinction between the 'handicapped' (in special school) and those with 'educational difficulties' who were helped by 'remedial services' in mainstream schools. The continuum of special educational needs would thus range from pupils with the most profound and multiple learning difficulties at one end to those with temporary and minor learning difficulties at the other.

The Warnock Report proposed that a small minority of pupils whose needs were particularly severe and complex should be given a statement or record of SEN, thus retaining a distinction in that only those with severe, complex and long-term disabilities were to have such a statement. Another recommendation was that pupils with special educational needs should be educated in mainstream schools, with certain provisos: that such provision was in accordance with the parents' wishes, that it was compatible with the education of other children in the class, and that it permitted the efficient use of resources.

The Warnock Report estimated, by looking at various studies, that approximately 2 per cent of the school population would require statements of SEN, while up to a further 18 per cent might at some time in their school career experience learning difficulties. For most of this latter group, their difficulties would be minor, temporary and transitory, and would be likely to disappear following short-term attention in mainstream school.

Observations

Three points may be noted here.

1   The 2 per cent and 18 per cent

Although the 2 per cent and 18 per cent of pupils having special educational needs have been much quoted, there is nothing absolute about them, since they were merely estimates based on epidemiological studies of the time, and the incidence of SEN depends on many factors both within the child and within the child's environment, including the school. Some areas of the country may determine that there are more than 20 per cent of pupils experiencing learning difficulties, while others have significantly less than 20 per cent.

2   Numbers of Pupils Identified

The inclusion of a wider group of pupils as having special educational needs led, in a positive sense, to a blurring or removal of the distinction between the 'handicapped' and the 'non-handicapped'. However, on the negative side, this wider definition led to a larger number of pupils being identified and labelled. This leads to a paradox in which on the one hand there is a desire to remove categories and labels, while on the other there is a move or a need to use a new label in order to access additional resources.

3   Handicap and SEN

Although the Warnock Report abolished the previous categories of handicap, these became replaced by a new terminology such as: severe learning difficulties, emotional and behavioural difficulties, and physical and neurological impairment, which, though conferring less of a negative label, none the less serve to categorise pupils. Since the passing of the 1981 Education Act, the Department for Education (DfE) has been unable to collect statistics by category of disability, so figures concerning incidence of particular SEN are dated.

The Education Act 1981

The 1981 Education Act may be seen as the legislative embodiment of the key recommendations of the Warnock Report. As such, it constituted the integration legislation of the UK. The opening section of the 1981 Education Act defined three terms: 'special educational needs', 'learning difficulty' and 'special educational provision'. A child has 'special educational needs' if he (sic) has a learning difficulty which calls for special educational provision to be made for him. The definitions have been re-enacted without change in the Education Act 1993.

A child has a learning difficulty if –

(a) he has a significantly greater difficulty in learning than the majority of children of his age,

(b) he has a disability which either prevents or hinders him from making use of educational facilities of a kind generally provided in schools, within the area of the local authority concerned, for children of his age, or

(c) he is under the age of five years and is, or would be if special educational provision were not made for him, likely to fall within paragraph (a) or (b) when over that age

(Section 156 (2) of the Education Act 1993)

'Special educational provision' means –

(a) in relation to a child who has attained the age of two years, educational provision which is additional to, or otherwise different from, the educational provision made generally for children of his age in schools maintained by the local education authority..., and

(b) in relation to any child under that age, educational provision of any kind
(Section 156 (4) of the Education Act 1993)

A child is not to be taken as having a learning difficulty because the language (or form of language) used at home is different from that used in school.

Observations

Three points may be noted here.

1   Special Educational Need

The Act establishes that a special educational need only exists when special educational provision is needed or called for. This is a relative matter, and depends on the provision available in the school and classroom in which the child is found. Special educational provision is defined as provision which is different from or additional to ordinary provision made generally for children of that age in the schools in that local education authority (LEA).

2   SEN Depend on Provision in Ordinary Schools

Whether a child experiences special educational needs or not is to an extent dependent on the provision made in the particular school or LEA. Since schools differ in their abilities to provide for children with different needs and LEAs differ in the extent to which they fund schools to make provision, two children with similar educational needs, in neighbouring schools or in neighbouring LEAs, could need and receive different provision under the Act. This makes it very difficult both to define and to quantify special educational needs.

3   SEN are both Relative and Interactive

In addition to being relative, children's special educational needs are interactive; children's strengths and deficits interact with their learning environment and may become more or less handicapping. An assessment of special educational needs must take into account factors within the learning environment as well as factors within the child. Two children with identical scores on tests and identical degrees of impairment may be able to function in very different ways which will result in different learning difficulties and SEN.

The Implementation of the 1981 Education Act

The 1981 Education Act was implemented in 1983 at a time when many countries of the Western world were passing legislation to promote integration of pupils with special educational needs. It was the only Act concerned with the integration of pupils with special educational needs in Western countries to be implemented without additional government finance (Wedell, 1990). Although the 1981 Act facilitated the integration of pupils with special educational needs into mainstream school, it was permissive rather than prescriptive. There were no clear incentives or financial procedures for ensuring a similar quality of provision in mainstream schools to that found in many special schools.

Following the implementation of the 1981 Education Act, most LEAs made considerable additional provision for children with special educational needs, even though they received no additional funding from central government. Many LEAs redistributed funds from other sources in order to be able to allocate more funds to SEN. This extra provision was intended both to support a larger number of pupils with special educational needs and to support pupils being integrated into mainstream schools. Moves towards integration had to be financed either from local funds or from a shift of resources from special schools to mainstream schools. In practice, there was little shift of funds, and considerable resources remained locked up in special schools while additional resources were required to support pupils in mainstream schools. In order to maintain choice between provision in special school and in mainstream school, the two systems need to be maintained, and at considerable expense. This has been criticized by the Audit Commission/HMI in their survey of provision for SEN (Audit Commission/HMI, 1992).

Additional provision by the LEA typically included peripatetic support teachers for children with learning difficulties, advisory teachers, on-site and off-site units for pupils with difficulties, individual support teachers and assistants (Goacher et al., 1988). LEA educational psychology services (EPS) expanded considerably and educational psychologists increased their involvement both in the new statutory work of formal assessment under the 1981 Education Act and in further interventions and preventative work in schools. Every LEA in the country has an EPS which is funded centrally by the LEA. This service is available to all state schools, at least for statutory work and for assessments at Stage 4 of the Code of Practice. Many EPSs offer other services to schools, either free of charge or through a service level agreement, or at a separate cost to the schools.

Observations

This expansion in special educational provision and the extension of the term 'special educational needs' to include a wider group of pupils meant that many more pupils were helped, mainly in their mainstream schools by LEA support services. These were pupils without statements who were identified by class teachers as having special educational needs in the wider sense described by the Warnock Report. In this way, the Warnock Report had the beneficial effect that more children were being identified and therefore being helped, but the possible negative effect that more children were being labelled as having special educational needs.

More children were identified by class teachers as having SEN and therefore in need of extra help, which led to a perception that more children were to be the responsibility of a specialist teacher rather than the class teacher and to be financed by the LEA rather than the schools. This led to a pressure for more resources for SEN from the LEA.

Paul Vevers of the Audit Commission (Vevers, 1992) suggested that:

The substance of the 1981 Act can be distilled into five main principles:

1 The most needy pupils should have the safeguard of a full assessment of their needs.

2 The extra help which they require should be provided with continuity for as long as necessary.

3 Children with special needs should generally be educated in ordinary schools, with certain provisos, as stated in the 1981 Act.

4 Parents' views should be taken into account.

5 The pupils with the greatest needs should be subject to regular review.

However, these principles can be fully implemented only if the three underlying problems which the report identified are addressed. Those problems are a lack of clarity, accountability and incentive.

LEAs had interpreted the 1981 Act in very different ways, and there was no agreement as to an operational definition of special educational need, nor any agreement as to the level of need or difficulty in a child which should trigger either extra attention or a formal assessment. There is nothing absolute about the definition or label special educational needs. Thus, as Vevers stated:

Firstly, parents are unclear when they are entitled to extra help for their child.

Secondly, the respective roles of schools and LEAs have not been defined, leaving room for conflict over who is responsible in any given case.

Thirdly,   LEAs have an open-ended commitment to an ill-defined group at a time when their resources are limited.

The 1988 Education Reform Act

The 1988 Education Reform Act introduced considerable changes to the education system which affected special education provision. The National Curriculum and a national assessment framework and Local Management of Schools (LMS) changed the context for making special educational provision. In addition, the changes which enabled schools to expand and to take on as many pupils as possible under open enrolment increased parental choice and paved the way for certain schools to flourish at the expense or even demise of others. At the same time opting out and the creation of grant-maintained schools reduced the scope and power of LEAs to plan educational provision for the area.

The introduction of the National Curriculum for all pupils means that pupils with special educational needs, both in mainstream and special schools, are entitled to participate in the same curriculum, thus making transfer of both pupils and teachers between systems much easier. For the first time it is possible for pupils to be placed in special school for a short period with a view to a planned return to mainstream. However, the National Curriculum and its assessment arrangements have put pressure on schools to demonstrate their success in league tables comparing pupils' examination performance. Schools may be less willing and have less incentive to support pupils with special educational needs who may do less well in national assessments.

LMS, in particular, has had a profound effect on SEN provision. The requirement to delegate the majority of the education budget to schools has meant that LEAs have had to reduce their central provision. Since schools receive the majority of their budget on the basis of numbers of pupils, they are under pressure to attract as many pupils as possible. In most LEAs, schools receive enhanced funding for pupils with special educational needs but the amounts are frequently considered insufficient to make adequate provision. There are a number of different ways in which LEAs allocate money for SEN; see Chapter 4. These include: through the formula for the delegated budgets to schools and specific elements within it, through LEA central support services and through statements of SEN. The introduction of a market into the education system may make pupils with special educational needs more vulnerable, as schools compete for pupils and high scores in the league tables.

The 1992 Audit Commission/HMI Report

In 1992, the Audit Commission and Her Majesty's Inspectorate (HMI) collaborated to produce a report about SEN. The timing of the report coincided with a period when LEAs and schools were implementing the 1988 Act, including provisions for LMS and delegation of most of the education budget to schools. This had resulted in a reduction of LEA support services for SEN and a corresponding increase in demand both by teachers and by parents for statements. More pupils were being identified as calling for individual support but LEA budgets had reduced substantially.

The report criticised the working of the 1981 Education Act:

> There are serious deficiencies in the way in which children with special needs are identified and provided for. These deficiencies are caused by three key problems.

> 1 Lack of clarity about what constitutes special educational needs and about the respective responsibilities of the school and LEA.

> 2 Lack of clear accountability by schools and LEAs for the progress made by pupils, and accountability by schools to the LEA for the resources that they receive.

> 3 Lack of incentives for the LEA to implement the 1981 Act.

1 The Lack of Clarity

The 1981 Act's relative definition of SEN led to a difficulty in defining or identifying which pupils had special educational needs and, in particular, what level of SEN should lead to a statement. Statement rates and the criteria by which statements were allocated varied considerably across the country, leading to widespread dissatisfaction and confusion over which children needed or deserved a statement.

The introduction of LMS shifted the responsibility for most provision from the LEA to schools. Many schools found themselves unable to provide for the needs of a greater number of pupils and, perceiving that a statement brought additional resources from the LEA, requested statements for a larger number of pupils. The Audit Commission/HMI report demanded more consistency and objectivity over the level of need which would trigger a statement or the 'statement threshold'. This will be referred to again on pages 65–71.

2 The Lack of Accountability

The report pointed out the varying and often lengthy time taken to assess pupils and issue statements, and the large numbers of parents of children in special schools who wished to move them to mainstream or other schools. It further pointed out the lack of accountability of schools in their provision for pupils with special educational needs and the lack of clear targets and monitoring of children's progress. This is particularly important in view of the fact that many schools now receive substantial funds intended for special provision.

3 The Lack of Incentives

LEAs had few incentives either to issue statements promptly or to fund integration adequately. The expense of maintaining special school provision in order to permit parental choice gave LEAs little room for providing a similar level of provision in mainstream schools.

The Education Act 1993

Many of these criticisms were addressed by the Code of Practice on the Identification and Assessment of Special Educational Needs (DfE, 1994a) produced by the Secretary of State following the passage of the 1993 Education Act. The Code of Practice attempts to clarify responsibilities, to reach a clearer definition of SEN and to formulate a staged approach to assessment of SEN.

The fundamental principles of the Code of Practice are that:

- The needs of all pupils who may have special educational needs must be addressed, and that there is a continuum of needs and a continuum of provision.
- Children with special educational needs require the greatest possible access to a broad and balanced curriculum, including the National Curriculum.
- The needs of most children will be met in mainstream schools without a statutory assessment or a statement. All children with special educational needs, including those with a statement, should be educated in mainstream schools, where appropriate and in accordance with the wishes of the parents.
- SEN provision may be necessary for children before the age of 2.
- The knowledge, views and experience of parents are vital in securing effective assessment and provision.

Parents' rights

The government published the first version of the Parent's Charter in 1991, giving parents 'the right to know' and 'the right to choose'. This was followed in 1992 by the Education White Paper 'Choice and Diversity', which contained five themes: quality, diversity, increased parental choice, greater autonomy of schools and greater accountability. Finally the Education Act 1993 repealed the Education Act 1981 and replaced it with the current legislation which aims to:

- Extend parents' rights over the choice of school.
- Reduce the time taken by LEAs in making assessments and statements of special educational needs.
- Make parents' rights to appeal LEA decisions concerning statements more coherent and extend those rights.

The 1981 Education Act extended the rights of parents of children with special educational needs. Since that time there has been a growth in parent power, parent pressure groups and parent advocacy. The 1981 Act entitled parents to involvement in the statutory assessment process, and gave them rights to make their own views known to the LEA. However, despite these rights, there has been criticism that parental involvement has been more rhetoric than reality. Parents have frequently found it difficult to understand the somewhat bureaucratic procedures of the assessment process, and have found themselves of little influence in the choice between mainstream and special school. This has been in part because LEAs have maintained both kinds of provision. The costs of maintaining special schools are high and LEAs have sometimes been unwilling to switch resources to mainstream schools. There have been situations where the only way for a parent to be assured of additional resources has been to agree to a special school placement.

The 1993 Act considerably strengthens the rights of parents of children with statements by giving them the right to express a preference of school, and extending the rights of appeal. This coincides with a general growth in consumerism and citizens' rights.

The most significant change arising from the 1993 Education Act and relevant to SEN provision is the introduction of the Code of Practice on the Identification and Assessment of Special Educational Needs. The Code of Practice proposes a staged approach to assessment, using five stages, and gives guidance in relation to statutory assessment previously provided by DfE Circulars 1/83 and 22/89.

Conclusion

Since the passage of the 1981 Education Act, there have been enormous changes and challenges in the provision for pupils with special educational needs. Prior to the 1981 Act, only a very small minority, approximately 2 per cent, of the school population were identified or labelled (as handicapped). The remaining 98 per cent of pupils were educated in mainstream schools, though frequently grouped by ability in either schools, streams, sets or bands.

The Warnock Report coincided with the almost universal introduction of comprehensive schooling in the 1970s and the widespread use of mixed ability teaching. The Warnock Report's wider concept of special educational needs led to a larger number of pupils being identified (around 20 per cent). This posed a series of potentially confusing questions: How many pupils should be identified as having special educational needs? To what purpose? Who should have responsibility for them? According to the 1981 Education Act, the definition of special educational needs implies those who require special educational provision. The question then becomes: What is SEN provision and who should provide it? SEN provision is defined as that which is additional to and different from the provision normally available in mainstream schools, but this does not give any indication of the nature and level of provision available or the nature and level of need to be met in mainstream schools.

Pupils' learning difficulties or special educational needs arise from an interaction between factors in the child and factors in the environment. The Warnock Report introduced the relative concept of SEN which was included in the 1981 Education Act, the 1993 Education Act and in the Code of Practice. Pupils' difficulties are dependent on factors within themselves, for example their degree of hearing impairment or physical disability, interacting with and in relation to their environment, including their home, their school, the teaching environment and so on. This interaction has been described as 'compensatory', since positive factors in the environment may to an extent compensate for weaknesses within the child, and vice versa.

Schools differ in their ability to provide for pupils with special educational needs. Therefore schools will differ in the number of pupils that they judge to have SEN. One of the benefits of the term 'special educational needs' was its move away from categories. One of its disadvantages was the lack of a clear definition of the concept. Therefore the judgement as to whether a child has special educational needs or not has to be relative, and to an extent subjective, depending as it does to a certain extent on the competence, judgements and expectations of the child's teachers. Whether the 'learning difficulty' is sufficiently severe to call for additional provision to be made is to an extent a question of judgement and of the capacity of the learning environment in which the child is found.

This point is then related to the question: Who has responsibility for pupils' special educational needs? If a pupil requires extra resources, who should pay for this? Prior to the 1981 Education Act, extra resources were usually allocated in the form of a place at a special school which cost considerably more than a place at an ordinary school. Following the 1981 Education Act, many LEAs made considerable additional provision for pupils with special educational needs. Thus, following the 1981 Act, pupils' special educational needs were met at three levels:

1 Through a statement of special educational needs (intended for around 2 per cent), either in special or in mainstream school.
2 Through help from LEA support services, usually in mainstream school.
3 Through support by the school from general resources.

The 1988 Education Act shifted the responsibility for meeting the majority of pupils' special educational needs from the LEA to the school by delegating the majority of the budget to the school. This largely removed the middle level of support. Schools found themselves with more pupils with special educational needs requiring help and less support from the LEA. There followed an increase in the numbers of pupils being put forward for statutory assessment in order to gain additional LEA resources. Now, the 1993 Education Act and the Code of Practice seek to define more clearly the responsibilities of schools and LEAs in relation to pupils with special educational needs.

The question of which and how many pupils have special educational needs leads on to the questions: Where should the resources for SEN be targeted? How should they be used? In the case of the small minority of pupils with statements who are placed in special school, one could say that the resources follow the pupil: the individual pupil receives the additional resources through placement in the special school. For pupils with a statement in mainstream school, the resources are targeted towards the individual pupil, often in the form of individual support from an assistant or teacher or specific specialist equipment. For other pupils with special educational needs, resources for SEN which may be allocated to the school through the LMS formula are usually targeted at a group of pupils or used for an additional member of staff for SEN or for specialist equipment.

The question of where resources are most effectively and appropriately targeted is complex. It has been argued (Dessent, 1987) that LEA and school resourcing policies should focus on 'increasing what is normally available' within mainstream education and that 'the thrust of...policy should be towards general as opposed to individual resource strategies'. According to this argument, the majority of additional resources should be allocated to schools to enhance their ability to meet the needs of all their pupils, the corollary being the identification of a minimal number of pupils in need of individually targeted resources. However, this poses a conflict with the Code of Practice which may be seen to lay an emphasis on individual identification and, by implication, a pressure for allocation of resources to individuals.

Ever since the implementation of the 1981 Education Act, there have been problems in defining which children have special educational needs and which children need or deserve a statement and therefore special educational provision to be arranged by the LEA directly rather than by the school from its delegated budget. There is no absolute measure or answer to this. Children's learning difficulties depend on factors within themselves and factors in their environment. Thus, however tempting it might be to look for absolute definitions or measures based on normative tests, this search is irrelevant. Whether the child has a difficulty in learning depends on many factors, all of which will need to be taken into account in the assessment.

In general, LEAs have responsibility for meeting the needs of the tiny minority of pupils who require statements – around 2 per cent of the child population. Schools themselves are responsible for the remainder of pupils with SEN through their delegated budget which is allocated according to the needs of different schools judged by the LEA.

This chapter has aimed to set the context for a consideration of SEN provision by tracing developments over the past 15 years. In particular, it has raised questions over the difficulty of defining SEN and identifying who needs a statement; it has emphasised some of the benefits and disadvantages arising from the Warnock Report and the 1981 Education Act; and it has highlighted some of the issues which need to be taken into account when considering provision for pupils with special educational needs.

It is difficult to decide which children have special educational needs and will require special educational provision, because this depends on factors both within the child and within the child's environment. Most children's special educational needs will be met by the school from its delegated budget. Schools are now required to state how they spend this budget and have become more accountable both to their governors and to parents, A very small minority of pupils will need a statement and individually targeted support. For the remainder of pupils with special educational needs, resources will be allocated to the school and it is up to the school to decide how they are to be used. LEAs should attempt to enhance schools' capacities to meet the needs of all pupils, with the aim of reducing the numbers of pupils who experience difficulties in learning.

CHAPTER 2

Identifying Special Needs

Introduction

The 1981 Education Act set up a procedure for identifying a child with special educational needs, carrying out an assessment of the child's needs and, where necessary, providing a statement and making provision. The 1993 Education Act follows this procedure. Adopting the stages of assessment put forward in the Warnock Report (DES, 1978), the Code of Practice of the 1993 Education Act (DfE, 1994a) has introduced a staged approach to the identification and assessment of pupils with special educational needs. In addition, the Code of Practice recommends the practices and procedures to implement its principles which are summarized as follows:

- All children with SEN should be identified as early and as quickly as possible

- Provision for children with SEN should be made by the most appropriate authority, which will usually be the child's mainstream school

- Where needed, the LEA must make assessments and statements in accordance with the time limits, must write clear and thorough statements, and carry out annual reviews of provision

- The wishes of the child should be taken into account considered in the light of his or her maturity and understanding

- There must be close cooperation with all the agencies concerned and a multi-disciplinary approach must be used.

(Paragraph 1:3 Code of Practice, DfE, 1994a)

This chapter will consider some of the issues involved in identifying and assessing children who may have special educational needs. It will start with a consideration of the issue of early identification and the professionals involved, then move on to consider the techniques frequently used to identify needs and some of the specific difficulties experienced by children.

The Stages of the Code of Practice

The stages outlined by the Code of Practice are summarized as follows:

Stage 1 The class or subject teachers identify a child's special educational needs and, in consultation with the child's parent and the school's SEN coordinator, take initial action including entering the child's name on a register of SEN in the school.

Stage 2 The school's SEN coordinator takes lead responsibility for gathering information and for co-ordinating the child's special educational provision, working with the child's teachers.

Stage 3 Teachers and the SEN coordinator are supported by specialists from outside the school.

Stage 4 The LEA consider the need for a statutory assessment and, if appropriate, make a multi-disciplinary assessment.

Stage 5 The LEA consider the need for a statement of special educational needs and, if appropriate, make a statement and arrange, monitor and review provision.

(Paragraph 1:4 Code of Practice, DfE, 1994a)

Moving through the first three stages of the Code of Practice involves the successive cycles of attempts to understand and meet pupils' special educational needs within a decision-making strategy:

It is important that the procedures set out in the Code are put into practice in a way which supports teachers and others in these attempts. The procedures of Stages 4 and 5 are quite different, since they serve to meet the LEAs' duty to be accountable in allocating limited resources,   (Wedell 1995).

Early Identification

If a parent or a teacher is concerned about a child's progress in learning or development, early identification is important. The earlier that difficulties are picked up, the more that may be done to help. The five stages of assessment aim to create a systematic framework for early identification. If a parent is concerned about a child it is a good idea to discuss this concern with the teacher at the earliest opportunity. The teacher may share the parent's concern and will try out various forms of support, and evaluate these. If concern continues, this may lead the teacher to consult the school's SEN coordinator. On the other hand, if the teacher does not share the parent's concern, there is opportunity for teacher and parent to listen and learn from each other.

The Code of Practice stages serve to systematize and record the actions taken by the class or subject teachers, emphasizing their central role in the assessment process. The stages of assessment are intended both to emphasize the central role of teachers in assessment, monitoring and record-keeping, and to enable progressive support from other professionals in the LEA and outside where needed. It is most helpful for the child if parent and school are working together and are communicating over their concerns; in this way, the child may be provided with a framework in which the learning difficulties are identified and helped early on, before they have a chance to become serious. The stages of assessment are intended to provide a framework for a continuous cycle of teaching-assessment-review. This is good practice in relation to all children, whether or not they have special educational needs.

Other Professionals Working with Schools

Probably the main other professional working with schools in this field is the educational psychologist. Though some pupils will have involvement with a social worker, a speech therapist, a physiotherapist, or another professional, all pupils with special educational needs who move from Stage 3 to Stage 4 will have some contact with an educational psychologist. All state schools have access to the services of educational psychologists who will provide an assessment and consultation service for pupils with special educational needs at least for statutory assessment.

Many pupils with more severe and complex special educational needs will have had their needs identified at the preschool stage. These pupils will include those with profound and multiple learning difficulties, those with profound visual or hearing impairment or severe communication disorders, or those with considerable physical and neurological impairment. These include both pupils who would previously have been placed in a special school (see Chapter 1), but may now be placed in mainstream school with support provided through a statement of SEN and those other children who are judged to be in need of special provision at the preschool age.

The Education Act 1993 requires the Health Authority to notify the LEA of any child who probably has special educational needs.[1] For children of preschool age, medical professionals may be extensively involved. These will include the health visitor, possibly a multi-professional child development assessment team, the paediatrician and other medical specialists. If it is thought that the preschool child has special educational needs and requires special educational provision, an educational psychologist will be asked to see the child and to make an assessment. The Code of Practice reiterates the need for multi-professional collaboration both between the departments of Education, Health and Social Services and, more particularly, between the individual professionals from these different departments.

Where the child is under 2, the LEA must carry out some assessment at the parent's request if any educational provision is necessary.[2] The same applies for a child who is over the age of 2 but under the age at which provision is made generally. If no provision is made generally by that LEA, then any provision is SEN provision.[3] Therefore in LEAs which do not have universal provision for nursery education, parents are entitled to expect that there should be nursery provision for children with special educational needs.

Assessments

Different professionals will use different techniques for gathering information about pupils who may have special educational needs. The 1981 and the 1993 Education Acts emphasized the importance of assessment being seen as a continuous process and carried out over time. Assessment techniques will include all or some of the following: detailed observation of the child, interviewing the child and parents, consideration of examples of work, informal and formal testing using different procedures, including standardised tests. Assessment through the Code of Practice stages may involve increasingly formal assessment techniques, until, at Stages 4 and 5 the process itself becomes formal assessment or statutory assessment. At the stage of formal assessment the 1993 Education Act requires that a child is assessed by at least a teacher, a doctor and an educational psychologist.[4]

Throughout the stages of assessment, the teacher is likely to draw on information from personal observations and teaching, as well as the results of National Curriculum assessment and other teacher evaluation. Teachers are in a good position to evaluate children's progress and difficulties over time and to engage in the cycle of planning, teaching and evaluation as set out in the Code of Practice.

Medical professionals are also likely to have access to records of previous medical examinations and therefore to make an assessment over time, though the medical examination is likely to be carried out for the purpose of formal assessment on a single occasion. Medical factors may not be relevant to the child's particular special needs, but it is important for all children who may have special educational needs to have a medical examination in order to integrate relevant information, and to record factors which may be contributing to the child's learning difficulties.

Educational psychologists will use a range of techniques for collecting information and will usually be in a position to make their assessment over a period of time. Educational psychologists should be involved to give advice as early as possible in the Code of Practice stages of assessment.

Observation

Much useful information may be gained by an experienced professional observing the child either in the classroom or at home. This frequently provides the opportunity to see how a child's learning difficulties may be impeding development or learning, and to record progress over time. It also provides a chance to see the child in a familiar environment and interacting with other children and adults and with the learning or play situation. Educational psychologists are trained in observation methods and use their expertise to make helpful observations and hypotheses about the child which inform their assessment of the child and the learning context. Speech therapists and physiotherapists may also use a period of observation as part of their assessment, using their experience and their training to draw some preliminary conclusions.

Interviews of the Child and Parent

Most assessment will involve some form of interview, both with the child and with the parent. Children usually have very valuable information about themselves and are frequently insightful about their own difficulties. Professionals have training and skills in interviewing which help to put children and young people at their ease and to gain the most useful information. Many professionals will start by taking some form of case history in order to gain information about the duration and the extent of the difficulties.

Educational psychologists will make extensive use of interviews in order to explore with the child or young person and their parents their views and understanding of the situation, how they feel about it, and their hopes and expectations. They will be particularly interested to find out about the young person's own views. Most professionals wish to find out information both about the child and the context, and may therefore also talk with other relevant people. The interview gives parents and others the opportunity to discuss fully their concerns and views and to put their point of view and their feelings.

Tests

There is a considerable range of tests used by different professionals. Most, though by no means all, educational psychologists will use either informal or formal tests as part of their assessment. Other professionals such as speech therapists and physiotherapists may also use tests as part of their assessment. There are a number of specialist tests of speech and language function and motor function available. Some commonly used tests include the following.

1   Reading tests

New McMillan Reading Analysis, Neale Analysis of Reading Ability, and Wechsler Objective Reading Dimensions (WORD). In these tests the child is required to read aloud passages of text of graded difficulty. The test will usually give a reading age or level (indicating a comparison between the reading of the individual child and an 'average' child of that age), and other information such as the child's understanding or comprehension, and the way the child attempts to read words and sentences.

2   Intelligence or Ability Tests

The most commonly used tests in this country are the Wechsler Intelligence Scales (WISC) and the British Ability Scales (BAS). However, there are a considerable number of tests of this kind. In these tests, the child is required to carry out a number of different puzzle-type tasks and answer comprehension-type questions. The tests give a comparison between the scores of the individual child with those of 'average' children of that age. The 'average' is the average of the particular population on which the test was standardized. For most tests this population was white American or white British, which means that comparisons with this 'average' or 'norm' must be made with caution.

3 More Specialized Tests of Specific Functions

Examples include the Movement Assessment Battery for Children (Movement ABC) which assesses children's motor function and ability and the Reynell Developmental Language Scales which assess children's receptive and expressive language function. These tests usually compare an individual child's score with a level of functioning which is expected of 'normal' or 'average' children of that age.

The value of tests is that they enable the professional to make comparisons and judgements of a child's performance either in relation to previous performance or as compared with other children of the same age or stage. Thus it may be possible to say that a child has made a certain amount of progress since an earlier assessment, or that a certain child may be three years behind his or her 'average' peers in a certain activity or domain.

The problems with tests are that they provide only a small sample of the child's functioning, they may be highly specific in the information that they can provide, and the test situation may not enable the child to perform at the best or even average level. There has been evidence to show that many tests are biased against some ethnic groups, partly because they have been standardized using a particular population which is predominantly white and middle class.

The fact that all children now follow the National Curriculum and take part in the national assessments means that it will be easier to carry out assessment over time and in relation to local norms and the performance of the majority of children in a particular school and community. The most important sources of information, at least at the initial stages of assessment, will be the National Curriculum assessment and the teachers' assessments over time. If needed, these will be supplemented by more detailed investigations by other professionals which focus on the areas of difficulty, and the particular learning difficulty which is preventing the child making progress and which is causing a 'special educational need'. It is very important that parents are aware both of the limitations and of the possibilities of different kinds of assessment.

There are two main types of test used by professionals such as educational psychologists: so-called attainment tests and ability tests.

Attainment Tests

Most educational psychologists will use a test of educational attainment such as a reading test (which may give some indication of the child's reading level compared with other children of that age), and possibly a mathematics test, in addition to having available the results of the National Curriculum assessments and any other assessment made by the school.

Attainment tests give the child's level of performance in the curriculum area under consideration. This may be expressed as a comparison with an average pupil (a normative test), or as a statement of attainment of a particular criterion (a criterion-referenced test). A reading age or level, a mathematics age or level, or a spelling age or level aims to compare the individual with other children of the same age, and is based on an assumption that an average 8-year-old will have a reading age of 8 years. Thus, for example, a 10-year-old with a measured reading age of 8 years would be said to be two years behind the average. These tests are norm-referenced or normative. One problem is that these tests have also been standardized on a particular population, which may be very different from that of the individual child who is being tested. However, norm-referenced attainment tests do give some indication of how the child compares with other children in the particular domain.

Criterion-referenced tests measure a child's attainment against given criteria. These tests give information on what a child is able to do and not able to do; for example, the test may show that the child is able to read a particular set of words, but not other words.

Ability Tests

Many educational psychologists will also use a test of cognitive ability such as an intelligence test; this will give a comparison with other children of that age of a child's performance on the particular test. These tests frequently give IQ (intelligence quotient) measures, which aim to compare the scores of the individual with an average score. The use of intelligence tests, however, is considered controversial by many professionals. It has been demonstrated that children from white middle-class backgrounds score more highly on IQ tests than children from other backgrounds for reasons which are unlikely to reflect educational ability or 'potential'.

The concept of 'intelligence' is not necessarily useful either to educational or psychological assessment, although performance scores from the items in such tests may form a useful part of a wider assessment. Intelligence is a hypothetical construct which is measured indirectly through tasks on an intelligence test, and the final IQ score may not be very meaningful or useful when one is seeking to define and identify special educational needs. Although 'intelligence' and 'general ability' are sometimes used interchangeably, and intelligence tests are used to measure something referred to as 'general ability', neither construct is necessarily relevant to the identification of learning difficulties where a more functional analysis of the learning tasks and the child's performance on them may be more useful.

One of the main reasons that many educational psychologists question the usefulness of IQ tests is that they do not in themselves demonstrate the existence or absence of a learning difficulty and thus special educational needs. SEN implies a gap between what the child can do and what most children of the same age are able to do or what the child is expected to do in the particular situation. For example, if the individual child is unable to read at the level required to access the curriculum while the rest of the class is able to read at a certain level, this child has a learning difficulty which calls for SEN provision to improve reading. This learning difficulty exists independent of any measures of 'general ability'.

A further problem arises over the question of which 'norm' or whose expectations pertain in the definition of the gap between what the child is able to do and what is expected of children of that age. This question is philosophical and political rather than educational and relates to questions of teaching organization and goals of education and provision. It is furthermore a political decision whether to define as in greater need of resources a child who appears verbally able, but who has a reading difficulty, rather than one who appears less able verbally and who has the same reading difficulties. Both of these children share the same goals of education, and both need help with their difficulties in reading. The 1993 Education Act does not specify how great the learning difficulty (in this case the difficulty in reading) has to be in order for the child to be eligible for additional resources. However, in neither case will the use of an intelligence test help to establish the extent of the learning difficulty or to decide whether the child should be entitled to extra resources.

Identification and Assessment of Different Needs

The term SEN is defined through the term 'learning difficulties'. As mentioned above, special educational needs implies a significant gap between what the child can do and what most children of the same age are able to do. SEN arise as a result of different forms of difficulty. As stated earlier, the majority of severe and complex learning difficulties are identified at the preschool stage. These may include physical and neurological difficulties, sensory difficulties such as severe hearing or visual impairment, more severe and profound learning difficulties, or some severe language and communication difficulties. At the preschool age, there will probably be a number of different medical and other professionals involved in the assessment. Children identified at this age will be provided for either in a special or a mainstream nursery, often as part of a further assessment over time and in interaction with other children. Preschool children identified as having severe and complex difficulties and SEN are likely to be put forward for formal assessment and may be given a statement at this stage, entitling them to additional resources.

Some learning difficulties may emerge over time during a child's school career. If parents have a concern about their child either before the child enters school or on entering school, they may request a formal assessment. It is important that parents' concerns are considered promptly so that children's difficulties can be identified and appropriate provision made as early as possible. The largest number of learning difficulties are in the areas of emotional and behavioural difficulties and of moderate learning difficulties. These difficulties are the most awkward to define, to assess and to determine the extent to which they should be met by the school without additional resources from the LEA.

A growing number of learning difficulties are identified in the area of specific learning difficulties (frequently referred to as dyslexia). It is hard to determine the nature and extent of these difficulties, in part because they are not solely dependent on factors within the individual child; they depend to a large extent on the child's interaction with the learning environment and other environmental factors.

Needs Calling for a Statutory Assessment

If a child has a specific reading difficulty (or any other difficulty) which is preventing access to the curriculum and learning, this child has special educational needs. Depending on the extent both of the difficulty and of the provision made by the school, there may be a need for a statement.

Although the 1981 Act and the 1993 Act provided a definition of SEN, they did not provide criteria for the level of need which would trigger a formal assessment, a statement and thereby additional resources arranged for the individual by the LEA. This has led, particularly in the area of specific learning difficulties and dyslexia, to confusion or disagreement over who should provide the additional help.

The percentage of children identified as having special educational needs which call for a statement has varied enormously between LEAs over the past decade. LEAs have increasingly struggled to find some form of standard level in order to achieve consistency of identification. Recently, some LEAs have attempted to return to the use of the notion of 2 standard deviations below an average (in the area under concern) or the concept of a significant discrepancy between scores in different areas. Decisions based on these measures may be partially useful, but should be used with caution since they do not provide reliable measures of SEN or of learning difficulty.

The Code of Practice gives guidance on the criteria to be used when deciding to make a formal statutory assessment:

> Where the balance of the evidence presented to and assessed by the LEA suggests that the child's learning difficulties and/or disabilities:
> – are significant and/or complex
> – have not been met by relevant and purposeful measures by the school and external specialists, and
> – may call for special educational provision which cannot be reasonably provided within the resources normally available to mainstream schools in the area
> the LEA should consider very carefully the case for a statutory assessment of the child's special educational needs.
>
> (Paragraph 3:74 Code of Practice, DfE, 1994a)

The Code goes on to describe the following categories of learning difficulty and to suggest the evidence that the LEA should seek in respect of them, including evidence of detailed provision by the school.

1 Learning Difficulties

Children with learning difficulties will have a

> general level of academic attainment ...significantly below that of their peers. In most cases, they will have difficulty acquiring basic literacy and numeracy skills and many will have significant speech and language difficulties. Some may also have poor social skills and may show signs of emotional and behavioural difficulties
>
> (Paragraph 3:55 Code of Practice, DfE, 1994a.)

2 Specific Learning Difficulties (for example Dyslexia)

Children with specific learning difficulties (for example dyslexia) may

have significant difficulties in reading, writing, spelling or manipulating number, which are not typical of their general level of performance.

3 Emotional and Behavioural Difficulties (EBD)

Children with emotional and behavioural difficulties (EBD)

may fail to meet expectations in school and in some but by no means all cases may also disrupt the education of others.

4 Physical Difficulties

Children with physical difficulties may have sensory impairments, neurological problems and learning difficulties. These may be the result of an illness or injury or may arise from a congenital condition.

5 Sensory Impairments: Hearing and/or Visual

Hearing loss may be temporary or permanent and can compound other learning difficulties. Visual difficulties range from relatively minor and remedial conditions to total blindness. One of the issues in assessing the child's needs will be the child's ability to adapt socially and psychologically as well as to progress in an educational context.

6 Speech and Language Difficulties

Children with speech and language difficulties will have significant speech and language difficulties which impair their ability to participate in the classroom by the time they start school.

7 Medical Conditions

Children with medical conditions may have poor academic attainment as a result of their medical condition.

Having described the categories of difficulty, the Code of Practice recommends that the LEA seeks to establish that:

i. there is a significant discrepancy between the child's attainment, as measured by National Curriculum assessments and tests, and teachers' own recorded assessments of a child's classroom work, including any portfolio of the child's work, and the attainment of the majority of children of his or her age.

ii there is a significant discrepancy between the expectations of the child as assessed by the child's teachers, parents and external specialists who have closely observed the child, supported, as appropriate, by the results of standardised tests of cognitive ability, and the child's attainment as measured by National Curriculum assessments and tests

The wording is formulated slightly differently under some of the categories of difficulty, but discrepancies are referred to with respect to all the categories except learning difficulties. These statements in the Code of Practice imply three points. First, that the child's difficulty will be compared with the 'average' or majority of children of the same age; this implies some comparison with a 'norm' or a normative assessment. Second, the child will be measured against expectations of performance. Third, it is suggested that a significant discrepancy between different measures is looked for. It is sometimes difficult to establish a significant discrepancy. The question must be asked: How significant a discrepancy is required? The Code does not spell out the extent of a significant discrepancy. Different tests will produce different discrepancies and can be manipulated to do so. The use of discrepancy definitions is therefore controversial, and may not be helpful either in seeking to identify learning difficulties or in determining which pupils should receive additional resources in respect of their special educational needs. The answer is a political matter which concerns the resource policy of the particular LEA.

> Few educational psychologists would be so naive as to imagine that the adoption of a discrepancy definition moves decision making from the realm of politics to the realm of science

> (Frederickson and Reason, 1995).

Allocating Resources to Children with Special Needs

The problem of deciding how many children with special educational needs to identify individually and to which children to allocate additional resources, and how much, provides a considerable challenge for LEAs and schools. The financial aspects of these decisions are described in Chapter 4. However, it is important to discuss here the various alternatives.

Most children with special educational needs will have their needs met in their mainstream school and from the resources of that school. Individual LEAs determine through the LMS formula how much money is to be allocated for pupils with special educational needs. Some LEAs also indicate how judgements of different needs (or numbers of pupils with special educational needs) will be made. There is considerable variation between LEAs as to total funding for SEN and how that funding is allocated to different schools.

On the one hand, an LEA might decide that most of its primary schools had about the same number of pupils with special educational needs, and the SEN budget should therefore be shared out equally. On the other hand, it could identify considerable differences between numbers of pupils with special educational needs in its schools, and allocate very different sums for SEN to different schools. Following the 1988 Act and LMS, the LEA is no longer able to earmark resources or to require schools to use them for a particular purpose. It is up to the school to use the resources as it sees fit. Although resources will be allocated according to numbers of pupils (for example, numbers of pupils eligible for free school meals), schools are unlikely to use the resources for individual pupils, rather they will use the resources to enhance the general provision for pupils with SEN.

However, the Code of Practice, which recommends placing individual pupils on the different stages of the Code, and then allocating additional resources to these pupils, either as a group, or as individuals, could mislead schools into expecting individually allocated resources for a larger number of individual pupils. It is important that the Code of Practice is used as a system of identification and assessment of SEN, and that systems of resource allocation for SEN are devised which permit schools both some flexibility and economy in their use, and some systematic means of monitoring their effect. It is therefore suggested that the Code of Practice is a useful document for identification, assessment, planning and evaluation, and less useful as a guide for allocating resources for SEN. These are two separate functions.

A child's needs may be of such severity and complexity as to merit a statement and therefore a decision in most cases to allocate resources individually from the LEA. This decision is intended for the tiny minority of children who would previously have been placed in special school, i.e. about 2 per cent. The problem is how to identify these children. They are likely to fall, by definition, among a group of children whose performance is more that two standard deviations below the mean or average in the domain under consideration. However, this is only part of the solution. It is important to adopt a functional approach and to acknowledge the interaction between the attributes of the child and those of the environment, and the fact that children's learning and progress depends on a multiplicity of factors, both in the child and elsewhere. Many children with apparent low 'ability' may make good academic progress and vice versa, and measures of child performance need to be taken into account with other areas of achievement.

This means that the LEA could be expected to provide additional resources to an individual who has a significant visual or hearing impairment more than two standard deviations below the mean, or that attainment in other areas such as general performance is significantly below the mean. The LEA has finite resources and a decision to allocate resources to one child may mean a decision not to allocate resources to another child. It is up to the LEA to develop a policy of allocating resources for special provision, balancing the needs of a small number of individuals who need statements with the educational needs of pupils generally.

An LEA could decide to allocate the majority of its additional resources to schools which have a large number of pupils with special educational needs, defined either by measures of social need or by measures of educational attainment (see Chapter 4). This would arguably be an efficient way of allocating resources provided that there is a means of calling schools to account for their expenditure of this additional money. Fortunately this is the case, since schools are required to report on their SEN policy, provision and expenditure (see page 37). The same LEA would identify less than 2 per cent of pupils who would receive individually allocated resources through a statement to provide highly specialized equipment or support, either in a special school or in mainstream.

It is possible for LEAs and schools to find themselves in a vicious circle. If schools have less resources to support pupils with special educational needs, more pupils will be identified as having learning difficulties which the school is not able to support, and which are put forward for LEA support through statements. The LEA then issues more statements and consequently further reduces the resources allocated to schools.

This may be turned into a more virtuous circle by ensuring that schools have the resources and support which enable them to provide for all their children, and which lead to minimum identification of children to whom resources are allocated on an individual basis. It is up to the LEA to make the decision as to how to resource schools for SEN, and therefore what level of SEN will trigger a statement. This in the last resort is a political decision, though with substantial educational implications.

Conclusion

This chapter has attempted to present some of the approaches to the assessment of SEN, to emphasize the fact that children's special educational needs arise from an interaction of factors within the child and factors in the environment, and to highlight the fact that decisions to allocate additional resources are essentially political decisions. The level of 'significance' of a learning difficulty which requires additional resources depends on the child, the learning environment, and the resourcing policy of the LEA. Although the Code of Practice seeks to clarify definitions and levels of SEN, in particular the level which should trigger a statement, it has not succeeded in what is likely to be an impossible task. This is because this decision is largely political rather than educational, and because such judgements are relative rather than absolute.

Notes

1 Section 176 (2) of the Education Act 1993.
2 Sections 175 and 156 (4) (b) of the Education Act 1993.
3 Section 156 (4) (a) of the Education Act 1993.
4 Section 167 (5) of the Education Act 1993, Paragraph 2 (2) of Schedule 9 to the Education Act 1993 and Regulation 6 of the Education (Special Educational Needs) Regulations 1994.

CHAPTER 3

Provision by the School

Introduction

This chapter describes the SEN provision which can reasonably be expected to be made by schools and the statutory duties of the Governing Body. These duties have been clarified by the recent legislation, DfE circulars and the Code of Practice

The 1988 Education Act provided that schools would be allocated a budget under Local Management of Schools (LMS) which may include an identified element for pupils with special educational needs (see Chapter 4). The school is expected to make provision from its delegated budget for all its pupils, including those with special educational needs. The school will receive assistance and usually some additional resources from the LEA for children with statements. These are expected to be used alongside continuing provision made by the school from the delegated budget at about the level that is reasonable for a child at Stage 3. A statement does not require the LEA to take over the entire responsibility for making SEN provision for the child concerned. Governing bodies should be aware of the total amount allocated to them for SEN each year and are required to be able to give an account as to how this amount has been spent.

The 1981 Education Act had the effect that a larger number of pupils with special educational needs received additional support from the LEA directly. With delegated budgets under LMS, schools are expected to be responsible for supporting the majority of these pupils. Recently, therefore, attempts have been made to clarify these responsibilities of schools and the level of provision that they are required to make (Audit Commission/HMI, 1992; DfE, 1994a). The challenge both for schools and for LEAs is summarized by Pumfrey (1995) as 'resources finite; priorities contentious; knowledge partial; demand infinite'.

The kind of provision which ordinary schools are able to make, and therefore the levels of SEN that they are able to meet from their own resources, depend both on the SEN budget and on the total budget. But

1	Shared leadership	Firm and purposeful A participative approach The leading professional
2	Shared vision and goals	Unity of purpose Consistency of practice Collegiality and collaboration
3	A learning environment	An orderly atmosphere An attractive working environment
4	Concentration on teaching and learning	Maximization of learning time Academic emphasis Focus on achievement
5	High expectations	High expectations all round Communicating expectations Providing intellectual challenge
6	Positive reinforcement	Clear and fair discipline Feedback
7	Monitoring progress	Monitoring pupil performance Evaluating school performance
8	Pupils' rights and responsibilities	High pupil self-esteem Positions of responsibility Control of work
9	Purposeful teaching	Efficient organization Clarity of purpose Structured lessons Adaptive practice
10	A learning organization	School-based staff development
11	Home-school partnership	Parental involvement

Table 3.1 Eleven factors for effective schools (after Sammons et al., 1995)

financial resources are not the only factor affecting the ability of a school to meet children's special educational needs. The policy and organization of the school have a vital role to play.

The literature on school effectiveness and school improvement emphasizes factors within the organization of the school which are important to its ability to provide for all pupils. Table 3.1 summarizes 11 factors for effective schools identified from the research literature in this field.

It has been shown that schools which are effective for the majority of pupils are also effective for pupils with special educational needs, and the 11 factors identified in Table. 3.1 are important for consideration by all schools.

In their survey of innovative practice for special educational needs, Clark and her colleagues identified four principles which are key to enabling schools to respond successfully to a wide range of diversity:

1   The creative deployment of resources to support the learning of all pupils.
2   The development of the school as an organisation able to respond to diversity.
3   Enhancement of the professional skills of all staff as the key agents of learning.
4   Providing a culture of collaborative support for staff and students by drawing on the widest possible resource base.

(Clark *et al.*,1995)

Statutory Duties of the Governing Body

Publication of Special Needs Policy

Regulations[1] require the governing body to publish an SEN policy which must be available to parents on request and to include information in the Annual Report to Parents about any changes to the SEN policy, how resources are allocated and the success of the policy over the last year.

The SEN policy must, amongst other things, explain how pupils with special educational needs are identified and their needs determined and reviewed, how resources are allocated amongst pupils with special educational needs, any special facilities for SEN that the school provides and how the governing body evaluates the success of the education which is provided for pupils with special educational needs. The policy must describe any arrangements relating to the treatment of complaints from parents about special educational needs provision in the school.

The Annual Report to Parents[2] must contain information about the success and effectiveness of the policy, significant changes in the policy, and how resources have been allocated to and amongst children with special educational needs over the year.

The detailed requirements for publication of a policy and annual reports impose significant duties on school governors in addition to the primary legislation. The financial information called for suggests that the governors should identify a sum which is allocated to the school by the LEA or Funding Agency for Schools for the purpose of meeting additional educational needs and describe how this sum is spent. This means that for the first time, schools are required to be accountable for the finance that they receive in respect of pupils with special educational needs. Parents and others will be able to find out how the school is using its additional resources, and how it is meeting the special educational needs of pupils.

The requirement to give information about the success of the policy is very challenging. There is, as yet, no guidance as to how this could be done. It is proper that those spending public money should be able to show that the money has been put to good use. However, it is very difficult to identify measures of the success of the SEN policy. Guidance on SEN policies may be found in DfE Circular 6/94 (DfE 1994b) and help in implementation is available in the Schools' Special Educational Needs Policies Pack (Stobbs *et al.*, 1995).

Best Endeavours to Secure Provision for the Children

The governing body are required by the 1993 Education Act[3] to:

(a) use their best endeavours, in exercising their functions in relation to the school, to secure that if any registered pupil has special educational needs the special educational provision which his learning difficulty calls for is made,
(b) secure that, where the responsible person has been informed by the local education authority that a registered pupil has special educational needs, those needs are made known to all who are likely to teach him, and
(c) secure that the teachers in the school are aware of the importance of identifying, and providing for, those registered pupils who have special educational needs.

The governing body are also required to ensure that children with special educational needs, so far as is reasonably practicable, engage in the activities of the school together with children who do not have special educational needs.[4]

These requirements lay considerable responsibilities on schools and their governing bodies. The responsible person is the head teacher, or the chair of the governors, or another governor appointed for the purpose. In practice the head teacher is likely to delegate the responsibility to a Special Educational Needs Coordinator (SENCO). Most schools have appointed a SENCO who is responsible for organizing SEN policy and provision.

The Code of Practice

As described in Chapter 2, the Code of Practice recommended a five-stage model of assessment of SEN. The 1993 Education Act[5] imposes on governing bodies a duty to 'have regard to the provisions' of the Code of Practice issued by the Secretary of State for Education.

Baroness Blatch, speaking for the government in the House of Lords, said:

> having regard to the Code does not mean that governors have a choice as to whether they implement it or not. Rather it means that if there are parts of the Code that the governors decide not to follow, then they should be able to demonstrate that what they chose to do was as good as or better than, the process set out in the Code.

However, where words in a statute have a clear meaning, the meaning cannot be changed by what a government spokesperson says in Parliament.

The meaning of 'have regard to' has been construed by the courts.[6] Mr and Mrs De Falco were European workers, entitled under European Law to equal treatment in the field of social services. They left their home in Italy and together with their baby came to stay in England with her brother. They both found work, but after three months her brother's wife became pregnant and the De Falcos had to move out. The local authority determined that he was intentionally homeless despite the words of the Code of Guidance (First Edition) applicable at that time:

> It would be inappropriate to treat as intentionally homeless a person who gave up accommodation to move in with relatives or friends who then decided after a few months that they could no longer accommodate him.

The court agreed with the local authority, saying:

> The council of course, had to have regard to the code...but, having done so, they could depart from it if they thought fit. This is a case in which they were perfectly entitled to depart from it. That paragraph may be all very well for people coming from Yorkshire or any other part of England. But it should not,

or, at any rate, need not be applied to people coming from Italy, or any other country of the Community.

The governors of a school must not ignore the Code of Practice, but they may make a reasoned decision not to follow parts of the Code of Practice. They do not have to do something as good as or better than the Code of Practice suggests. A decision by the governors not to follow the Code of Practice would not be open to challenge unless the decision was such that no reasonable governing body could ever have made such a decision.

LEAs' Special Educational Needs Policies

In addition to the requirements for schools to publish SEN policies, there are also duties imposed on LEAs to publish their SEN policies.[7] The policy should state:

- The arrangements for identifying children with special educational needs, including any staged approach as recommended in the Code of Practice, and the part to be played by schools, LEA central staff, the health services, social services and voluntary organizations.
- The role of primary, secondary and special schools.
- The arrangements for placing and monitoring pupils in independent and non-maintained special schools.
- The arrangements for coordination, including the management and availability of support services, and collaboration with neighbouring LEAs, the health service and social services.
- The arrangements for
  - monitoring the performance of LEA-maintained schools and LEA-provided support services;
  - ensuring that children with statements receive the provision specified in the statements;
  - reviewing statements annually.

The requirement for LEAs to publish details of their SEN policies, although not new (see Circular 7/91 and 2/94), provides the opportunity to see how LEAs are meeting their responsibilities, what provision is available from the LEA, and how provision is being monitored and evaluated.

Schools' responsibilities

The problem with the concept of special educational needs is that it is both relative and highly subjective and lacks an agreed operational definition. It is therefore very difficult to answer the question: What level of SEN should schools be expected to meet? The answer will depend both on the level of need of the child and on the ability of the school to meet children's needs. The Code of Practice attempts to begin to clarify the respective responsibilities of schools and LEAs, while continuing to emphasize the relative and interactive aspects of SEN. However, the definition continues to be potentially circular since schools are expected to meet the needs of those pupils they are able to meet from their own resources. It is important for the LEA to be able to distinguish and to clarify in its resourcing policy which children it is appropriate to resource individually, and for which children it is appropriate to support schools through targeting resources to the schools.

Schools have clear responsibilities for the first three 'school-based' stages which are designed to meet the needs of pupils for whom a statement is not required and for whom provision is to be financed by the school from its delegated budget. In the booklet entitled *Putting the Code of Practice into Practice: Meeting special educational needs in the school and classroom,* Klaus Wedell (1995) suggests:

> The three school-based stages of the Code involve successive decisions on finding out about pupils' SENs, and about how to plan effective help. These decisions are often made intuitively, but it is important to be aware of them, and of the strategies which drive them.

The Code of Practice states that:

> The majority of children will not pass through all three school-based stages of assessment and provision. In many cases action taken at one stage will mean that the child will not have to move on to the next....
>
> These stages will not usually be steps on the way to statutory assessment. Nor are they hurdles to be crossed before a statutory assessment can be made. They are means of helping schools and parents decide what special educational provision is necessary and to match that provision to the child's needs.
>
> (Paragraphs 2:23 and 2:24 Code of Practice, DfE, 1994a)

The stages of the Code of Practice provide the opportunity for the teacher to engage in a systematic cycle of early identification, exploring concerns, developing strategies for teaching and evaluation and monitoring of progress. This systematic cycle is likely to lead to the teacher being able to help the progress of the majority of pupils with special educational needs, particularly when helped by flexibility over staffing and the use of other resources (see below).

Schools need systems and procedures for coordinating, monitoring and evaluating their work with pupils with special educational needs. However, the education of any child calls for a similar procedure. A competent school need not be expected to introduce a different system for children whose needs are relatively minor but fall within the statutory definition of SEN.

With respect to less than serious special educational needs, there is no obvious reason to distinguish between special educational needs and other kinds of need. All children are entitled to individual attention from their teachers and to a learning approach that is suited to them. Children who are unhappy are entitled to special attention; so are children who are fast learners and get bored, children who are silent, children who could do better, children who upset or disturb other children, and children who make racist remarks. None of these children has special educational needs within the statutory definition.

The Code of Practice suggests the setting up of a separate register for all children with special educational needs: that is the notional 20 per cent of children. In schools which maintain a system for monitoring and recording the progress of all children, an additional register for one child in five would be unnecessary.

At Stage 1 information will be collected and additional strategies to help the child will be devised by the class teacher or form tutor, perhaps with advice from the SENCO. Additional strategies should build on the school's practice for all children. Clear targets for learning should be set, together with a procedure for monitoring and review. A differentiated curriculum may be needed. Parents can expect that the teacher will discuss the child's needs with them and give the child time and attention. All parents are entitled to expect that degree of attention to their child.

A minority of children will require more attention and will be moved from Stage 1 to Stage 2. At this stage the SENCO will take the lead in assessing and monitoring in close collaboration with the class teacher or form tutor, and building on the information and strategies used at Stage 1. The Code of Practice recommends that the SENCO ensure that an Individual Education Plan (IEP) is drawn up. The IEP provides a means for recording detailed information about the outcomes of Stage 1, the next steps and learning targets and a timetable and mechanism for reviewing progress. In many cases the IEP will be a more detailed version of the records which the class teacher already keeps on the progress of all children. The extent to which IEPs are necessary will depend on the quality of planning and record-keeping which is used for all children. The class teacher retains responsibility for teaching the child.

Only a minority of children who do not make sufficient progress will move to Stage 3, and at this stage the SENCO will involve other relevant professionals, such as the educational psychologist. There will be a new IEP, with new strategies and targets for the child. The Code of Practice suggests that SEN provision at this stage might include time with a specialist teacher or help from a classroom assistant.

At Stage 3 schools may need expertise from outside the school; possibly from the educational psychology service and other LEA support services, which could include learning support services and sensory impaired support services. LEAs vary in the extent to which they maintain such services. In some LEAs the services are centrally allocated to schools and paid from a central budget; in others the budgets have been devolved to schools. It then becomes the responsibility of schools to purchase necessary services from either the LEA or other providers.

The educational psychology service is a mandatory exception to delegation because of its statutory role in relation to the 1993 Education Act. Many educational psychology services also work in schools at the earlier stages of the Code of Practice: playing a more preventative role, contributing to consultation work with teachers, in-service training and the development of policy.

It is important for schools to be aware of the range of support services which are available, which are free and which may be bought in either from the LEA or from an alternative provider. Support for individual pupils is only one way in which SEN provision may be organized, and it may not be the most appropriate. It is up to the school to decide and to evaluate the effectiveness of different forms of support, including both educational outcomes and value for money and to allocate its resources appropriately.

The review at Stage 3 and the evidence of the SEN provision that has been made will usually provide the basis for the LEA's consideration at Stage 4 as to whether a statutory assessment is necessary.

Although there have been attempts to define levels of need or extent of delay in attainment to correspond with the stages of the Code of Practice, such attempts are inappropriate, since a child's progress in learning will usually depend on factors within the school at least as much as on factors within the child. The Code of Practice should therefore be used as a framework for identification and assessment by teachers, and not for allocating children to levels or categories, or for determining additional resources, other than for prioritizing within a school budget.

The Code of Practice aims to encourage and develop good practice in the identification and assessment of SEN, building on awareness of the benefits of early identification and systematic teaching, monitoring and record-keeping. Wedell's booklet referred to above describes aspects of good practice in teachers' systematic teaching and decision-making strategies. However, early on, he emphasizes that:

> Whole school policies are required, which enable schools to be responsive to the broad range of the needs of pupils in general. Teachers cannot otherwise give due attention to the special educational needs of the minority of pupils. The policies have to cover the curriculum, behaviour, further professional development of teachers, managing staff time, and allocating resources.
>
> (Wedell, 1995)

Pre-Warnock and Post-Warnock Thinking

A distinction has been drawn between pre- and post-Warnock thinking (Ainscow and Muncey, 1989). Ainscow and Muncey suggest that pre-Warnock thinking was characterized by an emphasis on placing children in categories in order to provide care that tended to be given in segregated settings; this thinking was based on the following assumptions:

- a group of children can be identified who are different from the majority
- only this relatively small group needs special help
- the problems of these children are a result of their disabilities or personal limitations
- special help can best be provided when separate groups of children with common problems are taught together
- once such a group has been provided for, the rest of the school population can be regarded as normal.

Post-Warnock thinking is suggested as being based on the following assumptions:

- any child may experience difficulties in school at some stage
- help and support must be available to all pupils as necessary
- educational difficulties result from an interaction between what the child brings to the situation and what the school has to offer
- teachers should take responsibility for the progress of all the children in their classes
- support must be available to staff as they attempt to meet their responsibilities.

Ainscow and Florek (1989) define a whole-school approach as one 'where attempts are being made to utilise all the resources of a school to foster the development of all its children'.

This definition depends on a school using all its staff, equipment and buildings to the maximum benefit of all its pupils including those with special educational needs. The amount of resources that the school receives depends on the resourcing policy and the LMS arrangements of the LEA. As is shown in Chapter 4, these vary widely across the country. The way in which resources are used by the school depends in very large measure on the school. This also varies widely both within and between LEAs.

Whole-school Approaches

The Code of Practice points out that:

> Provision for pupils with special educational needs is a matter for the school as a whole...all teaching and non-teaching staff should be involved in the development of the school's SEN policy and be fully aware of the school's procedures for identifying, assessing and making provision for pupils with special educational needs.
>
> (Paragraph 2:7 Code of Practice, DfE, 1994a)

Schools make provision for all their pupils of whatever age and ability within the context of their Development Plan. It is important that SEN provision is also made within this context and that the school's SEN policy is developed within the School Development Plan. Schools are expected to indicate in their Development Plans goals and expected outcomes for pupils; these could include improved reading levels, reduced level of exclusions, and improved SATs results. They could also include specific and more detailed goals and outcomes for pupils with special educational needs. The School Development Plan provides an opportunity for the school to achieve consistency over:

- management, discipline and behaviour policies
- curriculum organization and differentiation
- management of staff time
- further professional training.

These aspects are crucial in enhancing the school's ability to meet the needs both of pupils with special educational needs and of the majority of its pupils. A whole-school approach will include SEN within its plans for teacher training, for curriculum differentiation and organization, for pastoral care and discipline, for teacher induction and support, for management and communication, for partnership with parents and cooperation with other agencies, and in the goals and framework which inform the organization of the school.

Clark and her colleagues sought to identify and describe innovative practice, and to identify themes which are likely to contribute to success in meeting special educational needs (Clark *et al.*, 1995). The report includes examples of good practice which have enabled mainstream schools to enhance their provision for pupils with special educational needs. These have been described under the following headings each of which will be considered in turn:

1 Teaching and learning
2 Resource management
3 Managing change, managing roles
4 Professional development
5 Collaborative working.

1 Teaching and Learning

Some schools were 'actively seeking to develop a range of specific strategies that could be used to meet particular children's special needs'. These included developing a range of assessment strategies to inform teaching programmes for particular pupils, linking assessment closely with teaching and developing individualized teaching programmes or carefully differentiated curriculum plans. Many of the schools had developed responses to a range of special needs, and therefore their own confidence and acceptance of their responsibility and skill in this area.

The majority of these teaching strategies are of general application and of benefit to all children. These techniques are neither specialist nor different from ordinary teaching, and therefore encouraging teachers to develop a range of teaching skills is likely to benefit all pupils and to help teachers to address difficulties before they have become identified as SEN. Individualized and differentiated teaching and learning benefits all pupils of whatever abilities.

2 Resource Management

Since LMS, schools have had more flexibility in managing their own resources. In some LEAs, it has been possible for them to bid for resources to pump-prime particular projects or developments. They have been able to collaborate with other schools, sharing resources and benefiting from economies of scale and sharing of expertise, for example in cluster groups, and sometimes have been enabled to bid for resources from the LEA as a cluster to support a particular collaborative initiative. It is important that schools are able to identify resources dedicated to special needs as distinct from other resources, and that they are able to prioritize special needs in their Development Plan. A creative approach to the deployment of special needs teachers enables greater flexibility and the development of a more coordinated whole-school approach. Special needs teachers may teach alongside other teachers, may teach small groups or may release the class teacher to concentrate on pupils with special educational needs.

3 Managing Change, Managing Roles

The more innovative schools used their School Development Plans as dynamic documents to monitor, plan and review over a long period involving all staff. The SENCO and the head teacher or deputy head may play important roles in relation to managing change. For example, some schools in the survey reported that: 'The SEN coordinator was becoming a manager of organisational change and development' as well as working specifically with individual teachers and pupils. In some cases,

> head teachers...were able to create a framework within which special needs became a genuinely whole-school issue, special needs teachers could operate across the schools as a whole, and change and development became a part of the school's culture.

4 Professional Development

The most effective way of deploying resources is to support and invest in school staff, and to increase their expertise. Many schools are now pursuing strategies of school-based professional development both for teaching and non-teaching staff which have succeeded in reducing their dependence on outside specialists and in enhancing their own professional expertise to deal with special educational needs. This is equally important for classroom assistants whose contribution may be considerably enhanced and supported if they are given non-contact time to plan with teachers, to work on materials, to meet with parents, and have the opportunity to attend courses and training events.

5 Collaborative working

Many schools are now seeing the benefits of collaborative working, both within the school and between the school and parents and the school and other schools or agencies, including the LEA. Collaborative arrangements were reported which involved mutual respect and responsibility, and there was evidence of a more balanced partnership between school and LEA services which aimed to build on school policy and practice. Clearly there are tensions between competitive and collaborative pressures on schools. There have, however, been significant examples where collaboration between groups of schools has been successful in promoting schools' abilities to provide for pupils with special educational needs, particularly at the primary stage.

Some Tensions in the Code of Practice

The Code of Practice has accentuated some of the tensions in the resourcing of SEN. The main tension is that between resources targeted at schools and resources targeted at individuals. On the one hand, the Code of Practice states that:

> Effective management, disciplinary and pastoral arrangements and policies in schools can help prevent some special educational needs arising, and minimise others...Schools should not automatically assume that children's learning difficulties always result solely or even mainly from problems within the child. The school's practices can make a difference – for good or ill.
>
> (Paragraph 2:19 Code of Practice, DfE, 1994a)

On the other hand, the way in which the Code of Practice has been formulated has led, in some cases, to an expectation that it provides a framework for the allocation of resources to individual pupils. This is misguided for many reasons. The Code of Practice provides a framework for schools to develop their own ways of supporting teachers in their work with pupils with special educational needs. All children are entitled to individual attention from their teachers and to a learning approach that is suited to them. All teachers are expected to differentiate between the children in their class and to be able to adapt their teaching to the needs of the child. Mixed ability teaching depends on teachers being able to individualize the curriculum to meet the needs of different children. Developing an Individual Education Plan (IEP) is an extension of the normal system of assessment, record-keeping, planning and monitoring of progress which guides every teacher.

The Code of Practice does not provide a formula for allocating resources to individual pupils or to schools, though some LEAs have attempted to use it as such. It is up to the LEA to decide on the size of the budget for AEN (additional educational needs; see page 51) and SEN and on the formula for its allocation to schools. This may be done through an index of social need such as the number of pupils eligible for free school meals, or through an audit of educational needs, which may relate to the Code of Practice stages, or a combination of the two. The LEA should state clearly how much additional budget schools receive in respect of AEN and SEN, and the basis for this amount, but it is not permitted to earmark the budget or to stipulate how it should be used. It is up to schools to decide how to use their budget. The numbers of pupils on the different stages of the Code of Practice may provide both LEAs and schools with some indication as to the differing levels of need in different schools, but they provide no absolute indication of need for resources.

An awareness that special educational needs occur as a result of an interaction between factors in the child with factors in the child's learning environment should result in resources being targeted and used both for the individual child and for the learning environment. Bearing in mind the importance of the whole-school policy, the goal of a resource policy should be to enhance the ability of the school to meet the needs of all its pupils. This means enhancing the capabilities and understanding of all the staff, establishing effective systems for consistency in communication across the school, investing in materials and equipment which may be used by all staff, including information technology, effective use of outside agencies, and the possibility of collaborating with other schools in relation to pupils with special educational needs for example through cluster groups (Lunt *et al.*, 1994).

The needs of pupils on stages 1–3 of the Code of Practice are to be met from the schools' own budgets. The three school-based stages of the Code of Practice should be seen as:

> a continuous and systematic cycle of planning, action and review within the school to enable the child with special educational needs to learn and progress. As such, they are a natural extension of the work of schools with children generally.
>
> (Paragraph 2:61 Code of Practice, DfE, 1994a)

They should not be seen as stages of resource definition. Since the needs of pupils at stages 1–3 are to be met from schools' budgets, any differential accounting would be notional rather than actual, and schools need to plan how to use their own resources to meet the needs of different pupils with different levels of special educational needs. The pressures in schools to gain additional resources has led to inappropriate pressures for more pupils to reach Stages 4 and 5 of the Code of Practice, and to inappropriate attempts to allocate additional resources individually to a larger number of pupils.

Notes

1   The Education (Special Educational Needs) (Information) Regulations 1994 which are reproduced in full as Appendix 4. These are included in DfE Circular 6/94.

2   Section 30 of the Education (No 2) Act 1986 requires governors to produce an annual report to parents. Section 161 (5) of the Education Act 1993 requires the annual report to contain information about special educational needs. The Education (Special Educational Needs) (Information) Regulations 1994 gives details of that information.

3   Section 161 (1) of the Education Act 1993.

4   Section 161 (4) of the Education Act 1993.

5   Section 157 (2) of the Education Act 1993.

6   *De Falco v Crawley Borough Council* CA [1980] 1 QB 460.

7   Education (School Information) (England) Regulations.

CHAPTER 4

Funding of schools

Introduction

The way a Local Education Authority (LEA) distributes money to schools determines the budget that is available for additional educational needs (AEN). AEN encompasses special educational needs (SEN) and a range of other needs which are outside the statutory definition of SEN. The budget to a large extent determines the 'statement threshold', which is the maximum level of an individual child's needs which can reasonably be met from within the school's own resources. For resource allocation purposes, the statement threshold may be expressed in terms of cost, so that when the cost of making the necessary provision exceeds the statement threshold, the LEA has a duty to issue a statement of SEN.

The money available to schools for AEN varies dramatically from one LEA to another and, as a consequence, the statement threshold varies significantly from one LEA to another. The resources available to the school are the main matter to be taken into account by the LEA when deciding whether to issue a statement. The SEN Tribunal will be required to analyse the budgets of LEAs in considerable detail on a case by case basis when deciding appeals against a refusal to issue a statement.

A systematic approach is called for. This chapter describes the mechanism of funding schools, then identifies the AEN budgets in each LEA in England and finally suggests a mechanism for determining the statement threshold in any given LEA.

National Funding for Education

Funding for state schools is derived from three sources. On a national basis 23 per cent comes from local council tax, 28 per cent from the uniform business rate and 49 per cent from central government Revenue Support Grant (RSG).[1] These proportions are illustrated in Figure 4.1.

The sum allocated to each LEA by RSG is derived from Standard Spending Assessments (SSAs). An SSA is the government's assessment of the amount of expenditure which would allow the local authority to provide a standard level of service. The calculation of the SSAs depends on general principles applied equally to all local authorities and takes account of each local authority's demographic, geographic and social characteristics. Differences in SSAs between local authorities are solely due to differences in the measurements of underlying characteristics.

The SSA for the local authority is constructed by adding the necessary expenditure for each of the local authority's different functions. With respect to schools there are separate calculations for nursery, primary, secondary and post-16 education, which are given as SSAs per child.

The SSA for educating a child at school is composed of four elements; 1) a uniform national age-weighted sum per pupil; 2) a variable sum for AEN; 3) a variable sum for provision of free school meals (FSM) and 4) a variable sum for low population density. These elements are multiplied by an area cost factor which reflects, in the main, different wage levels. The average national SSA per pupil is based 79 per cent on the uniform sum per pupil, 16 per cent on additional educational needs, 3 per cent on the provision of free school meals and 2 per cent on low population density. These proportions are illustrated in Figure 4.2. The 1994/5 national average SSA for a primary child was £1,623 + £333 + £43 + £29 = £2028.[2]

The AEN element in the SSA and RSG is based on a national AEN index which contains three measures for each LEA. They are; 1) the proportion of children whose parents are income support claimants; 2) the proportion of children who are in single parent families and 3) the proportion of children whose parents were born outside the UK, Eire, the Old Commonwealth or the USA. The SSAs for AEN range from £18,200 to £82,200 per hundred primary children in different LEAs. That is a range of 9 per cent to 27 per cent of the total SSA for educating a primary child.

To summarize; about half the cost of education is met by central government. Central government estimates that the cost of making provision for AEN is a substantial proportion of the total cost of education and varies considerably from one LEA to another. The next section considers how the money is allocated by LEAs to individual schools.

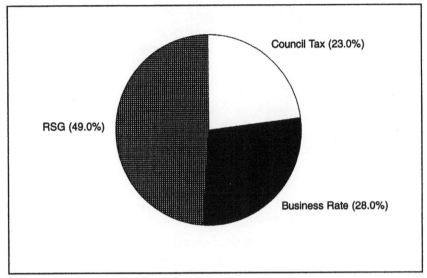

Figure 4.1 Sources of LEA finance

Formula Funding for Schools

LEAs are responsible for setting a general schools budget (GSB) and distributing that budget to schools. The local management of schools (LMS) legislation requires that LEAs delegate most of the GSB to individual schools.[3] A limited amount of the GSB may be spent directly by LEAs on central services. The remainder, called the Aggregated Schools Budget (ASB) is delegated to schools by means of a local management of schools formula (LMS formula). The LMS formula should be clear in its operation and fair in its result. Responsibility for spending the delegated budget shares lies with school governors.

In the case of grant-maintained (GM) schools, funding is managed by the Funding Agency for Schools (FAS). The FAS is a national body consisting of between ten and 15 members nominated by the Secretary of State. In most LEAs the GM schools are intended to receive exactly the same delegated budget as they would have received in accordance with the LEA formula together with a percentage allowance representing a share of the money that the LEA has retained for central spending.

This system of replication has proved difficult to operate fairly. There

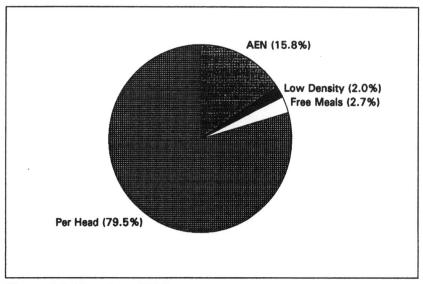

Figure 4.2 Allocation of RSG

have been a number of well-founded assertions that the GM schools have been over-funded in comparison to LEA schools.

The government intends that replication of the LEA formulae should be replaced by Common Funding Formulae (CFFs). CFFs were introduced for GM secondary schools in Calderdale, Essex, Gloucestershire, Bromley and Hillingdon for the financial year 1994/95. The scheme was extended to include GM secondary schools in Barnet, Brent, Cambridgeshire, Croydon, Cumbria, Ealing, Enfield, Hertfordshire, Kent, Kingston-upon-Thames, Lambeth, Lincolnshire, Surrey, Sutton, Wandsworth, Walsall and Wiltshire for the financial year 1995/96. The word 'common' is potentially misleading: CFFs are based on a combination of the SSA and the LEA formula and are different in each LEA.

The LMS formulae used by LEAs to allocate the ASB between different schools are complicated. At least 80 per cent is required to be pupil-led. That means allocated on the basis of pupil numbers. The allocation by pupil numbers may be a fixed sum per pupil or a different sum for pupils of different ages and may include a different sum for pupils with different levels of SEN. The remaining 20 per cent may be allocated on other measures. These are used to reflect, for example, the different levels of expenditure required to heat and maintain buildings of different ages or the higher cost of providing a full curriculum in a small school. This other expenditure may also include funding for SEN or AEN.

The total result of all the decisions of individual LEAs is that about 3 per cent of the funding delegated to schools is based on measures of AEN.[4] That may be compared with the 16 per cent allocated to LEAs by central government. The percentages for a selection of LEAs are given in Table 4.1. The LEAs given in each category are the highest, median and lowest. The full table containing all LEAs is at the end of the chapter.

Column B in Table 4.1 gives the percentage of the ASB that is delegated to schools on the basis of a measure of different levels of educational need in different schools. Column D shows that percentage

A	% School budgets AEN based	School budgets for AEN per 100 children
A	**B**	**D**
Inner London Education Authorities		
Greenwich	2.3	£4,879
Corporation of London	6.0	£18,082
Westminster	10.4	£23,367
Outer London Education Authorities		
Newham	0.0	£0
Bexley	3.7	£5,921
Barnet	5.5	£10,354
Metropolitan Education Authorities		
Doncaster	0.6	£1,012
Birmingham	3.1	£5,358
North Tyneside	11.3	£18,459
Shire County Education Authorities		
Suffolk	0.3	£570
Cambridgeshire	2.6	£4,051
Lancashire	6.3	£9,924

Table 4.1 Percentage of school budgets based on AEN

converted into £ per hundred children using 1995/96 budgets. It is the average for the whole LEA. Individual schools receive larger or smaller sums in accordance with the children's needs. For example, in Southwark, the average figure in 1994/95 was £15,979 per hundred children. The school with the highest allocation received £23,000 per hundred children and the lowest allocation was £3,000.

The information in Table 4.1 is published for each LEA in an annual 'Section 42' Budget Statement. LEAs are required, by Section 42 of the Education Act 1988 to ensure that the Section 42 statement is available for inspection in schools at all reasonable times. This statement includes the basic information about the money allocated to schools on the basis of a measure of AEN, but contains very little explanation. LEAs are also required to publish their local management of schools scheme (LMS scheme) which contains an explanation of the policy.

The allocations on the basis of AEN are very different in different LEAs. The differences are much larger than the differences in levels of AEN. The result is that in some LEAs schools have very substantial identified AEN budgets and in other LEAs schools have very small AEN budgets.

Schools should be expected to use the AEN budgets specifically for the benefit of children with additional educational needs and special educational needs, including, if necessary, making special educational provision for individual children. In the next section it is argued that schools cannot be expected to make further provision for individual children from their general funding, though they may choose to do so. The argument may be controversial.

Differences in School Populations

Within LEAs there are considerable differences between schools in the proportion of children who have special educational needs. This is brought about by a combination of parental choice and the mechanisms controlling the admission of children to schools.

Some special educational needs are related to social factors such as poverty, family break-down and flight from war or persecution in foreign lands. The nature of the population within the school's catchment area has a major influence on the proportion of children with special educational needs.

The old grammar schools and those GM schools which admit children on the basis of test results select against most children with special educational needs. Some selection may occur in entry to voluntary schools where admission is dependent on regular worship at a particular church or where admission is dependent upon an interview with the child and the parents.

A survey of the incidence of SEN in Lambeth primary schools showed a range from 0 per cent to 30 per cent of children having special educational needs.[5] A small study in Nottinghamshire gave a range of 0 per cent to 38 per cent in primary schools.[6] An audit of secondary schools in Kent shows a range from 0 per cent to 53 per cent.[7] The Kent audit in primary schools shows a range from 6 per cent to 86 per cent. An audit in Ealing shows a range of 10 per cent to 53 per cent in secondary schools and 6 per cent to 36 per cent in primary schools.[8]

An audit of SEN in Southwark found that in County primary schools 5.2 per cent of the children had special educational needs at or above Stage 3 of the Code of Practice, whereas the equivalent figure for Roman Catholic primary schools was 2.8 per cent.[9]

The widely different SEN levels in different schools means that it is unfair to allocate school budgets on the basis of pupil numbers alone. Meeting children's special educational needs both by whole-school strategies and individual attention costs money. If funding for SEN is to come from budgets allocated on the basis of pupil numbers, schools with a high proportion of pupils with special educational needs would be at a disadvantage compared to schools with low levels of SEN. This effect is exaggerated in LEAs where there are grammar schools or selective GM schools. About a quarter of the LEAs in England have selective schools

LEAs which allocate small sums on the basis of AEN might assert that further funding for Stages 2 and 3 of the Code of Practice is included in the money delegated on the basis of pupil numbers. Three lines of argument gainsay that assertion:

1 Central government has allocated money to the LEA on the basis of different levels of AEN. Central government expects that those differences will be passed on to schools. The Code of Practice states:

> Most mainstream schools should have within their delegated budget some funding which reflects the additional needs of pupils with special educational needs. LEA-maintained schools should receive this through local management schemes which are weighted for the incidence of special educational needs within the authority.
>
> (Paragraph 4:3 Code of Practice, DfE, 1994a)

2 The LEAs have published a sum allocated to each school for AEN or SEN based on a measure of different levels of educational need. Having identified an SEN allocation in this way, an LEA cannot

convincingly assert that schools in general ought to be spending further money on SEN provision for individual children.

3 The differences between schools make allocating money for SEN on the basis of pupil numbers alone unfair.

The second argument could be side-stepped by an LEA making no SEN allocation whatsoever. The London Borough of Newham is the only LEA in England that makes no SEN or AEN allocation to schools and makes no central provision for children at Stages 2 and 3 of the Code of Practice. Newham is relatively uniform in social geography which might lead to the differences between schools being small. However, the GCSE examination results from Newham's secondary schools show substantial differences between the schools. The percentage of children achieving 5 or more A to C grades at GCSE ranges from 5 per cent to 36 per cent in different secondary schools in Newham.[10]

The Corporation of London has only one school. The Corporation nevertheless allocates identified SEN funding on the basis of the number of pupils eligible for free school meals (FSM) and performance testing. It is highly unlikely that the SEN levels in all schools in Newham are the same. Even if they were, it is questionable whether that would be a justification for not allocating money for SEN. It may be noted that Newham schools receive the lowest level of funding of any LEA in England when the delegated sum per pupil is compared with the standard spending assessment per pupil.[11]

The conclusion is that schools in some LEAs should make substantial provision for children at Stages 2 and 3 of the Code of Practice from within the delegated budgets, but that in other LEAs only very limited provision can be expected.

Differential Measures in Funding Formulae

All LEAs in England, except the London Borough of Newham, allocate part of the schools' budget on the basis of estimates of different educational needs in different schools. In some LEAs the entire allocation is intended to fund provision for SEN. In others part of the sum is intended for general strategies to combat the educational effects of social and economic disadvantage. The method by which the money is allocated indicates how the money is expected to be spent. The LMS schemes describe the detailed methodology used by each LEA and sometimes explain the LEA's intentions. Various allocation factors are considered below.

Measures of Social or Economic Deprivation: Proxy Factors

A number of measures of social or economic deprivation are used by LEAs to achieve differential funding of schools. These include eligibility for FSM or clothing allowances, single parent families, child protection register, ethnicity and entry to the school at an age other than the usual age for entry. These measures stand in the place of direct measures of educational need and are referred to as proxy factors.

Eligibility for FSM is the most widely used proxy factor. A child is eligible for FSM if the parent receives income support. Though families eligible for family credit are not eligible for FSM, eligibility for FSM is a very good indicator of socio-economic disadvantage amongst the school population.

Where money is allocated differentially on the basis of proxy factors, the school may properly direct some of the money towards AEN as distinct from statutory SEN.

There are a great many aspects of school life in which children from economically deprived backgrounds need extra resources, but which do not fall within the statutory definition of SEN. There may be a greater need for pastoral care and time spent on disciplinary and behavioural difficulties. Being a bully or a victim is not of itself a special educational need. More staff time may be needed to attend case conferences with social service departments and to give evidence in family and criminal courts. Secondary schools may need to provide supervised facilities for homework. Primary schools may need to arrange greater support for home-school reading schemes. Children in the early years may need extra staffing to help them integrate with school life, dress themselves, go to the toilet and look after their property.

A school may also decide to spend some of the money on providing, without charge, opportunities which are in addition to the basic requirements of education. For example, it is common practice for schools to charge parents for school journeys and music lessons. A proportion of the money allocated on the basis of poverty measures might reasonably be used to provide music and school journeys for children who could not otherwise afford them.

The Education Act 1993 and in particular the Code of Practice have raised awareness of SEN. LEAs are emphasizing that money allocated on the basis of proxy factors is mainly for SEN. This approach assumes that a measure such as the proportion of children eligible for FSM is a reliable predictor of the proportion of children having special educational needs. It is important that LEAs which allocate money on the basis of FSM give consideration to the validity of that assumption.

A study carried out in 18 Nottingham primary schools in 1990[12] suggested that FSM was a reasonably good predictor of levels of SEN. The value of FSM as a predictor of SEN may be expressed mathematically as a correlation coefficient (r). A correlation coefficient is a measure of the degree of relationship between the two variables. For a perfect correlation r = 1.0: a measure of one variable can be used to predict the other variable with certainty. Where there is no correlation r = 0. The Nottingham study of the relationship between FSM and SEN gave correlation coefficients of r = 0.7 in primary schools and r = 0.86 in secondary schools. That data suggested that FSM is a reasonably reliable predictor of SEN. The Nottingham study is small, but appears to have had considerable influence on LEAs. Much larger data samples are now available.

Data from all primary schools in the London Borough of Ealing[13] are shown on a scattergram in Figure 4.3. The correlation coefficient r = 0.45. That is a weak correlation. The correlation between FSM and numbers of children at stages 2 and 3 of the Code of Practice is much lower. In secondary schools in Ealing there is a stronger correlation, r = 0.71, between proportion of children eligible for FSM and the proportion of children with special educational needs.

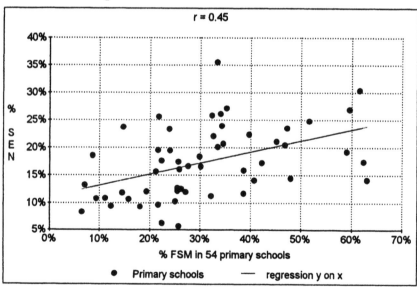

Figure 4.3 Ealing Primary Schools FSM and SEN, r=0.45

The London Borough of Southwark[14] carried out an audit of the number of children at or above stage 3 of the Code of Practice including children with statements in all schools in Southwark. The results are shown on Figure 4.4. There is a weak correlation, r = 0.47, between the proportion of children eligible for FSM and the proportion of children at or above stage 3 of the Code of Practice.

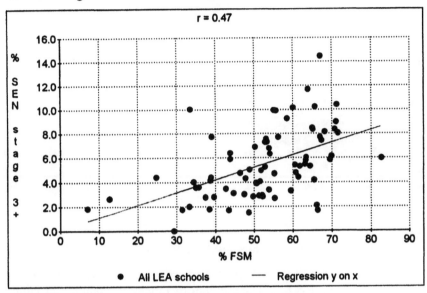

Figure 4.4 Southwark schools FSM and SEN 3, r=0.47

The most substantial and reliable data comes from the SEN audit in Kent which confirms the Nottingham figures. In primary schools the correlation between the proportion of children entitled to FSM and the proportion with SEN at all levels taken together is r = 0.73. In secondary schools r = 0.8. The results are shown on Figures 4.5 and 4.6.[15] Kent has a number of grammar and GM selective schools. These schools appear as a cluster in the bottom left-hand corner of Figure 4.6. They have very few or no children with SEN and very few children eligible for FSM.

It is concluded that the percentage of children eligible for FSM is a reliable predictor of the percentage of children with special educational needs in some LEAs, but not in all. Taking into consideration the observation that the percentage of children entitled to FSM is a remarkably reliable predictor of GCSE results as shown in Figure 4.7, there is ample justification for funding schools on the basis of FSM levels both as a proxy measure of SEN and to address other differences in educational needs.

Special Educational Needs Audit

A small number of LEAs make an estimate, or audit, of the number of

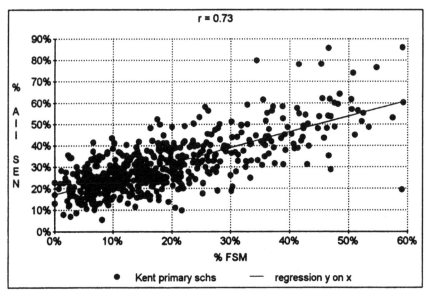

Figure 4.5 Kent primary schools FSM and SEN, r=0.73

children in each school having special educational needs at various levels and then allocate a specific sum of money per qualifying child. The audit procedure is time-consuming. The usual method is for the teachers to survey the children and allocate them to different levels of need. The LEA then moderates a random sample of the schools' results

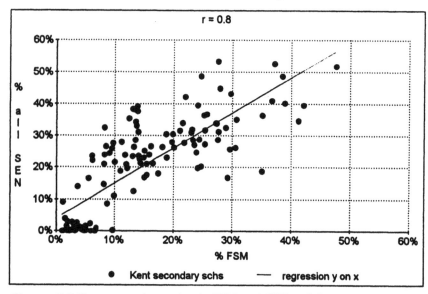

Figure 4.6 Kent secondary schools FSM and SEN, r=0.8

and adjusts the school's total figures accordingly. There may be significant differences in judgements made by different teachers in different circumstances. Audit funding cannot necessarily be assumed to be fair and consistent.

The audit method of differential funding is likely to be adopted by an increasing number of LEAs in the future. Where money is allocated on the basis of an audit, it would be extremely difficult for the school governors to justify spending that money on anything other than strategies to assist children with special educational needs. It would also be difficult to justify spending additional money on individual children with special educational needs. The money allocated may properly be described as the school's SEN budget.

Testing

Some LEAs test all children and allocate funds in favour of schools where the aggregate test scores are low. Tests used include the national standard assessment tasks (SATs), set by the government for all 7-, 11- and 14-year-olds, as well as reading tests and cognitive ability tests.

A child's performance in a test will depend on the educational opportunities experienced and the ease or difficulty the child has in learning. Test scores are thus affected by SEN but are probably dominated by educational opportunity outside school. This is illustrated by the remarkably strong correlation, $r = 0.88$, between the proportion of children whose parents claim income support and the proportion of children gaining 5 or more GCSEs at grade C or above. Figure 4.7 shows that correlation using FSM data and GCSE pass rates for every LEA in England. The reason that differences in GCSE performance are mostly explained by the proportion of income support claimants is likely to be different degrees of educational opportunity at home. It follows that tests do not provide reliable information about levels of SEN.

Where performance testing is carried out during a child's career at a particular school, as opposed to on entry, there is a risk of perverse funding: a school which fails to educate children adequately may be rewarded by increased funding.

Allocating money on the basis of test results resources schools in proportion to lack of educational opportunity at home. There is ample justification for doing that quite apart from differential funding for children with special educational needs.

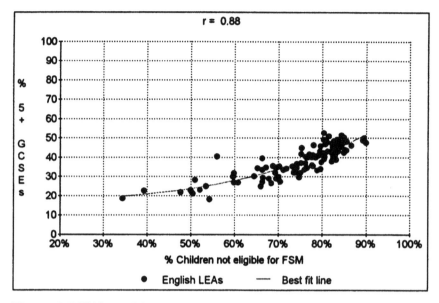

Figure 4.7 FSM and GCSE performance 1994, r=0.88

English as a Second Language

The proportion of children for whom English is a second language could be viewed as a proxy factor, but is also a measure of additional need which is expressly excluded from the definition of SEN by the 1993 Act:

> A child is not to be taken as having a learning difficulty solely because the language (or form of language) in which he is, or will be, taught is different from the language (or form of language) which has at any time been spoken in his home.

> (Section 156(3), 1993 Education Act).

Some children for whom English is a second language receive support under Section 11 of the Local Government Act 1966. The funding which is partly from central government and partly from local government is allocated on the basis of bids for projects. One element of a project may be language support in schools. Such in-school support must be controlled by the LEA as opposed to being delegated to schools. The existence of a Section 11 funded project within a school should be taken into account when considering the resources that a school has available for children with special educational needs.

In conclusion, a school's potential SEN budget is the money allocated differentially on the basis of a measure or estimation of additional needs.

If the only pupil needs differential factor is an SEN audit, all the money should be spent on SEN provision. Where proxy factors or testing are used a school may reasonably spend part of the money on strategies to combat disadvantage generally and part on SEN. Where money is allocated on the basis of fluency in English as a second language, that money should be used primarily to support those children, except where they are being adequately supported as part of a Section 11 project.

The emphasis that is currently placed on SEN by central government and LEAs in their LMS schemes suggests that it is reasonable to expect that 75 per cent of the potential SEN budget will be targeted towards discharging the school's responsibility for children with special educational needs.

School budgets and statements of SEN

It has been shown that SEN budgets vary considerably from one LEA to another. It has been argued that this gives rise to different expectations of the levels of SEN provision which schools can reasonably afford to make. It follows that the SEN budget determines to a large extent the level of need which will trigger the LEA's obligation to make a statement.

The Code of Practice stresses that resources are the primary matter which LEAs and the SEN Tribunal should consider when deciding whether it is necessary to issue a statement of SEN:

> The main ground on which the LEA may decide that they must make a statement is when the LEA conclude that all the special educational provision necessary to meet the child's needs cannot reasonably be provided within the resources normally available to mainstream schools in the area.
>
> (Paragraph 4:2 Code of Practice, DfE, 1994a)

The Code of Practice further emphasizes that principle by reference to the provision that schools can reasonably be expected to make from within their delegated budgets and the need to take into account arrangements for funding schools in the area (Paragraph 4:11 Code of Practice, DfE, 1994a). The approach has been approved by the court.[16]

Where the resources allocated for SEN are substantial, there will be less need for statements than where little money has been allocated for SEN. The SEN Tribunal will have to determine, on a case by case basis, the annual sum that schools in the particular LEA can afford to spend on SEN provision for a child for whom a statement might be necessary. The level of need which triggers the obligation to make a statement can be expressed theoretically in terms of cost. That sum is referred to by the authors as the 'statement threshold'. It is a constant within each LEA, but varies substantially from one LEA to another.

The legislation envisages statement thresholds which can be determined. A consistent approach to determining the statement threshold is highly desirable and feasible. Such an approach is described below.

A Fair Distribution of the School's SEN Budget

The statement threshold may be determined by distributing the SEN budget per hundred children fairly between the children with special educational needs in proportion to those needs. That exercise will produce an estimate of the maximum amount that a school can afford to spend on meeting the needs of a child at Stage 3.

It is inherent to the current approach to providing for children with special educational needs that there is a tension between financing individual and financing collective provision. The Code of Practice strongly advocates individual provision which has high administrative cost, is inflexible and may be uneconomical. The Code proposes that in general children at Stages 2 and 3 should have individual education plans (IEPs) which allocate resources on an individual basis. At Stage 3 the IEP is expected to specify additional staffing arrangements involving both school staff and external specialists. The IEPs at Stage 3 are intended to be similar to LEA statements of SEN so as to ensure a continuum of provision between the school-based stages and the LEA stages. A statement of SEN almost invariably allocates resources to an individual child. In future LEAs will not readily issue a statement unless the school has allocated individual resources by way of an IEP at Stage 3 and this has proved insufficient to meet the child's needs.

It is for LEAs and schools to decide the balance to be struck between individual and collective provision. LEAs can issue large numbers of statements at the expense of making provision for children generally or they may limit statements to those children who are or might be in a special school so as to permit better resourcing of schools generally. In the same way, having had regard to the Code of Practice, a school may decide that it is better to use general strategies both to make provision for SEN and to reduce the number of children requiring SEN provision as an alternative to allocating resources on an individual basis to large numbers of children.

Despite the different approaches that schools may properly take, it is possible to distribute the SEN budget between all the children with special educational needs at the different stages as a theoretical exercise. In order to do that it is necessary to ascertain the numbers of children at the different stages and to reach a view as to how much greater is the cost of providing for a child at Stages 2 and 3 compared with providing for a child at Stage 1

A number of LEAs using an SEN audit allocate a fixed sum of money in the school budget for each child at each stage of the Code of Practice. This may be the entire budget allocated on the basis of different needs or it may be in addition to funding on the basis of socio-economic deprivation. In considering a fair distribution of the SEN budget, the ratio between allocations per child at the different Stages provides an indication of expected cost ratios. The sums allocated per child at different levels of need in a number of LEAs which use audit funding are shown in Table 4.2

The cost ratio between children at stages 1, 2 and 3 of 1:4:10 which has been adopted by Kent, was derived by costing the levels of provision which are suggested for children at each of the three school-based stages described in the Code of Practice. A similar exercise carried out by the authors produced a ratio of 1:3:12 (Bibby and Lunt, 1994). The ratio 1:4:10 is adopted here as being a fair and reasonable basis for a notional distribution of the SEN budget.

Education Authority	Sum allocated to schools per child			Ratio
	Stage 1	Stage 2	Stage 3	
Southwark			£1293	
Hampshire	£96	£305	£1001	1:3:10
Kent	£97	£386	£967	1:4:10
Barnet	£62	£496	£682	1:8:11
Waltham Forest		£221	£662	
Ealing	£91	£182	£548	1:2:6
Solihull	£90	£270	£541	1:3:6
Hertfordshire		£119	£299	

Table 4.2 LEA budget allocations per child identified in SEN audit

Deriving statement thresholds

The cost ratios indicate the expected differences in resourcing required to meet different levels of need and so provide a fair way of notionally dividing the SEN budget between children at Stages 1, 2 and 3 of the Code of Practice. The ratios provide the basis for an equation which may be used to indicate the money that a school can reasonably afford to spend on an individual child at Stage 3, which is the statement threshold.

The statement threshold =

$$\frac{10 \times \text{the SEN budget}}{1(\text{no of children at Stage 1}) + 4(\text{no at Stage 2}) + 10(\text{no at Stage 3 or above})}$$

The budget available to implement the school-based stages of the Code of Practice or other SEN policy includes both the money allocated to schools on the basis of pupil needs differentials and any money retained by LEAs specifically for these pupils. Table 4.3, which is in the same format as Table 4.1, shows the centrally held (column C) and delegated budgets (column D) for children in mainstream school who do not have statements, in a selection of LEAs. The figures for every LEA in England are given at the end of this chapter. Column E (C + D) is the AEN budget per hundred children in that LEA.

In schools which have decided to implement the Code of Practice in full, the number of children at the various levels of need will have been ascertained by the school and each child registered. A parent or the SEN Tribunal can probably discover those figures. The figures can then be applied to the formula.

Estimating statement thresholds

It is possible to estimate the statement thresholds for all LEAs by predicting the levels of SEN in each LEA from the national AEN index. The estimated statement thresholds in every LEA in England are given in column G of Table 4.3. The estimated statement thresholds were derived as follows:

The Code of Practice accepts the concept that 20 per cent of children nationally may have special educational needs at some time within their school career and suggests that about 2 per cent of children will probably require statements. A notional national distribution of SEN levels assuming the 2 per cent and 20 per cent boundaries is suggested in Table 4.4.

About half of the children with statements are expected to be in

A	B	C	D	E	F	G

A   Education Authority

B   % of the budget delegated to schools on AEN or SEN differentials

C   *£ per 100 children held by LEA for non-statemented SEN*

D   *£ per 100 children delegated to schools on AEN or SEN differentials*

E   C + D £ per 100 children available for AEN or SEN spending

F   National AEN index adjusted to mean value 1

G   Estimated Statement threshold for LEA

A	B	C	D	E	F	G
Inner London Education Authorities						
Greenwich	2.3%	£32	£4,879	**£4,911**	1.7	**£455**
Corporation of London	6.08%	£0	£18,082	**£18,082**	1.4	**£1,998**
Westminster	10.4%	£0	£23,367	**£23,367**	1.7	**£2,152**
Outer London Education Authorities						
Newham	0.0%	£0	£0	**£0**	2.1	**£0**
Bexley	3.7%	£0	£5,921	**£5,921**	0.9	**£1,094**
Barnet	5.5%	£4,613	£10,354	**£14,967**	1.1	**£2,162**
Metropolitan Education Authorities						
Doncaster	0.6%	£1,037	£1,012	**£2,049**	1.0	**£311**
Birmingham	3.1%	£1,144	£5,358	**£6,502**	1.6	**£639**
North Tyneside	11.3%	£0	£18,459	**£18,459**	1.0	**£3,025**
Shire County Education Authorities						
Suffolk	0.3%	£352	£570	**£922**	0.6	**£233**
Cambridgeshire	2.6%	£2,210	£4,051	**£6,261**	0.8	**£1,232**
Lancashire	6.3%	£1,355	£9,924	**£11,279**	1.0	**£1,875**

Table 4.3 AEN and SEN budgets per 100 children in different LEAs

Stage/level of need	% of all children
Children not now requiring provision	4
Children requiring provision at level 1	7
Children requiring provision at level 2	4
Children requiring provision at level 3	3
Children requiring statements	2
Total	20

Table 4.4 Percentage of all children at various levels of need

mainstream schools and half to be in special schools. The 4 per cent given in the first row are the children who do not need provision at present, but for whom provision is required at some other time in their school careers.

In an LEA where the notional national distribution of children with special educational needs is applicable, the percentages given in Table 4.4 may be inserted into the statement threshold equation:
The statement threshold =

$$\frac{10 \times \text{the SEN budget per hundred children}}{1(7) + 4(4) + 10(4)}$$

which may be simplified to:

The statement threshold = the SEN budget per hundred children x 0.159

That formula will apply in an LEA where SEN levels are the notional national average. The SEN levels in a particular LEA may be estimated from the national AEN index for each LEA which is shown in column F of Table 4.3. The index has been calibrated to give a mean value of one so that an LEA with an AEN index value of one is expected to have the national average level of SEN. Where the AEN index value is two, the SEN levels are expected to be twice the national average. On that basis:
The estimated statement threshold =

$$\frac{\text{the SEN budget per hundred children x 0.159}}{\text{the AEN index.}}$$

The estimated statement thresholds are not completely reliable because the lower and upper limits of 2 per cent and 20 per cent are somewhat arbitrary as are the divisions within those limits. The actual national percentage of children with statements is about 3 per cent.[17] About 1.4 per cent of all children are in special schools. The upper limit of 20 per cent is conceptual. It underlies the definition of SEN: a child has special educational needs if the child has significantly greater difficulty in learning than the majority of children. The formulation supposes an upper limit to the proportion of children who can be said to have special educational needs, but does not identify the limit. The practice of individual LEAs or schools may produce different figures. For example in Kent 25 per cent of children are identified as having special educational needs at any one time, compared with the notional national figure of 16 per cent. However, the national index of AEN suggests that levels of additional need in Kent would be lower than the national average.

Further the method relies on the national AEN index as a predictor of SEN levels. It has been shown that FSM levels are not always reliable predictors of SEN. The relationship between FSM and SEN in Kent shown in Figures 4.5 and 4.6 and the relationship between FSM and national GCSE results shown in Figure 4.7 suggest, however, that the AEN index is adequate for estimating statement thresholds.

The estimated statement thresholds assume that the entire AEN budgets are allocated to children with special educational needs. It is clear however that, when money is allocated to schools on the basis of socio-economic indicators, test results or the proportion of children who are learning English as a second language, a part of the AEN budget may be expected to be spent on additional needs which are not SEN.

The estimated statement thresholds provide an indication of the sum that a school can reasonably afford to spend on an individual child for whom a statement is being considered. Detailed local information can provide a more precise statement threshold. In disputes over whether an LEA is obliged to issue a statement, the SEN Tribunal must determine whether or not the school can be expected to make the provision that is necessary from within the delegated budget. It would be reasonable for a parent to use the estimated statement threshold as a starting point. Where the LEA seeks to disagree, it would be up to the LEA to adduce evidence to show that the statement threshold differs from the estimate.

	A	B	C	D	E	F	G
A	Education Authority						
B	% of the budget delegated to schools on AEN or SEN differentials						
C	£ per 100 children held by LEA for non-statemented SEN						
D	£ per 100 children delegated to schools on AEN or SEN differentials						
E	**C + D £ per 100 children available for AEN or SEN spending**						
F	National AEN index adjusted to mean value 1						
G	**Estimated Statement threshold for LEA**						

A	B	C	D	E	F	G
Inner London Education Authorities						
Corporation of London	6.0%	£0	£18,082	**£18,082**	1.4	**£1,998**
Camden	7.8%	£2,940	£17,455	**£20,395**	2.0	**£1,643**
Greenwich	2.3%	£32	£4,879	**£4,911**	1.7	**£455**
Hackney	9.4%	£0	£19,522	**£19,522**	2.3	**£1,321**
Hammersmith-Fulham	8.6%	£1,199	£19,434	**£20,633**	2.0	**£1,635**
Islington	3.7%	£618	£8,362	**£8,980**	2.2	**£656**
Kensington & Chelsea	5.8%	£1,030	£13,422	**£14,451**	1.7	**£1,327**
Lambeth	7.6%	£0	£16,905	**£16,905**	2.3	**£1,160**
Lewisham	8.0%	£859	£16,510	**£17,370**	1.9	**£1,476**
Southwark	8.4%	£0	£17,046	**£17,046**	2.3	**£1,186**
Tower Hamlets	10.0%	£715	£21,647	**£22,362**	2.5	**£1,430**
Wandsworth	8.6%	£3,786	£16,249	**£20,035**	1.6	**£1,958**
Westminster	10.4%	£0	£23,367	**£23,367**	1.7	**£2,152**
Outer London Education Authorities						
Barking & Dagenham	1.4%	£2,867	£2,662	**£5,530**	1.3	**£682**
Barnet	5.5%	£4,613	£10,354	**£14,967**	1.1	**£2,162**
Bexley	3.7%	£0	£5,921	**£5,921**	0.9	**£1,094**
Brent	0.8%	£0	£1,448	**£1,448**	1.9	**£123**
Bromley	1.7%	£2,967	£2,716	**£5,682**	0.7	**£1,231**
Croydon	3.6%	£1,243	£6,482	**£7,725**	1.2	**£986**
Ealing	2.7%	£1,916	£4,893	**£6,809**	1.5	**£713**
Enfield	4.0%	£885	£6,972	**£7,857**	1.3	**£976**
Haringey	2.7%	£8,298	£5,442	**£13,740**	2.1	**£1,022**
Harrow	5.3%	£2,388	£9,967	**£12,355**	1.0	**£1,898**
Havering	1.7%	£816	£3,100	**£3,916**	0.8	**£808**
Hillingdon	1.6%	£1,853	£2,720	**£4,573**	1.0	**£719**
Hounslow	3.4%	£555	£6,492	**£7,047**	1.3	**£846**
Kingston upon Thames	4.6%	£0	£8,212	**£8,212**	0.8	**£1,590**
Merton	3.0%	£3,022	£5,443	**£8,464**	1.1	**£1,235**
Newham	0.0%	£0	£0	**£0**	2.1	**£0**
Redbridge	1.1%	£0	£1,973	**£1,973**	1.1	**£286**
Richmond upon Thames	1.5%	£1,533	£2,835	**£4,368**	0.7	**£1,024**
Sutton	4.9%	£0	£8,622	**£8,622**	0.9	**£1,568**
Waltham Forest	3.9%	£0	£7,541	**£7,541**	1.8	**£678**

Table 4.5 SEN budgets 1995/96 for all LEAs in England

A	B	C	D	E	F	G
Metropolitan Education Authorities						
Bolton	2.2%	£1,888	£3,463	**£5,351**	1.0	**£839**
Bury	1.8%	£619	£2,866	**£3,485**	0.8	**£660**
Manchester	4.1%	£1,765	£6,766	**£8,531**	2.1	**£655**
Oldham	4.2%	£2,468	£6,961	**£9,429**	1.2	**£1,294**
Rochdale	3.0%	£1,447	£4,715	**£6,161**	1.2	**£814**
Salford	6.8%	£953	£11,178	**£12,131**	1.3	**£1,474**
Stockport	1.1%	£1,068	£1,835	**£2,903**	0.7	**£626**
Tameside	1.2%	£2,839	£1,804	**£4,643**	0.9	**£792**
Trafford	1.0%	£1,356	£1,440	**£2,796**	0.9	**£502**
Wigan	3.5%	£2,035	£6,024	**£8,060**	0.8	**£1,519**
Knowsley	5.7%	£333	£9,501	**£9,834**	1.8	**£856**
Liverpool	8.6%	£2,181	£14,734	**£16,915**	1.7	**£1,580**
St Helens	4.5%	£0	£7,619	**£7,619**	1.0	**£1,189**
Sefton	3.5%	£1,109	£5,927	**£7,036**	0.9	**£1,185**
Wirral	7.1%	£0	£11,609	**£11,609**	1.2	**£1,531**
Barnsley	2.9%	£638	£4,153	**£4,791**	1.0	**£795**
Doncaster	0.6%	£1,037	£1,012	**£2,049**	1.0	**£311**
Rotherham	1.1%	£0	£1,808	**£1,808**	1.0	**£297**
Sheffield	4.2%	£2,917	£6,437	**£9,354**	1.1	**£1,323**
Gateshead	1.9%	£4,439	£3,158	**£7,597**	1.2	**£1,037**
Newcastle upon Tyne	5.0%	£0	£8,293	**£8,293**	1.4	**£922**
North Tyneside	11.3%	£0	£18,459	**£18,459**	1.0	**£3,025**
South Tyneside	2.6%	£1,988	£4,020	**£6,009**	1.2	**£813**
Sunderland	1.9%	£1,443	£3,162	**£4,605**	1.1	**£640**
Birmingham	3.1%	£1,144	£5,358	**£6,502**	1.6	**£639**
Coventry	2.6%	£1,517	£4,616	**£6,132**	1.3	**£737**
Dudley	3.0%	£1,577	£4,817	**£6,394**	0.9	**£1,180**
Sandwell	8.6%	£1,727	£13,332	**£15,059**	1.4	**£1,761**
Solihull	2.4%	£381	£4,379	**£4,760**	0.8	**£954**
Walsall	8.2%	£1,570	£13,092	**£14,662**	1.1	**£2,137**
Wolverhampton	2.4%	£1,787	£3,959	**£5,747**	1.4	**£663**
Bradford	3.2%	£322	£5,119	**£5,441**	1.3	**£652**
Calderdale	4.0%	£0	£6,244	**£6,244**	1.0	**£958**
Kirklees	2.0%	£156	£3,191	**£3,348**	1.0	**£516**
Leeds	3.1%	£33	£5,385	**£5,419**	1.0	**£886**
Wakefield	0.9%	£1,975	£1,368	**£3,343**	0.9	**£617**

Table 4.5 continued

A	B	C	D	E	F	G
Shire County Education Authorities						
Avon	2.9%	£1,004	£5,038	**£6,042**	0.8	**£1,138**
Bedfordshire	1.4%	£2,099	£2,256	**£4,356**	1.0	**£723**
Berkshire	0.8%	£882	£1,418	**£2,300**	0.8	**£462**
Buckinghamshire	2.7%	£1,288	£4,033	**£5,320**	0.7	**£1,151**
Cambridgeshire	2.6%	£2,210	£4,051	**£6,261**	0.8	**£1,232**
Cheshire	0.5%	£2,312	£801	**£3,133**	0.8	**£638**
Cleveland	5.1%	£3,150	£8,148	**£11,298**	1.2	**£1,520**
Cornwall	0.8%	£351	£1,291	**£1,642**	0.8	**£320**
Cumbria	3.3%	£367	£5,717	**£6,083**	0.7	**£1,319**
Derbyshire	1.4%	£0	£2,182	**£2,182**	0.8	**£460**
Devon	1.5%	£500	£2,420	**£2,920**	0.8	**£552**
Dorset	3.6%	£433	£5,435	**£5,868**	0.8	**£1,207**
Durham	0.5%	£0	£732	**£732**	0.9	**£125**
East Sussex	1.5%	£2,080	£2,554	**£4,634**	0.9	**£795**
Essex	3.2%	£439	£5,190	**£5,628**	0.8	**£1,106**
Gloucestershire	1.5%	£267	£2,226	**£2,493**	0.7	**£549**
Hampshire	3.5%	£70	£5,972	**£6,042**	0.8	**£1,235**
Hereford & Worcester	1.0%	£131	£1,546	**£1,678**	0.7	**£385**
Hertfordshire	2.9%	£329	£5,044	**£5,373**	0.7	**£1,170**
Humberside	3.6%	£5,890	£5,961	**£11,851**	0.9	**£1,991**
Isle of Wight	0.6%	£2,324	£969	**£3,292**	0.9	**£570**
Kent	4.9%	£3,111	£7,748	**£10,859**	0.8	**£2,091**
Lancashire	6.3%	£1,355	£9,924	**£11,279**	1.0	**£1,875**
Leicestershire	1.1%	£3,022	£1,707	**£4,729**	0.9	**£841**
Lincolnshire	0.7%	£1,841	£1,112	**£2,953**	0.7	**£642**
Norfolk	2.9%	£368	£5,021	**£5,389**	0.8	**£1,126**
Northamptonshire	1.6%	£1,059	£2,589	**£3,648**	0.8	**£748**
Northumberland	1.4%	£533	£2,289	**£2,822**	0.7	**£656**
North Yorkshire	2.9%	£1,814	£4,842	**£6,656**	0.6	**£1,724**
Nottinghamshire	3.5%	£3,054	£5,802	**£8,856**	1.0	**£1,460**
Oxfordshire	5.1%	£282	£8,634	**£8,916**	0.7	**£2,146**
Shropshire	4.3%	£88	£6,591	**£6,679**	0.8	**£1,413**
Somerset	1.6%	£1,476	£2,716	**£4,192**	0.7	**£976**
Staffordshire	3.1%	£0	£4,596	**£4,596**	0.7	**£987**
Suffolk	0.3%	£352	£570	**£922**	0.6	**£233**
Surrey	2.5%	£0	£4,300	**£4,300**	0.6	**£1,188**
Warwickshire	5.0%	£4,731	£7,815	**£12,545**	0.7	**£2,805**
West Sussex	1.3%	£2,190	£2,217	**£4,407**	0.7	**£963**
Wiltshire	1.2%	£2,930	£1,816	**£4,746**	0.7	**£1,079**

Table 4.5 continued

Notes

1   The figures are for 1994/95, Standard Spending Assessment Handbook, Department of the Environment, Local Government Finance Policy Directorate 1994, page 3.

2   The figures are for 1994/95, Standard Spending Assessment Handbook, Department of the Environment, Local Government Finance Policy Directorate 1994. The figures are derived from pages 113 and 115.

3   The principal legislation is in Chapter III of the Education Reform Act 1988.

4   The figure is derived by summing all the allocations to schools in England which are based on measures of AEN and expressing the result as a percentage of all the delegated budgets of all schools in England. The data come from 108 LEAs' Section 42 Budget Statements.

5   Result of Consultation on Special Educational Needs Review. Report to Lambeth Education Committee 3 February 1994, Appendix 5.

6   McConville Ray and others, Indicators of Special Educational Needs. Nottingham County Council, June 1990.

7   The figures were supplied to the author by Kent LEA. They are the moderated outcome of the SEN audit. The figures are published by being supplied to individual schools.

8   London Borough of Ealing Section 42 Statement for 1995/96 and further data supplied to the author by the Borough education department.

9   The data is published in Southwark's Section 42 Budget Statement for Schools 1995/96.

10   National league table of schools. Exam results for 1994 as published in *The Times* 22 November 1994.

11   The total sum delegated to schools in each LEA was divided by the total number of pupils in the schools using data from the Section 42 budget statements 1994/95 for each of the 108 LEAs in England. The SSA per pupil was calculated from data for 1994/1995 given in the Standard Spending Assessment Handbook, Department of the Environment, Local Government Finance Policy Directorate 1994. The SSA handbook gives SSAs separately for children aged 5–10, aged 11–16 and children at school aged 16+. The separate SSAs were multiplied by the number of children in each age range and divided by the total number of children to produce an average SSA for all children in each LEA.

12   McConville Ray and others. Indicators of Special Educational Needs, Nottingham County Council, June 1990.

13   The London Borough of Ealing funds schools partly by an SEN audit and partly by a fixed amount per child eligible for FSM. In 1995/96 Ealing allocated £90.95 per child at Stage 1, £181.91 per child at Stage 2 and £545.72 at Stage 3. The percentage of children eligible for FSM in each school may be calculated directly from data in the Section 42 statement. The allocations to children at Stages 1, 2 and 3 are aggregated in the Section 42 statement. Disaggregated data were supplied by Ealing Education to the author.

14   The London Borough of Southwark allocates £1,293 per child at Stage 3 or above on the basis of an audit and additional funds on the basis of an AEN index which includes the number of children eligible for FSM. The percentages of children at Stage 3 or above in each school may be calculated directly from the 1995/96

Section 42 statement. The percentages of children eligible for FSM in each school were supplied to the author by Southwark Education.

15   The figures were supplied to the author by Kent LEA. They are the moderated outcome of the SEN audit. The figures are published by being supplied to individual schools.

16   For example *R v Secretary of State for Education, ex parte Lashford* CA [1988] 1 FLR 72 at page 85 E.

17   Figure from The Audit Commission: Local Authority Performance Indicators, as published in *The Times Education Supplement* 31 March 1995.

CHAPTER 5

Local Authority Assessments

The Legal Duty

The 1993 Education Act[1] requires the LEA to carry out an assessment of
special needs for those children who are deemed to have special
educational needs which are so serious that it is probably necessary for
the LEA to arrange the SEN provision directly rather than relying on the
school. This formal assessment is intended for a very small minority of
children who may have severe and complex special needs. The Code of
Practice states that:

> The needs of the great majority of children who have special educational
> needs should be met effectively under the school-based stages, without the
> statutory involvement of the local education authority. But in a minority of
> cases, perhaps two per cent of children, the LEA will need to make a statutory
> assessment of special educational needs.
>
> (Paragraph 3:1 Code of Practice, DfE, 1994a)

The Code of Practice recommends that three school-based stages of
assessment are followed in a process of continuous assessment and
evaluation over time before formal assessment is initiated at Stage 4 or
a statement issued at Stage 5.

The Decision to Assess

The decision to assess is made by the LEA in whose area the child lives
following a referral by the child's school or other agency, or following a
formal request by a parent.

Referral by the School

When making a referral for statutory assessment, the school should state clearly the reasons for referral, and include the following information:

- the recorded views of parents and, where appropriate the child, on the earlier stages of assessment and any action and support to date
- evidence of health checks
- evidence relating to Social Services involvement where appropriate
- written Individual Education Plans (IEPs) at Stages 2 and 3
- reviews of each IEP indicating decisions made as a result
- evidence of the involvement of professionals with relevant specialist knowledge and expertise from outside the school.

This means that the school is recommended to produce evidence that the earlier stages of assessment have been followed, and that the child's progress and difficulties have been recorded and evaluated over time, and that the school has already used its own resources to support the child.

Request by the Parent

The parent has a right to request that the LEA carry out a statutory assessment.[2] The LEA must comply with such a request, unless it has already made a statutory assessment within six months of the date of the request, or it concludes on the basis of evidence that a statutory assessment is not necessary, in which case the parent may appeal to the SEN Tribunal against the LEA's refusal.

In the case of children already attending school a statutory assessment will only be appropriate after the staged approach has been followed by the school unless the circumstances are truly exceptional and the staged approach is clearly not in the child's best interests.

With respect to children entering primary school or seeking assessment before entry, the staged approach is neither necessary nor good practice. What is called for is prompt identification and provision. For children entering secondary school at the usual age or entering a primary or secondary school at an age other than the usual age, prompt identification and provision is again important. In any case past failure by a school should not cause or contribute to a delay in making a statement if it is necessary.

The LEA must make a decision on a parental request for an assessment within six weeks. A referral from a school does not impose any time limit on the LEA. Almost without exception the school will have sought the agreement of the parent before the school makes a referral. It is likely to save time if a referral is endorsed by the parent in plain words such as:

I, ..., the parent of .... hereby make a request under Section 172 or Section 173 of the Education Act 1993 that you carry out an assessment of my child.

Signed.................................Dated...............................

Time Limits

The procedure for a statutory assessment is set out in detail in the Education (Special Educational Needs) Regulations 1994 which are reproduced in full in Appendix 3. The Regulations contain a mandatory time limit for each stage of the assessment procedure. These are summarized in Table 5.1.

From	To	Time limit
Referral by school for assessment	Response from LEA	No limit
Request for assessment by parent	Decision by LEA	6 weeks
Decision to assess	Decision by LEA whether or not to issue a statement	10 weeks
Decision to issue a statement	Service of a proposed statement	2 weeks
Service of the proposed statement	Service of the final statement	8 weeks
	Total	**26 weeks**

Table 5.1 Time limits on stages of assessment

There are exceptions to the time limits. The exceptions to the six week time limit within which LEAs must tell parents whether they will or will not make a statutory assessment are:

- where the LEA has requested advice from a head teacher just before the school closes for a continuous period of more than four weeks, e.g. school holidays
- where there are exceptional personal circumstances affecting the child or parents
- where the child or the parents are absent from the area of the LEA for a continuous period of more than four weeks.

The exceptions to the ten week time limit within which LEAs must make an assessment are:

- in exceptional cases where further advice is needed following receipt of full advice
- where the parents want to provide advice for an assessment more than six weeks after the date on which the LEA's request for advice was received
- where the LEA requested educational advice during a period just before the school closes for a continuous period of more than four weeks
- where the LEA has requested advice from a health or social services authority and the authority has not replied within six weeks
- where there are exceptional personal circumstances affecting the child or parents
- where the child or parents are absent from the area of LEA for a continuous period of more than four weeks
- where the child fails to honour an appointment for an examination or test.

Statutory Assessment

Once the LEA has decided that there should be an assessment, it must send a formal notice to the parents setting out: the proposal to assess, procedures to be followed and a Named Officer to go to for further information; and the parents' rights to make representations about the proposal within 29 days of the date that the notice is served.[2]

This means that parents have 29 days to make representations to the LEA. The LEA will wait to hear from parents before going ahead. The Named Officer is a person in the LEA who will provide parents with further information concerning the statutory assessment procedure. There is no statutory right of appeal against an LEA's decision to make a formal assessment.

Having decided to carry out an assessment, the LEA will list the professionals whom it intends to ask for advice, and should ask parents for the names of anyone they wish to be consulted. Parents should also be given information about the full range of provision available in mainstream and special schools in the LEA, in order that they can consider the options from an early stage. Some LEAs arrange for the letter and other information to be delivered by hand in order that the parents are able to ask questions. In the case of parents who are not fluent in English an interpreter may be needed to ensure that the parents understand the procedure.

The LEA is required[3] to seek advice from the child's parent, a teacher, a doctor and an educational psychologist plus advice from the Social Services Department and 'any other advice which the LEA considers appropriate for the purpose of arriving at a satisfactory assessment'. The advice must be written and must provide information on:

(a) the educational, medical, psychological and other features of the case...which appear to be relevant to the child's educational needs (including his likely future needs)
(b) how these features could affect the child's educational needs, and
(c) the provision which is appropriate for the child in the light of those features of the child's case, whether by way of special educational provision or non-educational provision,...

Educational Advice

The educational advice will normally be provided by the child's head teacher or other teacher who knows the child, and will include the steps which have already been taken by the school to help the child, and the results of the Code of Practice earlier stages of assessment and the IEPs.

Medical Advice

The medical advice must be obtained from a registered medical practitioner who will normally be a specially designated school medical officer.

Psychological Advice

The psychological advice will be provided by an educational psychologist regularly employed by the LEA or engaged by the LEA as an educational psychologist in the case in question. The advice will be based on an assessment of the kind described in Chapter 3

When all the advice is assembled, the LEA may hold a case conference to decide whether to it is necessary to determine the special educational provision and to make a statement, or it may examine the evidence and decide on that basis.

The LEA then has a further two weeks either to write the draft or proposed statement or to draft a notice of the LEA's decision not to make a statement, containing the reasons for this decision and the evidence used to reach the decision. Attached to the draft statement will be all the evidence (advice) used by the LEA to draw up the draft statement, and a letter from the LEA explaining that parents may express a preference for a school.

The Code of Practice suggests that the LEA should consider issuing its decision not to make a statement in the form of a note in lieu of a statement. This note would probably follow the statutory format of a statement, but would have a different legal status. It informs the parent and school of the LEA's view of the child's needs and the appropriate provision. The school would not be obliged to make the provision suggested by the LEA.

The parents have 15 days by which to express a preference for a school, or to make representations to the LEA about the contents of the statement, or in which to meet with an officer from the LEA to discuss the proposed statement, and a further 15 days following such a meeting to require that further meetings be arranged with professionals with whose advice they disagree. The aim of this period is to ensure that parents express a preference for a school and understand the advice which led to the proposed statement.

Following the draft or proposed statement, the LEA has to consider parental representations and either make the statement of special educational needs unchanged or modified, adding the name of the school in part 4, or it may decide not to make a statement. In the latter case the LEA must inform the parents of the decision and their right to appeal to the SEN Tribunal.

Notes

1   Section 167 (2) of the Education Act 1993.
2   Section 167 (1) of the Education Act 1993.
3   Schedule 9 to the Education Act 1993 and Regulations 6 to 9 of the Education (Special Educational Needs) Regulations 1994.

CHAPTER 6
Statements of Special Educational Needs

Introduction

A statement of SEN may be issued by an LEA following a formal assessment (described in Chapter 5). The main purpose of a statement is to ensure that individual children with very serious difficulties have their needs assessed and the appropriate provision is identified and delivered. All children in special schools are expected to have statements as well as a small number of children in mainstream schools. A statement is a legal document which must be set out in accordance with detailed legislation. It obliges the LEA for the area in which a child lives to arrange the provision specified in it. When a child with a statement moves from one school to another or one LEA to another, the new school or LEA are bound by the statement.

Though the legislation defines a set of circumstances in which the LEA is obliged to make a statement, the definition is subjective and dependent on the policies of the particular LEA. The 1993 Education Act has increased the rights of parents with respect to the practice and procedure in drawing up statements and the Code of Practice stresses the importance of involving the child. The SEN Tribunal provides an independent national body to arbitrate in disputes between parents and LEAs about the decision to make a statement and the contents of a statement.

Normally a statement ensures that additional staff time and resources are allocated to an individual child. Any child is likely to benefit from such attention, but each decision to make a statement will transfer resources from educational funds in general to a specific child. A balance needs to be struck. In finding that balance there are bound to be disagreements between LEAs and parents and between LEAs and schools.

This chapter first describes the factors which affect the decision to issue a statement. It then describes the contents of a statement and finally discusses the effect of a statement in securing provision for the child.

Decision to make a statement

A statement of SEN is a description of a child's needs and a specification of the provision to be made for them. The LEA is obliged to arrange for the specified provision to be made and the child has a right to receive the provision. That right can be enforced. Having carried out an assessment the LEA must decide whether or not to issue a statement. If the LEA decides that a statement is necessary, the LEA issues a proposed statement for discussion with the parents. A final statement is only issued after the parental views have been considered.

Where the assessment shows that a placement in a special school might be necessary, the LEA should issue a proposed statement.[1] Where a mainstream school is the likely provision, the predominant factor which the LEA should consider when deciding whether to issue a statement is the cost of making the necessary provision:

> The main ground on which the LEA may decide that they must make a statement is when the LEA conclude that all the special educational provision necessary to meet the child's needs cannot reasonably be provided within the resources normally available to mainstream schools in the area.
>
> (Paragraph 4:2 Code of Practice, DfE, 1994a)

The Code of Practice calls for the decision to be based on an analysis of available resources. The resources are the school budget, the school buildings and any services which are provided by the LEA centrally. (An analysis of school budgets is discussed in Chapter 4.)

The severity or complexity of the needs are inextricably linked with the cost of the necessary provision. Taken alone the severity and complexity of the needs cannot determine whether a statement is necessary. However, the Code of Practice retains the concept that 2 per cent of children will require statements:

> The needs of the great majority of children who have special educational needs should be met effectively under the school-based stages, without statutory involvement of the local education authority. But in a minority of cases, perhaps two per cent of children, the LEA will need to make a statutory assessment of special educational needs.
>
> (Paragraph 3:1 Code of Practice, DfE, 1994a)

There is some contradiction between the 2 per cent notion which suggests a national standard level of need which calls for a statement to be made, and the resource-based approach which is expected to produce widely different results in different LEAs. The Code of Practice provides a suggestion of the level of provision which might necessitate a statement, but immediately qualifies this by drawing attention to the importance of funding arrangements in the LEA:

> but if, as a result of a statutory assessment, the LEA conclude that, for example, the child requires:
>
> – regular direct teaching by a specialist teacher
> – daily individual support from a non-teaching assistant
> – a significant piece of equipment such as a closed circuit television or a computer or CD-ROM device with appropriate ancillaries and software
> – a major building adaption such as the installation of a lift, or
> – the regular involvement of non-educational agencies
>
> the LEA may conclude that the school could not reasonably be expected to make such provision within its own resources and the nature of the provision suggests that the LEA should formally identify in a statement the child's needs, the full range of provision to be made and the review arrangements that will apply. The LEA's conclusions will, of course, depend on the precise circumstances of each case, taking into account arrangements for funding schools in the area.
>
> (Paragraph 4:11 Code of Practice DfE, 1994a)

In conclusion, all children who are or might be in a special school should have a statement. For children in mainstream schools the decision to issue a statement will be based predominantly on the funding arrangements for schools but some weight may be given to the 2 per cent figure. At present LEAs maintain statements on between 1.2 per cent and 5.2 per cent of children.[2] Where a child falls outside the 2 per cent, LEAs may be expected to make reference to that in the grounds for refusing to issue a statement. Adequate school-based provision for SEN should reduce the need for statements and therefore LEAs are likely to reduce the proportion of children for whom statements are issued.

Contents of a Statement

A statement must describe all the child's special educational needs and specify provision for those needs. Regulations describe the form and content of a statement of SEN in considerable detail.[3] The statement must be set out in six parts each of which is described below.

Part 1: Introduction

Part I contains the name and address of the child and of the parents and other such information..

Part 2: Special Educational Needs

Part 2 is required to set out the child's special educational needs, in terms of the child's learning difficulties which call for special educational provision. All the special educational needs of the child must be set out, including those which of themselves would not be sufficient to warrant a statement. Any dispute about that proposition was resolved by the Court of Appeal in *ex parte E*:

> A child has special educational needs if he has a learning difficulty which requires special educational provision. Of course, a child may have more than one learning difficulty. If the special educational provision which the child requires for all his needs can be determined, and provided, by his ordinary school then no statement ... is necessary. But once the local education authority have decided that they are required to determine that some educational provision should be made for him, they have to maintain a statement ... in respect of that child, not in respect of any particular learning difficulty that he may have. Then the statement must specify, in Part 2, the authority's assessment of the special educational needs of the child – ... - and, in Part 3, the special educational provision to be made for the purpose of meeting those needs.[4]

The gaps in the quotation above are references to the Education Act 1981. The material parts are unchanged in the Education Act 1993.

Part 3: Special Educational Provision

Part 3 is divided into three sub-sections: objectives, educational provision to meet needs and objectives, and monitoring.

Objectives

The LEA must specify the objectives which the SEN provision for the child should aim to meet.

Educational provision to meet needs and objectives

The LEA is required to specify all the appropriate facilities, equipment, staffing arrangements and curriculum and any appropriate modifications to or disapplications from the National Curriculum. That was emphasized by the Court in *ex parte* E and is repeated in The Code of Practice:

> the second sub-section should set out *all* the special educational provision that the LEA consider appropriate for *all* the learning difficulties identified in Part 2, even where some of the provision is to be made by direct intervention on the part of the authority and some is to be made by the child's school within its own resources. It may be helpful for the LEA to specify which elements of the provision are to be made by the school, and which are to be made by the LEA.
>
> The provision set out in this sub-section should normally be specific, detailed and quantified (in terms, for example, of hours of ancillary or specialist teaching support) although there will be cases where some flexibility should be retained in order to meet the changing special educational needs of the child concerned.
>
> (Paragraph 4:28, Code of Practice, DfE, 1994a)

A great many statements have been written which fail to meet this standard. A specification such as, 'she should have regular help with her maths work in class', is not only inadequate but also unlawful. The court in *ex parte E* said: 'The statement is no ordinary form. Part 2 may be compared to a medical diagnosis and Part 3 to a prescription for the needs diagnosed'.[5]

The sub-section should specify any speech therapy that is required as educational provision. The difference between speech therapy as educational provision and as medical treatment was defined by the court in *ex parte M*:

> To teach an adult who has lost his larynx because of cancer might well be considered as treatment rather than education. But to teach a child who has never been able to communicate by language, whether because of some chromosomal disorder as in the *Oxfordshire* case, or because of some social cause (e.g because his parents are themselves unable to speak, and thus he cannot learn by example as normally happens) seems to us just as much educational provision as to teach a child to communicate by writing.[6]

The Code of Practice merely acknowledges that speech therapy may be regarded as either educational or non-educational provision.[7] If a child requires speech therapy it is important that the therapy be specified in Part 3, because the LEA must arrange the provision specified in Part 3. Neither the LEA nor the health authority are obliged to arrange speech therapy if it is only specified in Part 6.

Schools must teach the National Curriculum to all children, but there are two exceptions for individual children. A headteacher may modify or disapply the National Curriculum for a period of up to six months[8] and a modification or disapplication may be specified in a statement.[9] This should rarely be necessary in a mainstream primary school. In a mainstream secondary school disapplication of one or more subjects may be used to permit concentrated work in other areas.

Children with special educational needs are entitled in some circumstances to assistance and concessions in public examinations. Concessions might include extra time in the examination, a person to read the exam paper, the use of a word-processor, or an amanuensis (a person to take down a dictated answer). Concessions are granted by the exam boards on the basis of an application from the school supported by evidence. A statement is not the only evidence that may be used but would usually be conclusive. If the child is approaching public examinations it may be helpful to specify appropriate concessions in the statement.

Monitoring.

The statement must specify arrangements for monitoring the child's progress towards the objectives and for the setting and monitoring of targets which are steps towards the objectives. The targets for the time being should not be described in the statement.

Part 4: Placement

In the proposed statement the LEA is forbidden from specifying a type of school or naming a school.[10] Instead the LEA asks the parent to state a preference for a school and give reasons within 15 days of service of the proposed statement. In the final statement the LEA must specify the type of school that is appropriate. such as mainstream, special or boarding and the name of a school.[11]

The school named in the final statement is of overriding importance. The name of a state school on a statement gives the child a right to attend that school and the governors must admit the child.[12] The LEA must name the school chosen by the parents unless:
  (a) the school is unsuitable for the child's age, ability or aptitude or to his special educational needs, or
  (b) the attendance of the child at the school would be incompatible with the provision of efficient education for the children with whom he would be educated or the efficient use of resources.[13]

If the parent does not express a preference for a school, the LEA must name an appropriate school in the final statement.

Those criteria are the same as the admission criteria which apply to schools generally,[14] except for one important difference: the right of religious schools to refuse admission on grounds of faith does not apply to children for whom a statement has been made.

'Ability and aptitude' refers to selective schools; either the old grammar schools or those grant-maintained schools which use some form of test or selection to chose which applicants to accept. The tests may be applied to children with statements in the same way as to other children.

'Incompatible with the provision of efficient education' means, roughly speaking, that the school is full for that year group.[15] In the case of a child with a statement seeking entry to a year group that is full, the LEA, having consulted the school governors, must balance the reasons given by the parent for preferring the particular school against the disadvantage to the children already at the school of having that additional child in their class.

A child with a statement naming a school which the child intends entering at the usual age, will take precedence over all other children seeking admission to that school. The decision to name the school on the statement takes place separately from the normal admission procedure. In the normal procedure, an oversubscribed school will survey all the applicants for places on a certain date and prioritize them in accordance with the published admission criteria. Provided the statement is made before that date, the attendance of the child at the school cannot be incompatible with the provision of efficient education for the children with whom that child would be educated because no such children have yet been ascertained. Therefore the LEA must name the preferred school in the statement.

It follows that parents who are able to ensure that a statement is issued or amended at the right time, can secure entry to any comprehensive state school of their choice, provided that mainstream education is appropriate for the child. It is reasonable to suppose that this opportunity, which has been granted to all children with statements, will be used to greater advantage by middle-class parents.

LEAs are obliged to provide free transport to school for children who must travel more than three miles from home to school, or more than two miles if the child is under 8 years old.[16] The obligation can be discharged by the LEA offering the child a place at a suitable school which is within walking distance. That rule applies even where the more distant school is specified in a statement.[17]

It is advisable for parents to raise the question of free transport at the time that the statement is being written and to ask the LEA whether free transport to the named school will be provided. There is nothing to prevent provision of free school transport from being entered in Part 6 of the statement as non-educational provision which the LEA intends to make. On the other hand there is nothing in the legislation or the Code of Practice which suggests that the question of free transport should be resolved in this way.

Part 5: Non-educational Needs

The LEA must specify the non-educational needs of the child, if some provision is required so that the child can benefit from the SEN provision specified in Part 3.[18] The Code of Practice suggests that:

> Part 5 should specify any non-educational needs of the child which the LEA either propose to meet or are satisfied will be met, by arrangement or otherwise, by the health services, social services department or some other body.
>
> (Paragraph 4:3 Code of Practice, DfE, 1994a)

There is no legal basis for the suggestion that non-educational needs should only be specified if the LEA is satisfied that they will be met. On the contrary the needs must be specified if the LEA considers provision appropriate whether or not provision will be made.

Part 5 should refer to the need for any medical treatment that is relevant to the school, such as drug treatments for asthma or epilepsy. It should refer to any need for aids such as spectacles, hearing aids and other aids for children with physical disabilities. Provision of this kind is generally agreed as being non-educational.

There are a number of types of provision that are on the borderline between educational provision and non-educational provision. Speech therapy has already been mentioned in this context. Counselling for children with behavioural difficulties may be on the borderline, as is physiotherapy in some circumstances. It is advantageous to have any borderline provision specified in Part 3 as educational provision.

Part 6: Non-educational Provision

The LEA must specify any non-educational provision which the LEA proposes to make available or which it is satisfied will be made available by a district health authority, a social services authority or some other body, including arrangements for its provision. Also to be specified are the objectives of the provision, and arrangements for monitoring the progress in meeting those objectives.[19] Before specifying non-educational provision in Part 6, the LEA should have the clear agreement of any other authority that the other authority intends to make the provision.

In this Part the mandatory requirement is for specification of provision that is going to be made. Where necessary the LEA is expected to request assistance from the health authority or social services authority. An authority whose help is so requested must comply with the request unless–

> they consider that the help requested is not necessary for the purpose of the exercise by the local education authority of those functions, or

> in the case of a District Health Authority, if that authority consider that, having regard to the resources available to them for the purpose of the exercise of their functions under the National Health Services Act 1977, it is not reasonable for them to comply with the request, or

> in the case of a local authority, if that authority consider that the request is not compatible with their own statutory or other duties and obligations or unduly prejudices the discharge of any of their functions.[20]

These authorities do not have to assist the LEA if they disagree with the LEA's assessment or if the assistance would cost too much or if resources are rationed by an established policy or criteria and the child does not meet those criteria. Conflict may be expected over the provision of speech therapy, physiotherapy and psychotherapy or counselling. Health and social service authorities are operating policies of allocating or rationing resources. Meeting the needs of a particular child would not be reasonable and would prejudice the discharge of functions, if meeting the needs was contrary to an existing policy or gave the child undue priority.[21]

Finally the statement must be dated and signed by a duly authorized officer of the LEA.

Arranging the Provision

The LEA must arrange the SEN provision specified in the statement, unless the parent has made suitable alternative arrangements.[22] The mandatory duty to arrange the SEN provision specified in Part 3 of the statement gives the child the right to that provision. Failure to arrange the SEN provision is a breach of statutory duty by the LEA.

The position with respect to provision specified in Part 6 is slightly different. Provision may only be specified if the LEA proposes to make it available or is satisfied that it will be made available. By entering the provision in this section the LEA is asserting that the provision will be made. The assertion is probably sufficient to give rise to a legitimate expectation. A legitimate expectation is a legal right which the court will recognize and enforce. (This is discussed further in Chapter 11.)

The meaning of 'arrange' presents something of a problem as the court acknowledged in *ex parte E*:

> The relationship between a local education authority and school governors is a thorny topic. In the absence of a specific example before the court, I do not think that it would be right to express a view as to what is required by the word 'arrange' ...; it may perhaps have been deliberately chosen as an expression that is different from 'procure' or 'ensure'. ... [I am not persuaded] that all the special educational provision in a statement must be such as is in the authority's business to provide.[23]

The difficulty arises because legislation and case law permit an LEA to write statements which purport to bind schools to make specific provision from within their delegated budgets, but the school governors do not have an express duty to comply. The relevant statutory duty imposed on governors is to:

> use their best endeavours, in exercising their functions in relation to the school, to secure that if any registered pupil has special educational needs the special educational provision which his learning difficulty calls for is made.[24]

Where the statement says the provision will be made or paid for by the LEA, there can be no doubt that the LEA must do what the statement says. Where the statement does not say who is to make the provision, the responsibility lies with the LEA to take some action to ensure that the provision is made. Where the statement says that the provision will be made by the school from within its own resources, that could be all that is required of the LEA. An LEA arranges education in general by setting up schools and giving them budgets. Provided the LEA has properly allocated funds to schools for making some of the provision for children with statements, the LEA may be said to have arranged the SEN provision. That logic is more difficult to apply to a grant-maintained school, because the school is not part of the arrangements made by the LEA.

If the specified provision is not being made, the parent may complain to the Secretary of State for Education, who will have to sort out where responsibility lies.

Annual reviews

The LEA may alter a statement at any time by notifying the parents of the proposed alteration, considering the parents' views and then making a decision.[25] In addition, there are two more complex and considered routes by which a statement can be amended: a further assessment and a review. A further assessment follows the same procedure as an original assessment and can be initiated by the LEA of its own volition or by the parent making a request.[26] The parent may appeal to the SEN Tribunal against the refusal of such a request.

The procedure for a review, which must be carried out annually,[27] is mandatory and very detailed. The following steps are required.[28]

1 The LEA initiates the review by sending a notice to the school.
2 The school seeks written advice from the parent, the relevant teacher or teachers and any one else appropriate.
3 The school sends the advice received to a representative of the LEA, the parent, the teachers and anyone else appropriate together with an invitation to a meeting.
4 The meeting makes recommendations in particular whether the statement should be amended. If the persons at the meeting cannot agree then dissenting recommendations are to be made.
5 The head teacher writes a report, which includes the head teacher's view on whether the statement should be amended and refers to any differences between the head teacher's views and those of the meeting.
6 The head teacher sends the report to the LEA and to everyone invited to the meeting and to anyone else appropriate.
7 The LEA review the statement in the light of the head teacher's report and other relevant information and make recommendations.
8 The LEA send copies of their recommendations to the school, the parent, everyone invited to the meeting and anyone else appropriate.

The head teacher may, and in larger schools usually would, delegate this duty to the SEN coordinator, who would chair the meeting.

The procedure for amending a statement after a review requires formal notification to be sent to the parents.[29] That notification could be combined with Stage 8 of the annual review, but the parents must be given a further opportunity to make representations to the LEA. Having considered those representations the LEA then notifies the parents of its decision. If the decision is to amend the statement, the LEA must inform the parents of their right to appeal to the SEN Tribunal.

Where, following an annual review, the LEA decides not to amend a statement, there is no appeal. The parent could seek a further assessment in order to bring the matter within the jurisdiction of the SEN Tribunal.

Once the meeting at the school with the involvement of the LEA, teachers, other specialists and parents has unanimously agreed that a statement should be amended in a particular way, the LEA ought to accept that recommendation unless there are good reasons for rejecting it. Where the LEA rejects a unanimous recommendation to amend a statement without adequate reasons or for unlawful reasons an application for judicial review is appropriate. It may be argued that, in setting out such an elaborate procedure for annual reviews, parliament intended the recommendations of the meeting at the school to be decisive.

Some support for that view may be found in the case of *ex parte M*. The case concerns a different area of local authority provision and a different procedure so the decision is not directly applicable. M, who was aged 22 and had Down's Syndrome, required a place in a residential home which Avon County Council were obliged to provide. M had set his mind on a particular home which would cost more than an alternative proposed by the Council. The matter was placed before an independent review panel.[30] The review panel, having heard evidence and cross-examined witnesses, concluded that M's entrenched view was a part of M's psychological needs which arose out of his disability. They recommended that M be placed in the home which he wanted. Avon Social Services committee rejected that recommendation. In quashing Avon's decision the court said:

> But the making of the final decision did not lie with the review panel. It lay with the social services committee. I would be reluctant to hold (and do not) that in no circumstances whatsoever could the social services committee have overruled the review panel's recommendation in the exercise of their legal right and duty to consider it. ... But I have no hesitation in finding that they could not overrule that decision without a substantial reason and without having given that recommendation the weight it required. It was a decision taken by a body entrusted with the basic fact-finding exercise under the complaints procedure. It was arrived at after a convincing examination of the evidence, particularly the expert evidence. The evidence before them had, as to the practicalities, been largely one way. The panel had directed themselves properly in law, and had arrived at a decision in line with the strength of the evidence before them. They had given clear reasons and they had raised the crucial factual question with the parties before arriving at their conclusion.

> The strength, coherence, and apparent persuasiveness of that decision had to be addressed head on if it were to be set aside and not followed. These

difficulties were not faced either by the respondents' officers in their paper to the social services committee, or by the social services committee themselves. ... It seems to me that you do not properly reconsider a decision when, on the evidence, it does not seem that that decision was given the weight it deserved. That is, to my judgement, what the social services committee failed to do here. To neglect to do that is not a question which merely ... impugns the credibility of the review panel, but instead ignores the weight to which it is prima facie entitled because of its place in the statutory procedure, and further, pays no attention to the scope of its hearing and clear reasons that it had given.[31]

Termination of a statement

A statement may only be terminated by a formal procedure, which is started by the LEA serving a notice on the parent of the decision to cease to maintain the statement.[32] There is no statutory opportunity for the parent to make representations; instead there is an immediate right of appeal to the SEN Tribunal.

Notes

1   Paragraph 4: 11, Code of Practice on the Identification and Assessment of Special Educational Needs, DfE, 1994a.
2   Audit Commission, Local Authority Standards of Performance indicators 1994 as published in the *Times Educational Supplement* 31 March 1994.
3   Regulation 13 of the Education (Special Educational Needs) Regulations 1994 requires that the statement is substantially in the form set out in Part B of the Regulations and shall contain the information specified in that form. The standard form in Part B is in six sections. Under each section is a short description of the information which must be included in a statement.
4   *R v Secretary of State for Education, ex parte E* CA [1992] 1 FLR 377, Balcombe LJ at page 388 F.
5   *R v Secretary of State for Education, ex parte E* CA [1992] 1 FLR 377, Balcombe LJ at page 388 B approving the words of Nolan J in the High Court.
6   *R v Lancashire County Council, ex parte M* CA [1989] 2 FLR 279, Balcombe LJ at page 301 G.
7   Paragraph 4:34, Code of Practice on the Identification and Assessment of Special Educational Needs, DfE, 1994a.
8   Section 19 of the Education Reform Act 1988.
9   Section 18 of the Education Reform Act 1988.
10   Paragraph 2 of Schedule 10 to the Education Act 1993.
11   Part B of the Education (Special Educational Needs) Regulations.

12   Section 168 (5) (b) of the Education Act 1993.

13   Paragraph 3 (3) of Schedule 10 to the Education Act 1993.

14   Section 6 of the Education Act 1980.

15   Section 27 of the Education Act 1988 set out a procedure for determining standard admission numbers for schools. Section 26 of the Education Act 1988 requires schools to admit pupils up to the admission number if there are sufficient applicants who are not disqualified by ability, aptitude or religious belief. Once the standard admission number has been reached, admission may be refused on the grounds that further admissions would be incompatible with the provision of efficient education.

16   Section 55 of the Education Act 1944.

17   See for example *R v Essex County Council, ex parte C* QBD (1993) 92 LGR 46. The court stated in *R v Dyfed County Council, ex parte S* CA [1994] *The Times* 25 July, that whether or not a school is suitable is a matter for the LEA to decide and not for the parents.

18   Part B of the Education (Special Educational Needs) Regulations.

19   Part B of the Education (Special Educational Needs) Regulations.

20   Section 166 (2) of the Education Act 1993.

21   A very similar provision was considered by the House of Lords in connection with provision of housing for homeless children in *R v Northavon District Council, ex parte Smith* HL [1994] 2 FLR 671. A housing authority has a duty to provide permanent housing for homeless families who have young children provided that the homelessness is unintentional. The housing authority decided that the Smith family was intentionally homeless and so the full housing duty did not arise. The Children Act 1989 imposes powers and duties on the social services authority to safeguard and promote the welfare of children, including a power to request help from a housing authority. Section 27 (2) of the Children Act imposes on the housing authority so requested a qualified duty to comply which is in the same form as Section 166 (3) (b) of the Education Act 1993. After the housing authority had determined that it had no duty to house the Smiths under the homeless provisions, the application was entered on the council housing waiting list along with 2,632 other persons. The social services department then made a request that the housing authority help the social services department by providing the family with permanent housing. The housing authority refused to comply. The House of Lords affirmed that the refusal was lawful. The Smiths were not entitled to priority over other homeless persons or other persons on the housing waiting list.

22   Section 168 (5) of the Education Act 1993.

23   *R v Secretary of State for Education, ex parte E* CA [1992] 1 FLR 377, Staughton LJ at page 392 D.

24   Section 161 (1) (a) of the Education Act 1993.

25   Paragraphs 9 and 10 of Schedule 10 to the Education Act 1993.

26   Section 172 (2) of the Education Act 1993.

27   Section 172 (5) (b) of the Education Act 1993.

28   Regulation 15 of the Education (Special Educational Needs) Regulations 1993.

29   The notice is required by Paragraph 10 of Schedule 10 to the Education Act 1993. The procedure is the same whether the proposal to amend follows an annual review or arises in another way.

30   Review panels are set up under the Local Authority Social Services (Complaints Procedure) Order 1990.
31   *R v Avon County Council, ex parte M* QBD [1994] 2 FLR 1006, Henry J at page 1019 F.
32   Paragraph 11 of Schedule 10 to the Education Act 1993.

CHAPTER 7

Local Resolution of Complaints

Introduction

The second part of this book deals with complaints about SEN provision for individual children. There are four different statutory complaints mechanisms. They are complaint to the Secretary of State, complaint to the Local Government Ombudsman, appeal to the SEN Tribunal and application to the High Court. The formal complaints procedures are described in the next four chapters. The selection of the appropriate complaint mechanism is not always straightforward. In the case of complaint to the Secretary of State and complaint to the Local Government Ombudsman, making the complaint is easy but the resolution of the complaint may take between one and two years. Appeal to the SEN Tribunal and application to the High Court require a considerable amount of work by or on behalf of the parent.

Reaching an agreement with the school or LEA at an early stage can save considerable time and trouble, but this may not be easy. In order to meet increasingly tight budgets in recent years, schools have increased the number of children in a class so reducing the amount of individual attention available from the teacher and increasing the demand for SEN provision. The levels of provision suggested by the Code of Practice will not normally be possible within current school budgets. Schools and LEAs which are performing reasonably well may nevertheless fail to meet parents' expectations.

The Class Teacher or Form Tutor

Any concern about a child at school should usually be raised in the first instance with the class teacher or form tutor. In primary school this is likely to be possible at the end of the school day without an appointment. In secondary school it is expected that making an appointment will be necessary. It would be highly unusual for a class teacher or form tutor not to arrange a meeting with a parent promptly following such a request. The expectation is that the school will welcome and encourage discussion with parents.

The class teacher or form tutor is responsible for how each child is taught in class. A teacher should be aware of the strengths and weaknesses of each individual child and to ensure that both teaching technique and expectations are appropriate and, as far as necessary, different for each child.

The Head Teacher or a Senior Teacher

Where extra individual help or equipment is needed for a child the agreement of a more senior teacher, the SEN coordinator or the head teacher will almost certainly be required. The appropriate person to agree extra provision will vary from school to school. It is expected that the right person will be pleased to arrange a meeting with a parent in the hope of agreeing about any extra help that is needed and can be provided.

The Governors

The head teacher is responsible for the day-to-day management of the school and will play a major part in policy making, but the governors have overall responsibility for most of the conduct of the school. It is the governors who hire and fire staff, direct spending within the school and create the school policy on curriculum, discipline and SEN.

In ordinary state schools (county schools), the governing body is made up of governors who are appointed by the LEA following the local council elections, together with parent governors who are elected by the parents, teacher governors elected by the teachers and various co-opted governors. No one of these groups will be so numerous as to have control of a county school. Each governor is appointed or elected for a period of four years. An election for a parent governor will be held when any parent governor's four-year term expires. The governing body must elect a chair annually. The chair has the power to make urgent decisions in between the meetings of the full governing body. The conduct of the governing body and its meetings is controlled the Education (School Government) Regulations 1989, Statutory Instrument 1503/89.

In the case of voluntary schools the governing body will be dominated by governors nominated by the foundation. Most of the voluntary schools are Catholic or Church of England schools and the majority of the governors are nominated by those churches. In addition to the powers of county schools, the governing body decides the admission criteria, though the criteria must be approved by the LEA if the school is to refuse entry to children when the school has available places.

In grant-maintained schools the governing body is self-perpetuating. The first governors appointed by the Secretary of State when the school became grant-maintained appoint their own successors. In addition there are parent and teacher governors elected as in county schools.

The governing bodies of schools are required to meet at least once a term and usually meet more often. Most governing bodies also have some sub-committees handling particular areas of responsibility. Some governing bodies have a sub-committee responsible for SEN. Some governing bodies have appointed an individual governor to ensure that the governors discharge their legal duties with respect to SEN.

Having met the class teacher or form tutor and the appropriate senior teacher, a parent who remains dissatisfied should approach the governing body. A good starting point is one of the parent governors. The names of all the governors and the way to contact them must be provided by the school and published in the Annual Report to Parents. Any governor, including the chair of the governors, should be willing to meet a parent, listen carefully to any problem and take steps to bring about a resolution. A meeting with the chair of the governors has good prospects of being effective.

Formal Complaint to the Governors

Schools are not required to have any formal mechanism for dealing with complaints, except in relation to admission, expulsion and a suspension of the requirements of the National Curriculum. In these areas a specific decision by a head teacher may be the subject of an appeal to the governing body. The governing body and/or the LEA must have a system for hearing such appeals.

Governors must publish information about 'any arrangements made by the governing body relating to the treatment of complaints from parents of pupils with special educational needs concerning the provision made at the school'.[1]

The DfE advises that a school's SEN policy:

should make clear to parents and children with special educational needs how they can make a complaint about the provision made for their child at the school and how that complaint will subsequently be dealt with by the school. Such information could include the time targets in which the school aims to respond.[2]

There is a strong expectation that schools will have a formal complaints procedure but no absolute requirement that they should do so. Many schools have extended their existing appeals procedure to deal with complaints or instituted a separate complaints procedure. A complaints procedure might be as follows:

Complaints Procedure

1   Any person with sufficient interest in the school including a pupil of the school may complain to the Governing Body about any matter relevant to them which is within the powers of the Governing Body.

2   A complaint must be in writing and delivered to the Clerk to the Governing Body.

3   The Clerk to the Governing Body shall deliver a complaint to the chair of the Complaints Sub-committee.

4   The chair of the Complaints Sub-committee may stay a complaint where reasonable steps have not been taken to resolve the dispute informally. Such a stay must be delivered to the complainant in writing together with an explanation of the informal steps which ought to be taken.

5   If the complaint has not been stayed, the Complaints Sub-committee shall hear and investigate the complaint. The Complaints Sub-committee shall make such findings of fact as are necessary to determine the issue and shall make such recommendations as appear suitable to resolve the issue. The Complaints Sub-committee shall set out the findings of fact and recommendations in writing and deliver them to the complainant, to the head teacher and to the chair of the governors.

6   A complainant who disagrees with a finding of fact may appeal to the remainder of the Governing Body by delivering a notice to the Clerk to the Governing Body within ten school days of receipt of the findings of fact.

7   Upon receiving an appeal, the remainder of the Governing Body shall either re-determine the facts itself or appoint a special sub-committee to do so.

8   Provided that no notice of appeal has been lodged the chair of governors shall accept the findings of fact and may take such steps as are ordinarily within the powers of the chair of governors to put the recommendations into effect.

9   The findings of fact and recommendations whether implemented or not shall be reported to the next meeting of the governing body.

In most schools the complaints procedure will not be so precisely and formally specified. A complaints sub-committee of the governing body is unlikely to have power to carry out substantive action in response to a complaint, particularly where the proposed action involves spending money. An informal meeting with a governor may be just as effective and quicker

Children with Statements

The primary responsibility for children who have or ought to have statements lies with the LEA. The procedure for drawing up a statement requires the parent to be kept informed and to be involved. When the LEA serves a proposed statement, it must consider any representations that the parent wishes to make and arrange a meeting on request with an officer of the LEA and arrange meetings with any of the persons who gave the advice on which the proposed statement is based.[3] The proposed statement must be accompanied by a letter giving the name of the officer responsible for the particular child's case (the named officer).[4]

Reaching agreement at the meeting with the named officer would be much quicker and easier than using any of the formal complaints procedures. If complete agreement cannot be reached, it may be helpful to identify the issues which are agreed and those which are not. A written note or a written agreement arising out of the meeting may serve to both reduce misunderstanding and assist in ensuring that matters which have been agreed are put into effect.

Most LEAs have a formal complaints procedure, but they are not required to do so. Provided that the procedure for drawing up a statement has been followed and any meetings requested have been held, a complaint about the contents of a statement is likely to best pursued through the SEN Tribunal rather than by way of an LEA's complaints procedure.

A failure to make the provision specified in a statement should be pursued in the first instance by contacting the named officer. If an oral complaint does not get the required result promptly, the complaint should be repeated in writing. If that is not successful then reliance on an LEA's complaints procedure alone is probably not sufficient.

Considerable difficulty may arise where the LEA asserts that the provision, which is specified in a statement but not being made, ought to made by the school and paid for from the school's own budget. In the case of county and voluntary schools the LEA is in a position to purchase the specified provision itself and subtract the cost from the school's delegated budget. In the case of a grant-maintained school the LEA may be able to purchase the provision itself and invoice the school under the power to provide goods and services in connection with SEN, but the legal position is uncertain.[5]

It is the LEA that has the duty to arrange the provision specified in a statement. Where that provision is not being made, regardless of any explanation given, it is the LEA that is responsible. The LEA may be compelled to act either by complaint to the Secretary of State or by application to the High Court.

Notes

1   Regulation 2 together with Schedule 1 of the Education (Special Educational Needs) (Information) Regulations 1994.
2   Department for Education Circular number 6/94 entitled *The Organisation of Special Educational Provision* at paragraph 49.
3   Schedule 9 to the Education Act 1993.
4   Regulation 12 of the Education (Special Educational Needs) Regulations 1994.
5   Section 162 of the Education Act 1993 and the Education (Payment for Special Educational Needs Supplies) Regulations 1994.

CHAPTER 8

Complaint to the Secretary of State

Legal powers of the Secretary of State

The Secretary of State for Education has the power to investigate complaints about LEAs and schools and to enforce remedial action. There are two separate powers contained in the Education Act 1944. The powers apply to duties of LEAs and schools which are laid down in subsequent Acts.

Section 68 of the Education Act 1944 empowers the Secretary of State to give directions to an LEA or school which is acting or is proposing to act unreasonably. In this context 'unreasonably' has a particular legal meaning: it means so unreasonably that no reasonable body could possibly have behaved in the way complained of. The meaning is based on the decision of the court in *Associated Provincial Picture Houses Ltd v Wednesbury Corporation*[1] and is referred to as *Wednesbury* unreasonableness.

Section 99 of the Education Act 1944 empowers the Secretary of State to make an order declaring that an LEA or a school has failed to carry out a statutory duty and to give directions to ensure that the duty is carried out. The directions can be enforced by an order from the High Court.

The two sections have considerable overlap. A *Wednesbury* unreasonable use of a statutory power is a breach of statutory duty within the scope of Section 99. It is not strictly necessary for the complainant to choose between them. The Secretary of State may invoke the statutory powers however the matter comes to light. A letter to the Secretary of State will be interpreted as a complaint under the appropriate section even if neither section is mentioned. The complaint must concern a live issue. The Secretary of State will not investigate a matter which has already been put right solely for the purpose of issuing a rebuke.

Grounds of Complaint

A number of common types of complaint about SEN provision which are within the powers of the Secretary of State are described below.

Failure to meet time limits for producing a draft statement

The Education (Special Educational Needs) Regulations[2] lay down time limits for each of the steps in carrying out an assessment of a child's special educational needs. Those time limits are mandatory. An LEA that fails to meet any of the time limits and which cannot rely on any of the exemptions mentioned in the statutory instrument is in breach of a statutory duty.

Delay in the statementing procedure has been a major source of complaint. Only about 25 per cent of all statements are completed within the six month time limit.[3] LEAs have recently put considerable effort into reducing the time taken to produce statements and it is likely that delay will be a less common cause of complaint. The first statutory time period runs from the day the parent presents a request for an assessment to the day when the authority gives notice of a decision on that request. The time limit is six weeks. If that time limit is not met, the parent has an immediate ground for complaint.

The express statutory time period does not begin to run where a school makes a request for a statutory assessment. The LEA is nevertheless under a duty to consider whether an assessment is necessary and by implication must do that within a reasonable period of time.

Failure to make the provision specified in a statement

It is the duty of the LEA to arrange that the special educational provision specified in the statement is made for the child.[4] If the provision specified in Part 3 of the statement is not being made, the LEA is in breach of its statutory duty.

It is not open to the LEA to say that the school or the health authority is responsible for making the provision. Equally it is not open to the LEA to say that there is no money left in this year's budget or that it is unable to find suitable staff. In the case of *ex parte M*, the LEA argued that speech therapy had not been provided because speech therapists are in short supply and not available. Stuart-Smith LJ said:[5] 'No doubt that is so. But, in my judgement, that does not affect the statutory duty on the local education authority to make provision for it.'

Writing a statement which does not adequately describe the provision

A statement is required to specify all the child's needs and the provision to be made to meet those needs. An LEA is in breach of duty if the statement fails to meet the required standard. Usually the remedy is an appeal to the SEN Tribunal. The SEN Tribunal Regulations 1994 place a time limit on lodging an appeal, which is two months from the date on which the final statement was served. Once that time limit has expired the SEN Tribunal can only hear an appeal in exceptional circumstances. Provided the statement is in breach of statutory duty, the parent may still complain to the Secretary of State. A breach of statutory duty does not necessarily arise where the cause of complaint is a disagreement about the kind of provision or the amount of provision that is specified. There is a breach of statutory duty where no provision or plainly inadequate provision is specified to meet an identified need.

Failure to make provision for a child who does not have a statement

The school governors have a duty to:

> use their best endeavours, ..., to secure that if a registered pupil has special educational needs the special educational provision which his learning difficulty calls for is made.[6]

The duty covers all children, not just those with statements. It is only a duty to use their best endeavours, so a breach may be difficult to identify. Where a child's needs are almost such as to necessitate a statement, the school should be expected to make some individual provision. A very strong case could be made if the school declines to make the provision specified in a note in lieu. A note in lieu may be issued by an LEA which has carried out an assessment but decided not to issue a statement.[7] The note in lieu could be as specific and detailed as a statement in describing the provision that should be made.

Failure to carry out orders of the SEN Tribunal

The SEN Tribunal is empowered to order an LEA to carry out a statutory assessment, or to make a statement or to amend a statement.

There are no statutory provisions concerning the effect of the SEN Tribunal's orders. There is no express statutory duty imposed on LEAs to obey the orders of the SEN Tribunal. The statute and subordinate legislation impose time limits on each stage of the assessment, but there is no time limit within which an LEA must consider an order from the SEN Tribunal.

It would be unreasonable of an LEA to ignore an order of the SEN Tribunal. It appears that a properly reasoned decision not to obey the SEN Tribunal's orders might not a breach of statutory duty. (The question is further discussed in the final section of Chapter 10.)

The Department for Education (DfE) takes the view that the Secretary of State should consider a complaint that an LEA had failed to comply with a Tribunal decision under the default powers contained in Section 68 or 99 of the Education Act 1944.[8] The DfE also correctly point out that it cannot give authoritative guidance on the interpretation of legislation.

An application to the High Court would be possible if the LEA has decided not to implement the SEN Tribunal's orders and has done so for no discernible reason or has done so for an unlawful reason such as that the LEA does not have the money or implementing the order would be contrary to a policy of the LEA.

Making a Complaint

The complaint is made by a letter addressed to the Secretary of State for Education, Department for Education, Great Smith Street, London SW1P 3BT. Any such letter is sufficient to impose on the Secretary of State a duty to consider the complaint. For the sake of speed it is advisable that the letter clearly identifies which statutory duty has been breached, by whom and in what way. The letter should be supported by copies of any relevant documents. The letter asserts the breach of duty. The documents are evidence that the assertions are true. A simple complaint might be phrased as follows:

Complaint under Section 99 of the Education Act 1944 concerning Sam Grant:

I am the mother of Sam Grant who was born on 15 December 1982 and is a pupil at Greendale School.

Sam has a statement of special educational needs issued by Feltshire Education Authority. I enclose a copy of the statement.

In Part 3 of the statement it is specified that Sam should have: 'access to a Tandy portable computer in English lessons and to assist his written work'.

Sam has no access to a portable computer. I enclose a letter from Ms Sandbach, who is the teacher in charge of special educational needs, saying that the school cannot afford to buy the computer and it is the responsibility of the education authority to provide it.

The education authority is therefore in breach of Section 168 (5) (a) (ii) of the Education Act 1993, in that the education authority has failed to arrange that the special educational provision specified in the statement is made for Sam.

Disposal of Complaints

The Secretary of State will acknowledge receipt of the complaint enclosing a leaflet describing the Secretary of State's powers. The complaint will be sent to the LEA for their reply. The reply or a summary of it may be sent to the complainant. Alternatively the Secretary of State may finally determine the issue without the complainant knowing what the LEA has said. Such a flexible approach may save time and avoid the risk of the Secretary of State becoming a postbox for a protracted exchange of letters between the LEA and the complainant. However, in an era of open government, it should be expected that parties to a dispute know what the other side is saying.

When sufficient information has been gathered from the parties the Secretary of State usually seeks professional educational advice from within the DfE. The Secretary of State's decision is then sent to the parties in the form of a letter setting out the reasons.

Where the Secretary of State determines the complaint in favour of the complainant, the usual practice is to indicate to the LEA that the Secretary of State is 'minded to' issue a direction or make an order unless the LEA makes amends of its own volition within a specified period. There has only been one recent SEN case in which the Secretary of State has issued a formal direction following the issue of a 'minded to' letter.

The Secretary of State does not publish any report of the complaints made or the results of investigations; however some information has been supplied about the number of complaints made concerning children with special educational needs.[9] Table 8.1 shows the disposal of complaints from April 1992 to September 1994.

Some 14 per cent of complaints were upheld, and a further 57.5 per cent resolved locally. In sharp contrast, the equivalent figures for the Ombudsman are 3 per cent upheld and a further 19 per cent resolved locally. In the 37 complaints under section 68 which were upheld, the Secretary of State determined that the LEA had behaved so unreasonably that no reasonable authority could ever have behaved in that way.

No of Complaints Decided		Outcome	
Section 68	**252**	Upheld	37
		Rejected	70
		Locally resolved	131
		Other	14
Section 99	**57**	Upheld	8
		Rejected	10
		Locally resolved	38
		Other	1
Section 68/9	**47**	Upheld	4
		Rejected	6
		Locally resolved	36
		Other	1
Total complaints	**356**	Upheld	14.0%
		Rejected	24.0%
		Locally resolved	57.5%
		Other	4.5%

Table 8.1 Disposal of complaints by Secretary of State, April 1992 to September 1994

In 1993/94 the average time taken to complete an investigation of a complaint was 27 weeks. The average time taken where a complaint is upheld is 39 weeks.[10] Experience reveals that some cases take substantially more than a year.

The Independent Panel for Special Education Advice (IPSEA) has found that the response of the Secretary of State to complaints is patchy and can take a very long time.[11] IPSEA has supported three complaints to the parliamentary ombudsman in the last year about the procedure adopted by the Secretary of State which has been inadequate and unfair. In one case there was a delay of 18 months, by which time the child had reached school leaving age.

The author is aware of complaints or appeals which were upheld having taken 12 months and 15 months, and one case which took 17 months to determine. In one case the Secretary of State suspended the investigation for six months without informing the parents and only recommenced investigation after the parents complained about the delay.

The present SEN complaints and appeals team at the DfE will be disbanded when the current backlog has been completed, because the appeals work will be carried out by the SEN Tribunal. In future complaints will be dealt with by other teams within the DfE. It is to be hoped that the response times will improve.

The subjects of complaints

Table 8.2 shows the complaints and SEN appeals which were addressed to the Secretary of State under the Education Act 1981 divided into various categories of SEN.[12]

Category of need	% of cases
Dyslexia (etc.)	51.0
Severe learning difficulties	24.0
Moderate learning difficulties	6.5
Visual impairment	5.5
Emotional/behavioural difficulties	5.0
Hearing impairment	3.5
Autism	3.0
Epilepsy	1.0

Table 8.2 Decided complaints and SEN appeals by category of SEN

The identification of discrete categories of SEN, which had a statutory basis following the 1944 Education Act, is now only carried out informally. There are no national statistics of the incidence of SEN either overall or in discrete categories and so a direct comparison between the incidence of particular needs and the frequency of complaints is not possible. However, experience suggests that the proportion of complaints concerning dyslexia is much higher than would be explained by the incidence of dyslexia alone. Appeals to the SEN Tribunal also show a similar over-representation of dyslexia. A possible explanation is that middle class parents are making more use of the complaints system than other parents.

Conclusion

The SEN Tribunal has no jurisdiction to deal with delay in carrying out assessments or failure to make the provision specified in statements. Both these concerns are likely to continue to generate complaints to the Secretary of State. In recent years the determination of SEN complaints has been slow. The determination of a complaint without the complainant knowing what the LEA has said may leave the complainant dissatisfied.

Publication of information about the work done by the Secretary of State is minimal. In comparison, the Local Government Ombudsman produces a comprehensive annual report and publishes reports of all completed investigations, having removed the names of the people concerned. Both LEAs and people working for children with special educational needs would be assisted by the equivalent information being published by the Secretary of State. Such information could be expected to raise professional and public confidence in the fairness of the procedure and justice of the outcomes.

Notes

1   *Associated Provincial Picture Houses Ltd v Wednesbury Corporation* CA [1948] 1 KB 223.
2   The Education (Special Educational Needs) Regulations 1994 (Statutory Instrument No 1047 of 1994).
3   Audit Commission. Local Authority Performance Indicators, 1995; published in the *Times Educational Supplement* 31 March 1995.
4   Section 168 (5) (a) (i) of the Education Act 1993.
5   *R v Lancashire County Council, Ex Parte M* CA [1989] 2 FLR 279 at page 289 G.
6   Section 161 (1) (a) of the Education Act 1993.
7   The note in lieu is described at Paragraphs 4:17 to 4:23 of the Code of Practice, DfE, 1994a.
8   Department for Education. Letter to the author from Pupils and Parents Branch, 16 January 1995.
9   Department for Education. Letter to the author from Pupils and Parents Branch, Appeals Team, 31 January 1995.
10 Department for Education. Letter to the author from Pupils and Parents Branch, Appeals Team, 18 May 1995.
11 The Independent Panel for Special Education Advice. Information supplied to the author, January 1995.
12 The figures are for the period April 1992 to September 1994. Department for Education. Letter to the author from Pupils and Parents Branch, Appeals Team, 31 January 1995.

CHAPTER 9

Complaint to the Ombudsman

Introduction

The Local Government Ombudsman investigates complaints about injustice caused by maladministration on the part of local authorities. If a complaint is well founded and not settled, the Ombudsman writes a report containing recommendations. The local authority is not obliged to implement the recommendations; however, the recommendations are implemented to the Ombudsman's satisfaction in 94 per cent of cases in which recommendations are made. The recommendations may include payment of compensation to a complainant. Unlike the Secretary of State, the Ombudsman may investigate complaints which have already been rectified. The Ombudsman makes no charge to complainants and may reimburse them for travel or incidental expenditure and pay an allowance for loss of earnings. The Ombudsman produces an annual report which is free in England. Reports of individual investigations are also available on request.

Complaint to the Ombudsman is relatively easy. All that is needed is to write a letter. The Ombudsman actively investigates complaints by visiting the complainant and the local authority. The most common grounds of complaint are delay or failure to take appropriate action. Complaint to the Ombudsman is the only complaints mechanism that can lead to the payment of compensation. Where a child has not had the benefit of SEN provision that should have been made by the LEA, payment of compensation to the child is a likely outcome.

Legal Powers of the Ombudsman

The Ombudsman is more formally called the Commissioner for Local Administration. There are four Local Government Ombudsmen. Three deal with separate areas of England and one deals with Wales.[1]

The Ombudsman has jurisdiction to investigate complaints alleging injustice caused by maladministration on the part of any local authority:

> ... where a written complaint is made by or on behalf of a member of the public who claims to have sustained injustice in consequence of maladministration in connection with action [elsewhere defined to include inaction] taken by or on behalf of an authority ..., being action taken in the exercise of administrative functions of that authority, a Local Commissioner may investigate that complaint.[2]

There are two important exceptions: 1) where the action or inaction complained of affects most or all of the people living in the area, 2) where the complainant has a right of appeal to a statutory tribunal or a Minister of the Crown or could gain a remedy by a court action and the person might reasonably be expected to appeal or commence a court action.

Maladministration causing injustice to children with special educational needs does not give rise to a private law action, except possibly if the maladministration is negligence by a professional. If the potential court action is a public law action by way of an application for judicial review, the Ombudsman is likely to accept jurisdiction. The Ombudsman has investigated numerous complaints on behalf of children with special educational needs in circumstances where an application for judicial review had or would have had good prospects of success.

It is highly unlikely that the Ombudsman would investigate a matter over which the SEN Tribunal has jurisdiction or would have had jurisdiction but for the expiry of the time limits. The right of Complaint to the Secretary of State under Sections 68 and 99 of the Education Act 1944 is not a right of appeal. In many circumstances it will be possible to make a complaint either to the Ombudsman or to the Secretary of State. It would be proper to complain to both where the complainant seeks a recommendation that compensation be paid for injustice in the past and a direction that the LEA puts right a continuing breach of duty.

The Ombudsman is prohibited from investigating any action concerning:

(a) the giving of instruction, whether secular or religious, or

(b) conduct, curriculum, internal organisation, management or discipline, whether in any school or other educational establishment maintained by the authority.[3]

That prohibits the Ombudsman from investigating a complaint about the provision made for a child with special educational needs unless the child has or ought to have a statement.

The Ombudsman is backed by substantial powers to compel the production of documents and cross-examine witnesses. Obstruction of the Ombudsman's investigation is equivalent to a contempt of court and may be dealt with by use of all the High Court's powers.

Following an investigation, the Ombudsman may make a report with recommendations. The report is sent to the parties. It is a public document, but it does not identify the complainant or anyone else by name. The local authority must consider the report within three months and inform the Ombudsman of the action to be taken. If the Ombudsman is not satisfied with the action to be taken, the Ombudsman may issue a further report and, if still not satisfied, may require the local authority to publish in a local newspaper a summary of the report and recommendations together with the local authority's refusal to implement the recommendations. The local authority may include its reasons for so refusing.

Grounds of Complaint

The essential ingredients of a well-founded complaint are maladministration and injustice. Maladministration is defined in the Ombudsman's leaflet:

> Maladministration can occur when the council does something in the wrong way, does something it should not have done, or fails to do something it should have done. Examples are unreasonable delay, muddle, bias, failure to follow proper procedures, and a decision badly made. The Ombudsman cannot question what a council has done just because someone does not agree with the council.[4]

The last sentence is based on the emphatic words of the statute:

> It is hereby declared that nothing in this Part of this Act authorises or requires a Local Commissioner to question the merits of a decision taken without maladministration by an authority in the exercise of a discretion vested in that authority.[5]

Injustice includes unfairness, harm or economic loss. In the context of SEN, a failure to provide for or a delay in providing for the needs in accordance with the statutory requirements is an injustice. The injustice must be more than trivial.

Making a Complaint

A complaint must be in writing and must specify the action or inaction alleged to constitute maladministration. It should be made within 12 months of the date on which the complainant first knew of the grounds of complaint. The Ombudsman may consider a complaint made after 12 months have expired if the Ombudsman thinks that it is reasonable to do so. The complaint should be supported by relevant documents.

The complaint should be sent to The Local Government Ombudsman:

21 Queen Anne's Gate, London SW1H 9BU (Telephone 0171 915 3210) if the complaint concerns an authority in London, Kent, Surrey and Sussex

The Oaks, Westwood Way, Westwood Business Park, Coventry CV4 8JB (Telephone 01203 695999) if the complaint concerns an authority in the South West, the South, East Anglia and most of central England

Beverley House, 17 Shipton Road, York YO3 6FZ (Telephone 01904 630151) if the complaint concerns an authority in the East Midlands and the North of England

Derwen House, Court Road, Bridgend, Mid Glamorgan CF31 1BN (Telephone 01656 661325) if the complaint concerns an authority in Wales.

Before proceeding to investigate the complaint, the Ombudsman must be satisfied that the authority complained of has had a reasonable opportunity to investigate and reply to the matters in question. The complainant should give the authority a fair chance before complaining to the Ombudsman and tell the Ombudsman that they have done so.

A complaint might be phrased as follows:

Complaint to the Local Government Ombudsman on behalf of Poppy Atutu.

I am the father of Poppy Atutu, who was born on 16 July 1989 and is a pupil at Bishop Markum school.

When she was two, Poppy was diagnosed as having a disorder within the range of autism. In September 1991, she was seen by a child psychologist, Dr Main at West Worsley hospital. Dr Main wrote to the Worsley Education Authority telling them that Poppy would need special help at nursery and at school. I enclose a copy of that letter and the report which was attached to it.

In July 1992 I took Poppy to see Bishop Markum School and had a talk with the head teacher about the extra help Poppy would need. In September 1993 she started going to the nursery at Bishop Markum school. She didn't get any special help, though there were several teachers.

In January 1994 she moved into the reception class. After a few days the teacher told me Poppy was very difficult and ought to have special help. The teacher said that the education authority should assess Poppy for a statement. I agreed to this and on 10 February 1994 the head teacher sent a form to the education authority requesting an assessment. I enclose a copy of the form.

On 14 April 1994 the education authority wrote to the head teacher saying they needed more information before deciding whether to carry out an assessment. I enclose a copy of that letter. The head teacher sent a report dated 26 April 1994, which is enclosed. On 8 June 1994 the education authority wrote back saying they would arrange for their educational psychologist to see Poppy, but nothing further has happened.

In July 1994 I telephoned Syd Greenaway, who is the Authority's head of special educational needs. I told him about the problem. He said he would sort it out as soon as possible and there had been some delay because the educational psychologist was on maternity leave. The educational psychologist still hasn't seen Poppy. She gets no extra help. Last term there were 30 children in her class and the teacher said she wasn't making any progress with Poppy at all.

Poppy should have had a full-time classroom assistant from when she first went to school and three hours a week of help from a specialist teacher. The Education Authority have known about her special educational needs since September 1991, but they have done nothing for her at all.

If the tale of woe is longer than Poppy Atutu's it may be advisable to assemble a bundle of documents with page numbers and an index. In this case the complaint alleges maladministration in that the authority did nothing after Poppy's needs were first brought to their attention in September 1991. The authority again did nothing after Poppy's needs were brought to the attention of the headteacher in July 1992. Finally the authority has not responded adequately or at all to the request for an assessment made by the school in February 1994.

It is not necessary for the complainant to specify the statutory duties to which the maladministration refers, but it may be helpful to do so. In this case Section 165 (3) (d) of the Education Act 1993 imposes a duty on the LEA to identify children who ought to have statements, who are over 2 years old and who are not yet at school but have been brought to the LEA's attention, and Section 167 (1) of the Education Act 1993 requires the LEA to carry out an assessment if the child should have or probably should have a statement.

Mr Atutu makes clear that he told the LEA about the complaint in the telephone call to Mr Greenaway. He goes on to specify the injustice which is that Poppy did not get any SEN provision.

Disposal of Complaints

Upon receipt of a complaint, the Ombudsman first determines whether the complaint is within the jurisdiction; about 19 per cent of complaints are outside the Ombudsman's jurisdiction. In those cases the complainant receives a letter of explanation.

Having accepted jurisdiction, the Ombudsman sends a copy of the complaint to the local authority. On receiving the local authority's reply the Ombudsman either decides that there was no maladministration leading to injustice (56 per cent of cases) or decides to commence a full investigation (8 per cent of cases). During this stage the remaining 17 per cent of complaints are settled locally.

The normal procedure in a formal investigation is for a member of the Ombudsman's staff to call on the people concerned in order to discuss the complaint and go through any relevant records kept by the local authority.

A draft report is sent to the people concerned setting out the findings of fact and asking for comments. A final report is then written taking those comments into account, drawing conclusions and, if appropriate, making recommendations. The recommendations may be directed towards satisfying the particular complainant or towards local authority procedures generally. A recommendation for the payment of compensation is common.

The investigation by visiting the complainant and the opportunity to comment on the draft report are of the highest value. None of the other complaints procedures provides such assistance to complainants. It is an outstanding advantage of making a complaint to the Ombudsman compared with other possible complaints procedures.

In the year 1993/94 the Ombudsmen in England determined 13,718 complaints. Only 446 of those led to the publication of a report following a formal investigation. In 2,606 cases the complaint was settled locally. In the remainder the Ombudsman either determined that the matter was outside the jurisdiction or decided at an early stage that there was no maladministration or no injustice. A break down of the figures is shown in Table 9.1.

All cases			
Complaints determined 13,718	No Jurisdiction 2,637	Complaint not brought to local authority's attention **1,865**	
		Alternative appeal available **674**	
		Alternative court action available **731**	
		Complaint not submitted within 12 months **508**	
		Other reason for no jurisdiction **671**	
	No maladministration apparent at an early stage **7,741**		
	Local settlement reached **2,262**		
	Formal investigation commenced **1,078**	Discontinued **632**	No maladministration **288**
			Local settlement reached **344**
		Report Issued **446**	Maladministration causing injustice **376**
			Maladministration but no injustice **36**
			No maladministration **34**

Note: Figures for England from Annual Report 1993/94. The sum of the figures in the third column exceeds the figure in the second for no jurisdiction because in some complaints there was no jurisdiction for more than one reason.

Table 9.1 Disposal of complaints by Ombudsman 1993/94

A matter of considerable concern is the time taken by the Ombudsman in carrying out and reporting a full investigation. For the year ending 31 March 1994, the average time taken to complete a full investigation, including those which were discontinued without the need for a formal report, was 17 months. The average time to complete reports must be longer. Some cases will take longer than the average. The author is aware of complaints in which neither the school nor the parent has been interviewed by the Ombudsman's staff 13, 14 and 16 months after the complaint was received by the Ombudsman. In another case, the draft report from the Ombudsman was not completed until 20 months after the complaint was first made.

The very long delays bring the Ombudsman's office into disrepute. An LEA which is told that it is guilty of maladministration for having taken more than six months to complete a statement, may justifiably shrug its shoulders if the Ombudsman took 18 months to reach that conclusion. Officers of the LEA and teachers at the school have difficulty recalling what occurred over such long time spans. The officers of the LEA will be able to tell elected members that everything is very different now, whether or not that is true. Some cases will involve continuing maladministration which is depriving a child of SEN provision.

Complaints Concerning SEN

The number of complaints concerning education has grown significantly over the last few years, as is shown in Table 9.2. In common with complaints generally, only a very small fraction result in a full investigation and a report.

Year	Education complaints lodged	Education reports published	SEN reports published
1989/90	331	14	5
1990/91	331	20	6
1991/92	571	13	5
1992/93	617	19	10
1993/94	888	45	37

Table 9.2 Complaints about education and SEN

In the Annual Report for 1993/94 all three Ombudsmen in England made specific mention of complaints about SEN. Mrs Thomas (Northern England) stated:

Councils often identify a shortage of resources as the reason for a delay – for example a shortage of educational psychologists whose reports are needed in order to assess a child's needs. However, providing a council has made reasonable efforts to provide the professional advice which is necessary, then delays caused in this way may not be unreasonable and thus not regarded as maladministration. I am more concerned about another aspect of rationing: the practice of identifying as a child's special educational needs only those needs which the council has the resources to meet. I do not believe this to be the right approach. The aim of the statement should be to ensure that the educational needs of the child are specified. Instead, the approach I criticise effectively seeks to specify only what the council can provide.

Mrs Thomas expresses the point mildly. Such behaviour by a council is unlawful. In addition, Mrs Thomas identified delay in the production of statements as being a cause of concern.

Mr Osmotherly (Central and West England) stated:

The other area where complaints have burgeoned is education, and especially special educational needs. This office has issued 13 reports on this subject over the last year.

Sir David Yardley (South East England) stated:

In the last two annual reports I referred to the way councils have dealt with children with special educational needs. This year I issued 11 reports about problems experienced by such children and their parents, compared with six last year. I also discontinued three investigations when the council agreed to settle the complaint.

Three cases illustrate one particular problem. When there is a disagreement about the contents of a draft statement of a child's special educational needs it is natural for the council to seek to reach a settlement with parents. But the council must not allow such disputes to run on for too long without resolution lest the interests of the child are prejudiced ....

In a third case it took the London Borough of Richmond upon Thames over two years to issue a final statement. Again the Council had been negotiating with the parents – but until a final statement has been issued parents are unable to exercise their statutory right of appeal. I pointed out that there comes a time when a council must accept that no agreement is likely to be reached and should then issue a statement.

Six other investigations showed delay in dealing with the process. The effect on a child of delays in providing special education can often be very serious and difficult to remedy. To avoid such delays councils should issue clear deadlines for action and monitor the process closely in order to ensure that the difficulties faced by these children and their parents are not made even greater.

There is now a mandatory time limit of eight weeks from the service of a proposed statement to the service of a final statement,[6] but this can be extended if the parent is raising questions about the content of the statement or seeking a meeting with the LEA.

The common complaint of delay is illustrated by the report of an investigation against Avon County Council issued in December 1993 (No 92/B/0648). The case was chosen as an example because it includes a number of usual grounds of complaint. The child, who is referred to as James, had a learning difficulty within the spectrum of dyslexia. His difficulty with reading and writing caused him to become restless, easily distracted and eventually contributed to behavioural problems which further impeded his progress. The sequence of events found by the Ombudsman was as follows.

April	1980	James born
Sept	1984	James started at primary school
Sept	1986	James began having four half hour sessions per week in maths and English with a specialist teacher outside the classroom
Sept	1988	Support reduced to half an hour per week, because of shortage of resources
Feb	1989	Parent arranged for James to be tested by the British Dyslexia Institute who identified a specific learning difficulty
April	1989	Parent met the LEA's educational psychologist
Sept	1989	Support stopped altogether because James 'clowned around and the limited time available would be better spent on other pupils'
July	1990	The Council's educational psychologist carried out a non-statutory assessment and reported that James' reading age was three years behind his chronological age and that he showed anxiety and lack of confidence
Sept	1990	Parent made a written request for a statutory assessment
Sept	1990	One session a week with a specialist teacher outside the classroom was resumed
March	1991	Parent complained to the local MP
March	1991	Parent arranged for James to be seen by an educational psychologist at their own expense, who reported general and specific learning difficulties and emotional and behavioural problems
April	1991	Sessions with a specialist teacher outside the classroom increased to three each week

May	1991	The council decided not to carry out a statutory assessment but did not inform the parent of the decision.
Sept	1991	James started at secondary school
April	1992	Parent complained to Ombudsman
May	1992	A statutory assessment was commenced at the request of the secondary school
Oct	1992	A draft statement was issued. The parent objected on grounds that the draft was inadequate in many respects.
Oct	1993	The Council issued a final statement
Dec	1993	Ombudsman completed report.

The Ombudsman found maladministration in that the council failed to make any SEN provision from September 1989 to September 1990 and further maladministration in the delay in the statementing procedure. In common with other reports, the Ombudsman does not identify the date when the complaint was first made. In this case it possible to infer that the complaint was made in April 1992.

The Ombudsman recommended payments be made to the parent as follows:

- £250 for time and trouble, and
- £489 for the cost of the educational psychologist and various private lessons and incidental expenses incurred by the parent. The Ombudsman further recommended payments be made to James in trust as follows:
- £500 for 1988/89 when there was some support, and
- £1000 for 1989/90 when there was no support, and
- £1500 for 1992/93 to compensate for the delay in issuing a final statement.

Conclusion

The Ombudsman provides some satisfaction in cases of maladministration. The predominant kind of maladministration in respect of children with special educational needs is delay on the part of LEAs in carrying out the statutory procedures to produce a statement and delay in commencing the statutory procedures in particular where there has not been a parental request for a statutory assessment.

The majority of complaints lodged are either outside the Ombudsman's jurisdiction or do not disclose a well-founded allegation of maladministration which has caused more than minimal injustice. It is necessary that the complainant make clear the nature of the alleged maladministration and the extent of the injustice, loss or harm that has been caused. If the complaint concerns the contents of a statement so that Special Educational Needs Tribunal has or had jurisdiction, the Ombudsman may be expected to decline jurisdiction. The LEA must have been given a chance to put matters right before the complaint is made to the Ombudsman.

Once a well-founded complaint has been made, the Ombudsman has shown a willingness to investigate maladministration continuing or arising after the date of the original complaint.

The most serious concern about the handling of complaints by the Ombudsman is the very long time, some 17 months on average, that it takes to complete a full investigation. A full investigation is always necessary for a well-founded complaint which is not settled locally. It is of the highest importance that central government and the Ombudsman take action to eliminate the injustice that is caused by these unacceptable delays. The administrative system under which complaints are investigated needs to be streamlined. It is more than likely that the Ombudsman's office is underfunded. There is an arguable case for charging a defaulting authority with the cost of the investigation as a fair way of increasing the funding for the Ombudsman.

Notes

1   The Local Government Ombudsman's powers derive from Section 23 to Section 34 of the Local Government Act 1974. Section 23 sets up the Local Government Commission and gives the Ombudsman the formal title of Commissioner for Local Administration.

2   Section 26 (1) of the Local Government Act 1974.

3   Paragraph 5 (2) of Schedule 5 to the Local Government Act 1974.

4   *How to complain to the Local Government Ombudsman.*

5   Section 34 (3) of the Local Government Act 1974.

6   Regulation 14 (3) of the Education (Special Educational Needs) Regulations 1994 imposes the eight week time limit, but Regulation 14 (4) provides an exception when the parent is seeking to make representations to the authority or requesting meetings with the relevant officer of the authority.

CHAPTER 10

Appeal to the SEN Tribunal

Introduction

The Special Educational Needs Tribunal was set up by the 1993 Education Act to hear appeals by parents against LEA decisions concerning statements. It replaces the previous system of appeals to committees set up by the LEAs themselves and further appeals to the Secretary of State. That system was criticized for being inconsistent, slow and unfair because the local appeals committee lacked independence.

The procedure and practice of the SEN Tribunal are to a large extent modelled on the Industrial Tribunals, but with the important difference that the SEN Tribunal has powers permitting it to gather evidence on its own initiative. The SEN Tribunal is required to conduct hearings in an informal manner. The English legal system generally is based on an adversarial approach in which opposing parties uncompromisingly argue the best case they can, with the court or tribunal acting only as referee and final arbiter. Each word of the law is presumed to have a precise meaning which can be discerned by detailed analysis of the whole of a statute, other statutes and decided cases. Legislation is drafted with that approach in mind and attempts to cover every possible combination of circumstances with the result that statutes are often almost incomprehensible. The legislation concerning SEN is no exception. The SEN Tribunal will have considerable difficulty in finding a balance between informality and accessibility on the one hand and the traditions of the English legal system on the other.

This chapter sets out to describe the procedure that is followed by the SEN Tribunal, the law that applies and some ways in which parents can improve their chances of success. The procedure of the SEN Tribunal is governed by the Special Educational Needs Tribunal Regulations which are set out in full at Appendix 5 on page 202.

Decisions Subject to Appeal

Parents can appeal to the SEN Tribunal against a refusal to carry out an assessment, a refusal to issue a statement, the contents of a statement or a decision to amend a statement. Whenever a right of appeal to the SEN Tribunal arises, the LEA must inform the parents. There are six separate chunks of legislation defining the rights of appeal: four in the main body of the 1993 Education Act and two in the Schedules to the Act. The separate rights are described below.

LEA refusal to carry out an assessment

A parent may appeal against a decision by the LEA not to carry out a statutory assessment. The assessment must have been requested by the parent. A request from a school does not give rise to a right of appeal. Where the parent and the school have agreed that a statutory assessment would be a helpful way forward, it is advisable that the request to the LEA should be made by or on behalf of the parent. The SEN Tribunal may either dismiss the appeal or order the LEA to carry out an assessment (Section 173 of the Education Act 1993).

LEA refusal to carry out a further assessment

The procedure for requesting an assessment and appealing against a refusal may be repeated after six months. This applies in respect of children who have statements, children who have had an assessment but no statement and children who have been refused assessments (Section 172 and 173 of the Education Act 1993).

LEA refusal to issue a statement after an assessment

The parent may appeal if, after carrying out an assessment, the LEA decides not to make a statement. The SEN Tribunal may dismiss the appeal, or order the LEA to make a statement or remit the question to the LEA to reconsider. Where the SEN Tribunal orders a statement or remits the question, the SEN Tribunal can exert further influence on the LEA by giving detailed reasons for that decision (Section 169 of the Education Act 1993).

Appeal against the content of a statement

The parent may appeal about any disagreement concerning the description of the child's needs (Part 2 of the statement), the provision specified for those needs (Part 3 of the statement) and the school named in the statement (Part 4 of the statement). The right of appeal does not extend to non-educational needs (Part 5 of the statement) or non-educational provision (Part 6 of the statement).

The right of appeal arises when a statement is first made or when an LEA amends a statement or when an LEA determines not to amend a statement following a second or subsequent statutory assessment.

The SEN Tribunal may dismiss the appeal, order the LEA to cease to maintain the statement or order the LEA to amend the statement. Amendments may be made to the description of the child's needs or the provision specified to meet the needs and any consequential amendments. In effect the SEN Tribunal has the power to rewrite a statement (Section 173 and Schedule 10 Paragraph 10 to the Education Act 1993).

The power to make consequential amendments could be used to specify whether the school or the LEA is to pay for a particular item of provision. The Code of Practice advises that:

> The second sub section [of Part 3 of the statement] should set out all the special educational provision that the education authority consider appropriate for *all* the learning difficulties identified in Part 2, even where some of the provision is to be made by direct intervention on the part of the authority and some is to be made by the child's school within its own resources. It may be helpful for the education authority to specify which elements of the provision are to be made by the school, and which are to be made by the education authority. The education authority will be responsible for arranging all the special educational provision specified in the statement.
> (Code of Practice para 4: 28, DfE, 1994a)

It is now widely accepted that provision specified in statements will usually be purchased in part by the school and in part by the LEA. The SEN Tribunal has the power to order that the statement specify who is to pay for which elements.

The SEN Tribunal may order the LEA to change or insert the name of a school in Part 4 of the statement. The school could be a mainstream school or a special school; it could be a state school or a private school. Once a state school is named in the statement the child is absolutely entitled to attend that school.[1] The Tribunal is empowered to order the naming of a school which is proposed by the parent at any stage of the proceedings, including during the hearing.[2]

LEA refusal to agree a subsequent change of school

Any parent has a right to move their child to a different mainstream state school which is suitable and can accommodate the child.[3] Should the chosen school refuse to accept the child, the parent may appeal to a local school entry appeal committee.[4] Parents of a child with a statement have an additional right to request the LEA to change the name of the state school specified in a statement, provided that more than 12 months have passed since the previous opportunity to change the name of the school. The LEA must change the name of the school unless the preferred school is unsuitable or cannot accommodate any more children. The parent may appeal to the SEN Tribunal against an LEA decision not to change the name of the school. The SEN Tribunal may dismiss the appeal or order the LEA to change the name of the school (Schedule 10 Paragraph 8 to the Education Act 1993).

LEA decision to cease to maintain a statement

The LEA must inform the parent of a decision to cease to maintain a statement. The parent may appeal. The SEN Tribunal may dismiss the appeal or order the LEA to continue to maintain the statement in the existing or an amended form. It is uncertain whether the LEA is obliged to maintain the statement pending the appeal. The use of the word 'continue' suggests that parliament intended the statement to remain in force until the appeal is decided (Schedule 10 Paragraph 11 to the Education Act 1993).

Legal Advice and Assistance

The SEN Tribunal will be dealing with contentious decisions made by LEAs which are short of money in a complicated area of law. Even though the SEN Tribunal has an investigative role enabling it to assist the parties, parents are likely to benefit from advice and representation at the hearing.

Legal aid is not available to pay for representation at the hearing, but it is available for legal advice and assistance prior to the hearing, provided that the parent is in receipt of income support or family credit or their income is very low. A solicitor can give advice and assistance for up to two hours without seeking approval of the Legal Aid Board. Should more preparatory work be needed, an application for legal aid is made by the solicitor. Legal aid should be granted where the parent meets the income requirements and the case has sufficient merit. The legal merits test applied by the Legal Aid Board may be summarized as: does the appeal have reasonable prospects of success and if so would a solicitor advise an applicant to bring the action privately if the applicant had the means?

Not all solicitors are prepared to work for people who are poor. The Citizens Advice Bureau or a law centre will provide a list of local solicitors who do accept legal aid work. Those organizations also give assistance themselves and may be able to suggest other sources of advice.

How to Appeal[5] contains a useful lists of voluntary organizations who may be able to assist parents. A similar list is to be found in *Special Educational Needs a Guide to Parents.*[6]

The Named Person

The Code of Practice introduces the concept of an independent Named Person to advise and assist parents. This may cause some confusion because such a Named Person was not envisaged by parliament when the relevant legislation was passed. LEAs are not required to identify such a Named Person. The Code of Practice states that:

> When the LEA send the parties the final version of the statement, they must inform the parents in writing of the name of a person who in future can give the parents advice and information about their child's special educational needs. This is the parents' **Named Person**.
>
> (The Code of Practice paragraph 4:70, DfE, 1994a)

> The Named Person, who should usually be identified in cooperation with the parents, must be someone who can give the parents information and advice about their child's special educational needs. He or she may be appointed at the start of the assessment process and can attend meetings with parents and encourage parental participation throughout that process. The Named Person should normally be independent of the LEA and may be someone from a voluntary organisation or parent partnership scheme.
>
> (The Code of Practice, Glossary page 128, DfE, 1994a)

If the parents decide that they do not wish to suggest a Named Person, the LEA must still give them the name of someone from whom advice and information can be obtained. There is no statutory restriction on the identity of the Named Person. Normally, however, there will be advantage in that person being someone who is independent of and who is not employed by the LEA. The role of the Named Person is not the same as that of the Named

LEA Officer. Both help parents. But the Named Person acts as an independent advisor, while the Named LEA Officer acts as a source of information within the LEA.

(Code of Practice, Paragraph 4:73, DfE, 1994a)

Parliament did not have in mind a Named Person who was to act as friend and independent advisor to the parent in the way suggested by the Code of Practice. The statutory requirement is:[7]

Where a local education authority make a statement they shall serve a copy of the statement on the parent of the child concerned and shall give notice in writing to him–

(b) of the name of the person to whom he may apply for information and advice about the child's special educational needs.

The identical words appeared in the Education Act 1981,[8] whereas the Named Person as friend and independent advisor to the parent appeared for the first time in the final version of the Code of Practice. There was no mention of the Named Person in the Draft Code of Practice published in October 1993.[9]

The statutory requirement would be met by the LEA naming either the officer who has been dealing with the child or the head teacher or the SEN Coordinator of the relevant school. That is surely what parliament intended.

Some LEAs are setting up schemes to identify potential Named Persons, but it is unlikely that either a sufficient number of volunteers can be found or that the money will be available to pay Named Persons.

Time Limits

An appeal is started by a written notice of appeal which must be delivered to the SEN Tribunal[10] within two months of the day on which the parent received the decision complained of, together with a notice of their right to appeal. For example, if the parent receives the decision on 10 May the last day on which the notice of appeal must reach the SEN Tribunal is 10 July.

The time limit is strict and can only be extended in exceptional circumstances.[11] If the time limit is about to expire, actual delivery should be ensured as opposed to relying on the postal service. A notice can be sent by fax.[12] It is not necessary to use the printed appeal form. An incomplete notice of appeal received on time is more likely to be accepted than a complete notice that is late.

The Notice of Appeal

The SEN Tribunal produces a booklet entitled *How to Appeal*[13] which contains a standard form notice of appeal. A notice of appeal must state the name and address of the parent, the name of the child, the name of the LEA, the date the parent was notified of the decision and the grounds of appeal.[14] It must be signed by the parent and accompanied if appropriate by a copy of the LEA's decision letter and the child's statement.

The grounds of appeal may be in short form such as; 'the provision specified in the statement is inadequate'. The notice of appeal is likely to be the first document read by the SEN Tribunal. The applicant will get off to a better start if the grounds of appeal set out precisely what the parent wants and explain why the child is entitled to it.

Steps before the Hearing

Upon receipt of a notice of appeal the Secretary of the SEN Tribunal sends the notice to the LEA. The LEA has 20 working days in which to reply. Days in August do not count as working days.[15] The reply must include the facts relating to the disputed decision and the reasons for it as well as stating whether the LEA intends to resist the appeal and, if so, the grounds on which it relies.[16] A copy of the reply will be sent to the parents, who may send a response to the reply within 15 days.[17]

Further and Better Particulars

The President of the SEN Tribunal may give directions requiring a party to provide a further explanation of the notice of appeal or reply.[18] A direction may be given either on the President's own initiative or at the request of a party. Before seeking a direction a party ought to have asked the other party for the required further and better particulars. The usual practice of the Tribunal is to refuse requests for the equivalent order if the other party has not been asked first. The President may be unwilling to give directions until the other party has failed to respond to a request.

Discovery and Disclosure

The President may order a party to identify and permit inspection of documents either on the President's own initiative or at the request of a party. The President can order documents to be sent to the SEN Tribunal.[19]

The power which applies to a request from a party is the same as that which applies in the County Court. As with further and better particulars, the first step should be to write and ask for the documents.

There are two steps in the formal procedure though they are often rolled into one. The first step is discovery, which means listing all the relevant documents that are in the possession or control of a party. The second step is disclosure, which means providing an opportunity to inspect the documents and take copies.

An order for disclosure would not be framed as an order to send photocopies but as an order to allow inspection and permit copies to be taken at a reasonable charge. The documents must be necessary to dispose of the proceedings fairly or to save costs. Saving costs includes saving time at the hearing.

An LEA would not be required to produce documents that are protected by legal immunity. Legal immunity covers documents created for the purpose of defending an appeal such as advice from a lawyer. Some documents may be protected from disclosure by public interest immunity. Public interest immunity could arise in respect of documents held by a social services department which concern a child in need of protection from serious harm.

The party is the LEA. A county school is part of the LEA. With respect to a child at a county school documents held by the school are discoverable. The position of voluntary schools which are mainly church schools is not clear. A recent court case suggests that they are not part of the LEA.[20] grant-maintained schools are not part of the LEA.

Summoning Witnesses

The President of the SEN Tribunal may issue a summons for a witness to attend the hearing.[21] A parent wishing to call a witness should ask the person well in advance of the hearing if they are willing to attend and only if the person declines apply to the President for a witness summons.

It is usual for doctors not to attend tribunals unless summoned. Some employees may wish to be summoned to ensure that their employer will allow the time off work. Where a person is expected to give evidence against their employer a witness summons is valuable as some protection to that person. Volunteering to speak against the employer appears different from being compelled to attend the SEN Tribunal and tell the truth.

A request for a witness summons should summarize what the witness will say, explain why the evidence is necessary and state that the witness is unwilling to attend unless summoned.

The Hearing

The SEN Tribunal consists of three persons: a legally qualified chair and two others with knowledge of local authorities and/or special educational needs. The SEN Tribunal will sit in a place convenient for parents such as a church or village hall. For parents in the London area the SEN Tribunal will sit at the Tribunal's headquarters in Victoria Street.

The hearing takes place in private unless the LEA and the parent request that the hearing be in public or the SEN Tribunal decides that the hearing should be in public. The SEN Tribunal is required to make hearings reasonably informal.[22] It is intended that everyone will sit round one big table. At the beginning the chair will explain how the hearing will proceed. The present practice of the SEN Tribunal is for the chair to take each aspect of the case separately. The LEA is asked to speak first and then the parent. The Tribunal may intervene to a considerable degree in questioning the parties or their witnesses.

The SEN Tribunal decides the issues as though it were the LEA making the decision for the first time. It considers the needs of the child at the time of the hearing which may be different from the time when the decision complained of was made.[23] The decision is made on the basis of the evidence submitted to the Tribunal. The parties need to produce sufficient evidence to prove each relevant issue in a logical series of steps which lead inevitably to a conclusion in their favour. It is notable that in two cases in the first Digest of Decisions[24] produced by the Tribunal, the Tribunal specifically referred to the lack of evidence:

> No evidence was offered to the Tribunal of the level of funding provided under the statement or Stage 3, nor whether the school would be able to continue X's current level of support from its own resources; and

> The Tribunal, noting that no evidence had been given about the efficient use of resources, ordered that the grant-maintained school be named in X's statement.

Evidence may be presented by written statement and orally. Neither party may call more than two witnesses to give oral evidence unless permission has been granted in advance by the President or is granted by the SEN Tribunal at the hearing.[25] The SEN Tribunal has interpreted this regulation as meaning two witnesses in addition to the parents themselves.[26]

The child may attend and speak. Both parents are entitled to attend even if only one of them signed the notice of appeal. The parties are entitled to cross-examine witnesses. Any evidence is admissible provided that it is relevant. Since the SEN Tribunal is empowered to seek evidence on the President's initiative, the SEN Tribunal is expected to play an investigative role where necessary.

The SEN Tribunal must give its decision in writing and with reasons. The SEN Tribunal may in addition give the decision orally at the end of the hearing, but the present practice of the SEN Tribunal is not to give oral decisions. The reasons are in summary form, but they must be adequate. They must be intelligible and they must deal with the substantial points raised. They should be sufficient to show whether or not the decision is open to challenge on appeal. Significant disputes of fact should be resolved in the reasons.

The Parent's Case

The parent will need to ensure that the SEN Tribunal is presented with the best available evidence to support their case. The relevant issues are different for an appeal at each of the stages of the statutory procedure. Some issues in particular kinds of appeal are discussed below.

Refusal to Carry out an Assessment Following a Parental Request

A statutory assessment must be carried out if the child's needs are probably such as to require provision which would cost more than the school can reasonably afford. In effect the parent must show what the result of a statutory assessment would probably be. The facts to be established are, 1) the extent of the needs, 2) the level of provision that is appropriate for those needs; and 3) the statement threshold, which is the maximum sum that a school in the area can reasonably afford to spend on provision for an individual child

1 The extent of the needs

In order to decide not to carry out a statutory assessment an LEA must have carried out some informal assessment of the child. The parent might expect to have a report from the school and a fairly brief report from the LEA's educational psychologist (EP). It is likely to be necessary to contradict what the EP has said. In most circumstances that will require a report from an independent expert arranged by the parent.

The Code of Practice strongly suggests that the extent of provision that has been made by the school at stages 2 and 3 should be crucial to the decision as to whether a statutory assessment is necessary. What the school has or has not done is not of itself a relevant issue. The relevant issue is the child's needs. What the school has or has not done can only be relevant as evidence of those needs. A failure by a school to make adequate provision at stages 2 and 3 cannot be turned into grounds for refusing to carry out an assessment, where an assessment is called for by the terms of the Education Act 1993 itself.

2 The level of provision that is appropriate for those needs

Evidence from an expert is likely to be the only way for a parent to contradict the LEA about the level of provision that is necessary. Having identified the need the expert should be asked to describe the appropriate provision in terms of materials and hours of work with a classroom assistant and/or a qualified or specialist teacher so that the cost may be ascertained.

3 The statement threshold

The main ground on which an LEA is expected to decide whether or not a statement is necessary is whether mainstream schools in the area have sufficient delegated resources to pay for all the provision required by the child.[27] The quantified provision recommended by the expert needs to be costed. Precise figures for staff costs at the particular school should be sought from the head teacher.

The amount that a mainstream school can afford to spend on an individual child, or the statement threshed, needs to be demonstrated in evidence given by or on behalf of the parent. (Ascertaining statement thresholds was discussed in Chapter 4.) If possible, a witness should be asked to explain the LEA funding of schools in the area and the use of the SEN budget by the school.

Refusal to Issue a Statement Following an Assessment

A statement must be issued if the child's needs are such as to require provision which would cost more than the school can reasonably afford. The relevant issues are the same as for an appeal against a refusal to carry out an assessment. Again an independent assessment of the child is likely to be required.

The parent will have copies of the statutory advices. The advice from the school may well contain a suggestion of the level of provision that would be appropriate; the advice from the EP is much less likely to do so. The EP is employed by the LEA. Many LEAs have told EPs not to quantify provision in their advice. There is, however, a mandatory requirement that the advice should relate to the provision that is appropriate for the child.[28]

There is some conflict between the LEA psychologist's duty to serve their employer and their duty to give independent professional advice. In cross-examination it may be revealing to ask the EP to give a professional opinion as to the level of provision that would be best for the particular child. Questioning on this line will probably require considerable skill.

Disagreement about the Contents of a Statement

It is a mandatory requirement that any special educational needs identified in the advice must be set out in Part 2 of the statement and adequate provision specified for every need in Part 3 of the statement.

If a need has been identified in the advice but is not mentioned in Part 2 of the statement, the parent has to show that it is a special educational need. A child has a special educational need if the child has significantly greater difficulty in learning than the majority of children of that age and the difficulty calls for special educational provision to be made.[29] Significantly greater difficulty in this context may be taken to mean that 80 per cent of all children have less difficulty. Special educational provision is provision that is not made generally for children in mainstream schools. Special educational provision is called for if the learning difficulty is likely to be ameliorated by the provision. The parent's success on appeal is likely to be as much dependent on the argument put to the SEN Tribunal as on additional evidence.

Once a need has been identified in Part 2 of a statement, it is certain law that some provision must be specified in Part 3 to meet that need.[30] The parent should succeed on that point at the SEN Tribunal even if they do not adduce any evidence. Evidence however is likely be needed to show the nature and extent of the provision that is necessary.

The standard of specification of provision was described by the court as being comparable to a medical diagnosis and a prescription.[31] The Code of Practice suggests that:

The provision set out in this sub-section should normally be specific, detailed and quantified (in terms, for example, of hours of ancillary or specialist teaching support) although there will be some cases where flexibility should be retained in order to meet the changing special educational needs of the child concerned.

(Code of Practice, paragraph 4:28, DfE, 1994a)

The detailed specification that is determined by the LEA or SEN Tribunal can only depend on expert opinion. The SEN Tribunal is itself knowledgeable or expert on both children's needs and LEA finances and is expected to apply that experience. The SEN Tribunal should not be expected to allocate more than a fair share of resources to an individual child despite the somewhat open-ended duty that is imposed on the LEA.

Costs and Expenses

The Secretary of State will pay an allowance for attendance at the SEN Tribunal to the parents and the witnesses. The SEN Tribunal will provide an application form for allowances. The allowance available to parents is limited to travelling expenses. The allowance available to witnesses includes a sum in respect of loss of earnings. The sums are £23 per day for any time off work up to four hours and £44.80 per day for any time off work over four hours. These allowances might be available to contribute towards the cost of an independent professional witness but, if such a witness is being paid by the parents, they would not ordinarily incur a loss of earnings.

The SEN Tribunal will not normally order a party to pay the costs of the other party, but may make such an order against a party that has acted frivolously or vexatiously or whose conduct in making, pursuing or resisting an appeal was wholly unreasonable.

In addition, costs may be awarded against an LEA which failed to reply to the original notice of appeal or where the SEN Tribunal considers that the disputed decision was wholly unreasonable.[32]

Appeal from the SEN Tribunal

A dissatisfied parent can appeal to the High Court, but only on a point of law and with leave of the Court.[33] An appeal is not a rehearing. The facts found by the SEN Tribunal are not open to challenge, except in very unusual circumstances. The exercise of discretion by the SEN Tribunal is not open to challenge. Professional legal advice is almost certainly necessary to mount such an appeal. Legal aid would be available provided the parents qualify under the income rules and the case has sufficient prospect of success. The appeal must be brought in the name of the parents. Consequently it is the parents' income, as opposed to the child's income, which governs eligibility for legal aid.[34]

Effect of the SEN Tribunal's Orders

The is doubt as to the effect of the SEN Tribunals orders, because the legislation makes no mention of how they affect at LEA. This is contrary to usual legislative practice. An LEA is apparently expressly forbidden from directly implementing the Tribunals orders in certain circumstances.

It is usual legislative practice to give express effect to the decisions of a tribunal. For example immigration officers are bound to comply with directions from the adjudicators and the Immigration Appeal Tribunal by clear words in the statute:

> Where an appeal is allowed, the adjudicator shall give such directions for giving effect to the determination as the adjudicator thinks requisite, and ...it shall be the duty of the Secretary of State and of any officer to whom directions are given under this subsection to comply with them.[35]

LEAs are expressly bound by the decisions of school admission and expulsion appeal committees with the words:

> The decision of an appeal committee on any such appeal shall be binding on the local education authority ...and ...on the governors of any county or controlled school at which the committee determines that a place should be offered to the child in question.[36]

The appeal committees also heard appeals against the contents of statements of SEN under the Education Act 1981. The appeal committees only had the power to confirm the special educational provision or remit the case to the LEA for reconsideration. Thereafter the parent could appeal to the Secretary of State, who was empowered to 'amend the statement',[37] thereby overriding the LEA. In contrast the SEN Tribunal is only empowered to order the LEA to amend the statement.

The Education Act 1993 is silent as to the effects of such an order. The statute and subordinate legislation impose time limits on each stage of an assessment of a child's special educational needs. There is no time limit within which an LEA must consider an order from the SEN Tribunal.

An order means an instruction which must be obeyed. The court could readily imply a duty to obey an order, but for the presence in the statute of an express provision prohibiting an LEA from directly implementing the SEN Tribunal's orders in certain circumstances.

An LEA is expressly prohibited from immediately implementing an order to amend a statement by Paragraph 9 and 10 of Schedule 10 to the Education Act 1993. Paragraph 9 (1) provides that: 'A local education authority may not amend, or cease to maintain, a statement except in accordance with paragraph 10 or 11 below.'

Paragraph 9 (2) disapplies that rule in certain circumstances including where the SEN Tribunal orders an LEA to cease to maintain a statement, but does not disapply the rule where the SEN Tribunal orders an amendment to a statement except if the amendment is to change the name of the school specified.

Paragraph 10 requires that:

(1) Before amending a statement, a local education authority shall serve on the parent of the child concerned a notice informing him –

    (a)   of their proposal, and

    (b)   of his right to make representations under sub-paragraph (2) below.

(2) [right to make representations]

(3) The local education authority –

    (a)   shall consider any representations made to them under sub-paragraph (2) above, and

    (b)   on taking a decision on the proposal to which the representations relate shall give notice in writing to the parent of their decision

Upon receipt of an order from the SEN Tribunal to amend a statement, the LEA is obliged to consult the parent on whether or not to amend the statement and to take the parent's views into account.

If Parliament had intended the SEN Tribunal to be able to effect changes in a statement it could have either empowered the SEN Tribunal to amend the statement or imposed a duty on LEAs to give effect to the orders of the SEN Tribunal. It would clearly be unreasonable of an LEA to ignore the SEN Tribunal altogether, but a properly reasoned decision not to obey the SEN Tribunal's orders is not a breach of an express statutory duty. It will be difficult for the court to hold that there is an implied statutory duty binding LEAs to obey an order to amend a statement in the face of the express statutory requirements.

The SEN Tribunal's booklet says: 'By law the Local Education Authority must keep to the SEN Tribunal's decision. If the Local Education Authority do not do so, you can write to complain to the Secretary of State for Education'. The Department for Education (DfE)

takes the view that the Secretary of State should consider a complaint that an LEA had failed to comply with a SEN Tribunal decision under the default powers contained in Section 68 or 99 of the Education Act 1944. The DfE also correctly points out that it cannot give authoritative guidance on the interpretation of legislation.[38]

If the SEN Tribunal's orders were effective, the SEN Tribunal would be directing the spending of public money. Parliament has not entrusted the SEN Tribunal with that power. The result is unfortunate in requiring further delay after an SEN Tribunal has promulgated an order. The result will infuriate parents who are likely to believe that an order from the SEN Tribunal is the final determination when it is not.

Decisions of the SEN Tribunal

The SEN Tribunal publishes summaries of selected decisions and statistics about the number of appeals lodged. The summary decisions are very terse. They give some indication of the Tribunal's view on statement thresholds. In particular in seems that the Tribunal is taking a local approach which can lead to a statement being necessary for a child in one LEA area but not necessary if that same child is in another LEA area. They also give some indication of the approach to disagreements about whether a mainstream or special school is appropriate in all the circumstances.

At least in the early years of the Tribunal's operation, it would be helpful if more decisions were published and perhaps if the full decision was published rather than a summary. This can readily be done in anonymous form. It is unfortunate that both the name of the child and the name of the LEA have been removed from the summaries. Parliament decided that the Tribunal was to meet in private to protect the parents and children. It is not obvious that LEAs should have such protection. Decisions by the Tribunal should be consistent within each LEA. Publication of the name of the LEA would not only encourage such consistency but also give people confidence in the fairness of the Tribunals decisions.

The SEN Tribunal statistics issued in June 1994 showed that appeals were being lodged at the rate of 30 per week. The parents were successful in between 50 per cent and 60 per cent of cases. The average time taken to complete a case was between four and five months. The appeals were distributed between the various types of appeal, as shown in Table 10.1.

Type of Appeal	%
Against refusal to issue a statement	29
Against contents of a statement	25
Against refusal to carry out an assessment	21
Against school named in a statement	18
Against decision to discontinue statement	5
Against refusal to change school named	1
Against failure to name school	1

Table 10.1 Distribution of types of appeal

The children's needs have been categorized by the Tribunal and are distributed as shown in Table 10.2. Specific learning difficulty may be taken to be the same category as 'dyslexia (etc)' used by the Secretary of State (see Table 8.2). Once again appeals concerning dyslexia are over-represented compared to the incidence of dyslexia amongst children as a whole.

Category of need	% of cases
Specific learning difficulty	51.0
Severe learning difficulties	7.0
Moderate learning difficulties	7.0
Speech and Language	7.0
Emotional/behavioural difficulties	7.0
Physical handicap	3.0
Hearing Impairment	3.0
Autism	1.0
Epilepsy	0.5
Visual impairment	0.5
Other	13.0

Table 10.2 Appeals by category of SEN

Notes

1   Section 168 (5) (b) of the Education Act 1995.
2   Section 170 (4) (b) of the Education Act 1993.
3   Section 6 of the Education Act 1980.
4   Section 7 and Schedule 2 to the Education Act 1980.
5   *How to Appeal* is available from the Special Educational Needs Tribunal at 71 Victoria Street, London SW1H OHW (Telephone 0171 925 6925).
6   *A Guide to Parents* is available from Special Educational Needs, Department for Education, Freepost 435, London EC1B 1SQ (Telephone 0181 533 2000).
7   Paragraph 6 of Schedule 10 to the Education Act 1993.
8   Section 7 (9) (c) of the Education Act 1981.
9   Draft Code of Practice on the Identification and Assessment of Special Educational Needs, Department for Education, October 1993.
10   Notice of Appeal should be addressed to the Secretary of the Special Educational Needs Tribunal at 71 Victoria Street, London SW1H OHW (Telephone 0171 925 6925).
11   Regulation 42 (1) of the Special Educational Needs Tribunal Regulations 1994 (Statutory Instrument No 1910 of 1994).
12   The fax number of the SEN Tribunal is 0171 925 6926.
13   *How to Appeal* is available from the Special Educational Needs Tribunal at 71 Victoria Street, London SW1H OHW (Telephone 0171 925 6925).
14   Regulation 7 of the of the Special Educational Needs Tribunal Regulations 1994 (Statutory Instrument No 1910 of 1994).
15   Regulation 2 of the Special Educational Needs Tribunal Regulations 1994 (Statutory Instrument No 1910 of 1994).
16   Regulation 12 of the Special Educational Needs Tribunal Regulations 1994 (Statutory Instrument No 1910 of 1994).
17   Regulation 8 of the Special Educational Needs Tribunal Regulations 1994 (Statutory Instrument No 1910 of 1994).
18   Regulation 21 of the Special Educational Needs Tribunal Regulations 1994 (Statutory Instrument No 1910 of 1994).
19   Regulation 22 of the Special Educational Needs Tribunal Regulations 1994 (Statutory Instrument No 1910 of 1994).
20   *Fidge and Others v Governing body of St Mary's Church of England Aided Junior School and Others* EAT [1994] *The Times* 9 November.
21   Regulation 23 of the Special Educational Needs Tribunal Regulations 1994, (Statutory Instrument No 1910 of 1994).
22   Regulation 29 (2) of the Special Educational Needs Tribunal Regulations 1994 (Statutory Instrument No 1910 of 1994).
23   Direction to members of the Tribunal issued by the President on 15 March 1995.
25   Special Educational Needs Tribunal. Digest of Decisions. March 1995 decisions number 95/3 and 95/6.
26   Regulation 30 (1) of the Special Educational Needs Tribunal Regulations 1994 (Statutory Instrument No 1910 of 1994).
27   Paragraph 4:2 and Paragraph 4:12 of the Code of Practice, DfE 1994a.
28   Regulation 6 (2) (c) of the Education (Special Educational Needs) Regulations 1994 (Statutory Instrument No 1047 of 1994).

29   Section 156 of the Education Act 1993.

30   For example see *R v Secretary of State for Education and Science, Ex parte E* CA [1992] 1 FLR 377 Balcombe LJ at page 387 H said: 'The law, as I understand it, is simply this, that if the need is serious enough to appear in the statement, then it necessarily qualifies for special educational provision.'

31   *R v Secretary of State for Education and Science, Ex parte E* CA [1992] 1 FLR 377, Balcombe LJ at page 388 B approved the words of Nolan J in the court below: 'The statement is no ordinary form. Part II may be compared to a medical diagnosis and Part III to a prescription for the needs diagnosed. It is axiomatic that Part III must deal fully with Part II, ...'.

32   Regulation 34 of the Special Educational Needs Tribunal Regulations 1994.

33   Section 181 of the Education Act 1993 adds the SEN Tribunal to the Tribunals which are covered by the Tribunals and Inquiries Act 1992. Section 11 of the Tribunals and Inquires Act 1992 both limits appeals to a point of law and requires that leave be granted by the High Court or the Court of Appeal.

34   *S v Special Educational Needs Tribunal and The City of Westminster* HC [1995] Unreported 25 July.

35   Section 19 (3) of the Immigration Act 1971. Section 20 (3) goes on to apply the same words to the decisions of the Immigration Appeal Tribunal.

36   Section 7 (5) of the Education Act 1980.

37   Section 8 (7) (b) of the Education Act 1981.

38   Department for Education. Letter to the author from Pupils and Parents Branch, 16 January 1995.

CHAPTER 11

Application to the High Court

Introduction

There are some circumstances in relation to children with special
educational needs where the court is likely to provide the most effective
remedy. While use of the courts requires considerable skill and precision
often necessitating the hire of solicitors and barristers, there is a steady
rise in number of people appearing in the higher courts in person. This
chapter briefly describes the process and procedure of the court in
relation to SEN complaints. A more thorough description is to be found
in *Effective use of Judicial Review* (Bibby, 1985).

The High Court has a supervisory jurisdiction over schools, LEAs, the
local government ombudsman, the SEN Tribunal and the Secretary of
State, which is exercised in proceedings known as judicial review.
Judicial review may be invoked by a person who is adversely affected by
the misuse of public power, provided that there is no other available
satisfactory remedy and an application to the court is made promptly.
The High Court has the power to quash an unlawful decision by an order
of certiorari and the power to compel a public body to carry out its duty
by an order of mandamus.

Judicial review proceedings have two stages. The first stage is an
application to the court for leave and the second stage is the application
for review itself. In order to be granted leave the applicant must show
that there is an arguable case that a remedy will be granted. At the full
hearing the applicant must show, on balance of probability, that their
interests have been harmed by a failure to discharge a public duty. The
court then has discretion to grant a range of remedies which can be
tailored to ensure that the applicant's rights are vindicated. In many cases
the grant of leave at the first stage will be sufficient to persuade the
public body complained of to mend its ways.

Judicial review will only be granted if the failure complained of is unlawful. The proper exercise of discretion is not unlawful. The lawful range of discretion in the exercise of public power is wide. The court will not intervene unless the exercise of discretion is so unreasonable that no reasonable person could ever have reached the decision complained of. The wide discretion is the basis for the frequently stated proposition that judicial review is not concerned with the merits of decisions made in the exercise of public power, instead it is only concerned with procedure.

In practice the scope of judicial review is somewhat larger than is suggested by that proposition. The court may intervene where the body complained of is in breach of duty by failing to take any action. This avoids raising a question of merits since there is no exercise of discretion.

Where there has been an exercise of discretion, the decision may be attacked on the grounds that it was founded on an error of law. That is the same jurisdiction as exercised by an appellate court to which appeal lies exclusively on a point of law. The decision may also be undermined by attacking the procedure used in exercising the discretion. The court expects high standards of procedure in public decision making. The legislation covering procedure for carrying out assessments, making statements and reviewing statements is precise in terms of timetables and notices to be served. The court will expect public bodies to follow the statutory procedure to the letter.

The administration of judicial review is carried out by the Crown Office. Anyone aggrieved by an abuse of public power can fill in a form, pay £20 and have a High Court judge decide whether they have an arguable case. If the aggrieved person is poor, a law centre or solicitor will help with the form and charge the legal aid board under the green form scheme. The application for leave is usually dealt with on paper. There is no need for oral argument and so no need for an advocate.

Commencing an application for judicial review is not particularly difficult, though most people would be assisted by professional advice. Once leave has been granted the Legal Aid Board may be expected to grant legal aid to pay for a barrister at the full hearing. This chapter describes the kind of circumstances in which judicial review may be invoked and explains how to make the initial application for leave. Parents may not be able to pay a lawyer to do this part of the work for them and so be obliged to act in person having had some advice. The further stages of a application for judicial review are not described because, if the case is worth pursuing, legal aid will probably be available in the child's name.

Exhaustion of Remedies

The High Court will not grant leave for judicial review if the applicant has available an alternative means of redress which is likely to be convenient and effective. If the matter complained of is within the jurisdiction of the SEN Tribunal, an application for judicial review would almost always be inappropriate. The High Court has however on occasion given leave for judicial review in the face of a suitable and available appeal. In *R v London Borough of Camden, ex parte B* QBD [1994] ELR 490, leave to apply for judicial review was granted despite the presence of a statutory appeal to the Secretary of State under the provisions of the Education Act 1981, now replaced by the Education Act 1993 appeal to the SEN Tribunal. May J said at page 493 D:

> It seems to me that this is a case where the applicant's case is on the face of the present evidence well-founded. The facts apparently all do go one way. The outcome of a successful judicial review in those circumstances ought to be that the council would swiftly take steps to reconsider and implement the recommendations of the appeal committee. I am far from satisfied that this court cannot bring the matter on, if it is expedited, with reasonable speed. It would be a policy of despair to suppose that where the consideration of these children's needs has now been going on since the spring of 1990, matters cannot be brought forward with proper speed so that a determination takes place at least as quickly if not more quickly than an appeal to the Secretary of State.

Judicial review was refused at the main hearing. The grant of leave was criticized. The case is not likely to be followed.

The Secretary of State's default powers contained in Sections 68 and 99 of the Education Act 1944 will in some circumstances act as a discretionary bar to the grant of a remedy by way of judicial review. If the subject of complaint is within the jurisdiction of both the High Court and the Secretary of State, the court is likely to grant a remedy by judicial review either if the action complained of is ultra vires or if judicial review would on balance provide the more convenient remedy.

Ultra vires

The court has drawn a distinction between a failure to discharge a duty (nonfeasance) and a decision which is unlawful (malfeasance). If the complaint is of a failure to discharge a duty, invoking the default powers is the appropriate way forward. If the complaint is that a decision has been made which is unlawful or beyond the powers of the body complained of (ultra vires) then judicial review is probably appropriate.

The division between nonfeasance and malfeasance is not always easy to identify. In *Bradbury v Enfield Borough Council* CA [1967] 1 WLR 1311, the Council proposed to reorganize education by closing grammar schools and opening comprehensive schools. In the case of eight schools, ministerial approval had not been sought for significant changes in character; in the case of many other schools such ministerial approval had been granted but the school premises did not comply with prescribed standards. A number of parents sought a declaration that the proposals were ultra vires and an injunction to restrain the Council from implementing the proposals. The court granted the injunction with respect to the eight schools, but with respect to the other schools determined that the failure to carry out the duty was one of nonfeasance, and that the duty was only enforceable by the Minister invoking the general default power.

It is nonfeasance for an LEA to fail to arrange the provision specified in a statement. If however the LEA has given an unlawful reason for not arranging the provision, such as shortage of resources, the decision may be characterized as malfeasance.

Balance of Convenience

There have been a number of cases where the court has granted judicial review where an alternative remedy has been available, but the alternative would be less effective, or slower or more expensive. For example in *R v Hillingdon London Borough Council, Ex parte Royco Homes Ltd* QBD [1974] 1 QB 720, certiorari was granted to a developer to quash a decision to attach a condition to a planning permission. A statutory appeal would have led to a public inquiry. The condition was plainly ultra vires. The applicant was assured of success by either route. Certiorari was quicker and cheaper.

In *R v Devon County Council, ex parte Baker and another case* CA [1995] 1 All ER 73 at page 92 f, Simon Brown LJ, referring to a similar default power in law of social services, said:

> Which of two available remedies, or perhaps more accurately, avenues of redress, is to be preferred will depend ultimately upon which is the more convenient, expeditious and effective. Where ministers have default powers, application to them will generally be the better remedy, particularly where, as so often, the central complaint is in reality about the substantive merits of the decision. The minister brings his department's expertise to bear on the problem. He has the means to conduct an appropriate factual inquiry. Unlike

the court, moreover, he can direct a solution rather than merely leave the authority to redetermine the question. Where, on the other hand, as here, what is required is the authoritative resolution of a legal issue, then, in common with Dillon LJ, I would regard judicial review as the more convenient alternative remedy.

There are problems of delay in the determination of complaints by the Secretary of State, which are sufficient to base a well-founded argument that the court should exercise its discretion to grant judicial review. The following case is an example.

A statement was issued in July 1993. In Part 3 of the statement, the section dealing with educational provision, regular speech therapy was specified. The LEA declined to arrange the speech therapy asserting that it was a matter for the health authority. The health authority refused to arrange speech therapy because it was the health authority policy not to provide speech therapy for children in mainstream schools. In December 1993 the parent complained to the Secretary of State that the LEA was in breach of the duty to arrange the speech therapy which was specified as educational provision.

The Secretary of State commenced an investigation and asserted that the complainant would be kept informed of the progress of the case. In March 1994 the Secretary of State suspended or abandoned the investigation without telling the complainant. In September 1994 the parent inquired as to the progress of the complaint. The Secretary of State said that consideration of the complaint had been suspended because the LEA had decided to carry out a further statutory assessment.

In response to the parent's persistence, the Secretary of State reopened the investigation and on 8 December 1994 upheld the complaint. However, instead of issuing a direction to the education authority, the Secretary of State gave the authority three weeks in which to confirm that the authority was prepared to provide the speech therapist. On 19 December 1994 the LEA served a new statement in which the specification of specify speech therapy as educational provision had been deleted. The Secretary of State then concluded that the question of compliance with the previous statement had become academic and so no direction would be issued.

With hindsight, the parent would have been better advised to apply to the High Court for an order of mandamus requiring the LEA to provide the speech therapist. It could have been argued that the LEA had made a decision not to provide a speech therapist and that the decision was ultra vires. It could have been further argued that complaint to the Secretary of State would not provide an effective remedy, though the parent would have been faced with the difficulty of establishing that proposition in advance of it having been plainly demonstrated.

Time Limits

An application for judicial review must be made promptly and in any event within three months from the date when grounds for the application first arose, unless the Court considers that there is good reason for extending the period within which the application shall be made.

An application which is made within three months may fail for not being made promptly where third party rights might be affected or where quashing a decision could have consequences which would be detrimental to good administration. These considerations are not likely to arise in respect of an application concerning the special educational needs of an individual child. They would be relevant, for example, where a parent sought an order quashing a decision to close a special school.

Grounds for Review

Judicial review may be used to challenge a decision, a failure to make a decision, or the existence of a rule on a number of different and loosely defined grounds. These are conventionally separated into three categories: illegality, irrationality and procedural impropriety which are explained in the following sections.

Illegality

The term 'illegality' is used in a narrow sense, meaning an error of law. In the wider sense an irrational or procedurally improper decision is also illegal. Decision makers in public law act within a set of rules which describe the limits of their powers. Where a decision maker goes outside those limits, or outside the scope of their jurisdiction, the decision is unlawful and for most purposes of no effect or void. With respect to children with special educational needs, the powers and duties of schools, education authorities and the Secretary of State for Education are set out in the Education Acts and Statutory Instruments. Those duties are mandatory. Judicial review is the appropriate remedy where a public body decides not to carry out a statutory duty or, when purporting to carry out a statutory duty, exceeds the scope of the particular power. The Code of Practice is not mandatory and is not enforceable. But the Education (Special Educational Needs) Regulations 1994, which are included at the back of the Code of Practice is a statutory instrument which is mandatory.

Local authorities have a mandatory duty under Regulation 11(3) of the Education (Special Educational Needs) Regulations 1994 to make a decision within six weeks of receiving a request from a parent for a statutory assessment. Unless a failure to make a decision falls within one of the exceptions contained in Regulation 11 (4), the failure is a breach of statutory duty. If, after the six weeks has expired, the LEA tells the parent that it is unable to make the decision because the LEA has not received sufficient evidence from the school, an immediate application for judicial review is a possibility.

Irrationality

The court will review a decision on its merits on what are referred to as the 'Wednesbury' principles which were laid down in the case of *Associated Provincial Picture Houses Ltd v Wednesbury Corporation* CA [1948] 1 KB 223. The corporation decided to attach to the grant of cinema licenses under the Sunday Entertainments Act 1932 and the Cinematographic Act 1909 a condition that children under 15 should not be permitted to attend performances on Sundays. Associated Provincial Picture Houses challenged the condition but were unsuccessful. Lord Greene at Page 229 said:

> It is true the discretion must be exercised reasonably. Now what does that mean? Lawyers familiar with the phraseology commonly used in relation to exercise of statutory discretions often use the word 'unreasonable' in a rather comprehensive sense. It has frequently been used and is frequently used as a general description of the things that must not be done. For instance, a person entrusted with a discretion must, so to speak, direct himself properly in law. He must call his own attention to the matters which he is bound to consider. He must exclude from his consideration matters which are irrelevant to what he has to consider. If he does not obey those rules, he may truly be said, and often is said, to be acting 'unreasonably'. Similarly there may be something so absurd that no sensible person could ever dream that it lies within the powers of the authority.

Lord Greene rephrased the last sentence at page 234:

> it may still be possible to say that, although the local authority have kept within the four corners of the matters which they ought to consider, they have

nevertheless come to a conclusion so unreasonable that no reasonable authority could ever have come to it. In such a case, again, I think the court can interfere.

Decisions that are so unreasonable that no reasonable authority could have reached such a conclusion are relatively rare. Decisions taking account of irrelevant matters or failing to take account of relevant matters are more common. Automatically applying a policy without considering the possibility of making an exception in the particular case usually amounts to either taking into account an irrelevant matter or failing to take into account a relevant matter. A policy of not including a particular kind of provision in statements on the grounds that the LEA cannot afford to make that kind of provision is unlawful. Equally, a failure to make the provision that is specified in a statement because the annual budget for children with statements has been exhausted is unlawful.

Procedural impropriety

Making a fair decision entails scrupulous care over the procedure that is followed. Public law has imposed high standards on all the stages of a decision-making process. Statutory instructions as to time limits and the service of notices must be adhered to rigorously. Where consultation is required, the person or persons consulted must be given adequate information and time to formulate a fully thought out response. The decision maker must not be biased or have prejudged the issue. Everything relevant must be properly heard and taken into account. When reasons for a decision are required, the reasons must deal with all the issues and be expressed so that they can be readily understood,

Infringements of the statutory procedures which affect the interests of the parents or the child are likely to render a subsequent decision void and the decision may be quashed on an application for judicial review. In these circumstances judicial review would normally be available even where the SEN Tribunal has concurrent jurisdiction.

Legitimate Expectations

Where a public body gives a clear undertaking concerning a person's rights, that person has a legitimate expectation that the undertaking will be honoured. The court has given legitimate expectations a status equivalent to legal rights and will normally require the public body to honour the undertaking. The public body may sometimes resite from the undertaking but only in a manner that is fair.

A good example of a legitimate expectation being enforced by the court is *R v Home Secretary, ex parte Khan* CA [1984] 1 WLR 1337. The applicant was granted certiorari quashing the Home Secretary's refusal to grant entry clearance to a child coming to England for adoption. The prospective adopters had received a standard letter from the Home Secretary setting out the conditions for the grant of entry clearance to a prospective adoptee. Those conditions were met by the applicant. The Home Secretary subsequently introduced a further condition which the applicant did not meet and for that reason refused entry clearance. The court held that the applicant had a legitimate expectation that entry clearance would be granted.

The duty to perform an undertaking and the grounds on which a public body may resite from the undertaking were described by Lord Denning in *R v Liverpool Corporation, ex parte Liverpool Taxi Fleet Operators' Association* CA [1972] 2 QB 299. The Corporation assured the taxi drivers that an existing regime of licensing would not be changed without consulting them and that it would not be changed until legislation controlling mini-cabs was in place. Lord Denning at page 308 D said:

It has been said that a corporation cannot contract itself out of its statutory duties ...

But that principle does not mean that a corporation can give an undertaking and break it as they please. So long as the performance of the undertaking is compatible with their public duty, they must honour it. And I should have thought that this undertaking was so compatible. At any rate they ought not to depart from it except after the most serious consideration and hearing what the other party has to say: and then only if they are satisfied that the overriding public interest requires it. The public interest may be better served by honouring their undertaking than by breaking it.

An LEA may only specify non-educational provision in Part 6 of a statement if the LEA proposes to make the provision itself or is satisfied that it will be made by someone else. It is submitted that a parent has a legitimate expectation that the provision specified will be made. That legitimate expectation may be enforced by application for an order of mandamus in judicial review proceedings.

Remedies Granted in Judicial Review

The remedies available in judicial review are declaration, certiorari, prohibition, mandamus, injunction and damages. A combination of remedies may be granted. The prerogative orders, certiorari, prohibition and mandamus are exclusive to judicial review. Declaration, injunction and damages are the remedies available at private law which have been incorporated in the unified proceedings known as judicial review. It is usual to seek several of the potential remedies. The court has a discretion whether or not to grant a remedy to a successful applicant.

Declaration

A declaration is likely to be sought in any application for review because the factors going against the grant of a declaration will have less weight than for any other remedy. A declaration may explain the relevant law or identify a breach of the law. A declaration has no legal effect, apart from clarifying the law.

A declaration is available to deal with errors of law in the Code of Practice because the Code is intended to guide decision makers. A declaration is the appropriate remedy because there is nothing which can be quashed by certiorari.

Certiorari, prohibition and mandamus

Certiorari is an order to quash a public decision. Prohibition is an order not to carry out an illegal act. Mandamus is an order to carry out a specific public duty. An order of certiorari alone may not advance the complainant's cause, since the decision maker may reach the same conclusion again but this time by a lawful procedure. An order of mandamus must be clearly and precisely framed so that the body to whom it is directed knows exactly what it must do.

Injunction

Where the Court finally decides to order a public body to act or not to act in a particular way, the decision will be framed as an order of mandamus or prohibition. In some cases it is possible for the court to grant an interim order during the application for leave. That order would be an interim injunction. An interim injunction is intended to maintain the status quo until trial of the main issue. For example, where a parent challenges the legality of their child's expulsion from school, the court may grant an interim injunction requiring the school to continue teaching the child until the matter is finally decided. In most cases concerning SEN provision for an individual child, an interim injunction would not be appropriate. If an interim injunction is sought, the application for leave would normally be made orally. Most parents would need a lawyer to make such an application.

Damages

Damages are not available for breach of statutory duty in the field of SEN. In *E v Dorset County Council and another case* CA [1994] 4 All ER 640, a claim for damages based on the failure of an LEA to provide for a child's special educational needs was struck out by the court. The court accepted that a claim in private law of negligence might succeed.

Procedure

An application for judicial review has two distinct steps, an application for leave and, if successful, a substantive hearing. The application for leave is a quick perusal by a High Court judge to determine whether the applicant has an arguable case. It is intended to protect public administration from trivial and improper applications. In many cases a public authority, against whom leave has been granted, will remedy the defect complained of rather than proceed to a final determination by the court.

Letter before action

Judicial discretion in the grant of remedies emphazises the necessity of high standards of conduct at all stages. It is important to act fast and to act openly. As soon as an application for judicial review is contemplated, it is proper to inform the intended respondent and other interested persons in writing. The respondent may change their decision or supply information that alters the proposed application or shows that it would not succeed. A formal letter before action is a necessity. Insofar as is possible the letter should set out the full grounds of the application for leave. The words 'letter before action' appear in the heading. The letter states that the complainant intends to lodge an application for leave for judicial review unless the matter complained of is remedied by a named date.

Legal Aid

Judicial review proceedings concerning SEN provision are brought in the name of the child by the parent acting as next friend. With respect to income the child may be expected to qualify for legal aid.

A solicitor can give the parent initial advice and assistance on the green form scheme with no cost to the parent. The solicitor then makes an application for legal aid. An applicant must satisfy the Legal Aid Board that there are reasonable grounds for commencing the action. The Legal Aid Board guidance notes interpret reasonable grounds as meaning that: 'the solicitor would advise an applicant to bring the action privately' if the applicant had the means and that there are 'reasonable prospects of success'. Legal aid will not be granted if 'the proceedings are not likely to be cost effective, i.e. the benefit to be achieved does not justify the costs'. This cost-effectiveness test may be conceptualized as; would a private client of moderate means pursue such a action? In *R v Legal Aid Board, ex parte Hughes* CA (199) 142 NLJ 1304, the court stated that the legal aid test is the same as the test for granting leave for judicial review. That rule is likely to apply in the majority of cases.

An application for legal aid and an application for leave to apply for judicial review are in practice very similar and could be identical. Time can be saved by applying for leave for judicial review before applying for legal aid.

Application for leave

The application for leave is made in a standard form (Form 86 A). The form, together with guidance notes for completing the form, is available from Crown Office, Royal Courts of Justice, Strand, London WC2A 2LL (Telephone 0171 936 6000, extension 6205). The application is normally dealt with on paper by a single judge. The application form must be supported by an affidavit from the applicant, and others if necessary, setting out all the facts and annexing all the documents in support. The completed form and accompanying documents must be lodged with the Crown Office at the above address and a complete copy sent to the respondent. The following sections give guidance on filling in Form 86 A.

Decision impugned

In this section it is necessary to identify as far as possible a specific decision taken on a known date. Where a decision was made by a person on behalf of the respondent organization, the person should be named and/or identified by their position in the respondent's organization. Any written decision should be annexed to the applicant's affidavit. Where the complaint is of a failure to take any action, the request for action

should be specified, including how and when the request was delivered
and to whom it was addressed.

Relief sought

The substantive relief sought should be listed and specified as precisely
as possible. Any remedy which might be granted should be included.
Typically the applicant will seek a declaration and/or certiorari and/or
mandamus. The separate items of relief sought are given numbers and
connected by 'and/or'. Certiorari is sought with the words 'An Order of
Certiorari to remove into the Queen's Bench Division of the High Court
of Justice and to quash ...'

Grounds

The grounds must be complete. No question should be left unanswered,
no reasonable alternative view of the facts should be left available. The
grounds set out at this stage are expected to be the grounds at the
eventual hearing of the motion. A good practice is to lay out the grounds
under separate headings: the facts, the law, the grounds for review and
other matters

The facts: a short resume of the facts. This should exclude evidence of
the facts. The affidavit will include both the facts and the evidence for
them.

The law: under this heading cite the relevant statutes and sections and
either quote the relevant parts or, if too long for convenience, summarize
them. Then continue with statutory instruments and the Code of Practice
as necessary.

The grounds: these are grounds of review discussed above. They
should be separated into individual sub-headings such as illegality,
irrationality and procedural impropriety. The grounds may need to be
supported by reference to decided cases. These should be fully cited. It
may be helpful to identify the relevant page number and quote the words
relied on. Citations normally follow a proposition of law in sentences
commencing with, 'The applicant will rely on ....'

Other matters: under other matters any potential bars to the
discretionary grant of a remedy should be dealt with. Consideration
should always be given to exhaustion of remedies. If the respondent is a
school or LEA then an explanation must be given as to why complaint to
the Secretary of State under Section 68 or Section 99 of the Education
Act 1944 would not provide an effective remedy. For example: 'the

decision of the LEA is outside the LEA's statutory powers and is ultra vires and/or experience has shown that the Secretary of State often takes more than a year to determine complaints, but the applicant needs provision for her special educational needs as a matter of urgency.'

Delay: if there has been any delay the reasons must be explained. Time taken in pursuing alternative remedies is not likely to be a bar to the grant of leave for judicial review, since that would be contradictory to the doctrine of exhaustion of remedies. In *R v Rochdale Metropolitan Borough Council, ex parte Cromer Ring Mill Ltd* [1982] 3 All ER 761, at page 764 j, Forbes J said:

> It is plain from that exercise performed by the applicants that they had sought to exhaust all possible remedies and that is the reason why there has been delay .... It is wholly understandable and wholly due to that effort to exhaust alternative remedies.

An application for judicial review might properly be made after lodging a complaint with the Secretary of State, but before that complaint has been determined, if it is apparent that the Secretary of State has not determined the complaint within a reasonable period of time.

Affidavits

The facts asserted in the application for leave must be supported by an affidavit. An affidavit is a sworn written statement. Any County Court will hear a person swear a statement and stamp the statement accordingly for no charge. The affidavit at this stage may contain hearsay, but this should be avoided if at all possible because this affidavit will also go forward to the main hearing at which hearsay in affidavits is not acceptable. Hearsay is anything that is not known to the maker of the affidavit (deponent) by personal observation.

The Decision on the application for leave

The test applied at the leave stage is: does the applicant have an arguable case that a remedy will be granted? That calls for a rapid analysis of the grounds put forward together with any matters which might, in the particular case, cause the court to exercise its discretion not to grant a remedy.

The next steps

The next step, assuming leave is granted, is for the applicant to serve notice of motion on the respondent and on all persons directly affected by it in Form 86. A copy of Form 86 is sent by the Crown Office to the applicant with the grant of leave. The notice of motion should be accompanied by a copy of the original application for leave and all the affidavits and exhibits. The applicant must, within 14 days of service of the grant of leave, file the notice of motion in the Crown Office together with an affidavit of service on the respondent.

At this stage the applicant can expect legal aid to be granted. Solicitors and barristers can be engaged to continue the proceedings and represent the applicant at the full hearing.

Costs

At the conclusion of the main hearing, the court will decide whether one party should be ordered to pay the costs of the other party. An applicant who is granted a remedy would normally be awarded costs. The Court will not order a legally aided applicant to pay the costs of the respondent.

At the leave stage, an unsuccessful applicant would not expect to have costs award against them provided the matter was decided on paper. Where the dispute is resolved before reaching a full hearing it is unlikely that an award of costs will be made unless the application has been deliberately made academic by a party in order to avoid defeat.

The award of costs is always discretionary. Any failure to act honestly, openly and promptly will expose a party to a risk that costs will be awarded against them. A failure to send a letter before action will be viewed seriously by the court.

Conclusion

An application for judicial review is a powerful mechanism for enforcing a child's rights to SEN provision. The initial application for leave is usually carried out on paper, but it is much more difficult than making a complaint to the Secretary of State or Ombudsman. Where a child is suffering due to a failure by an LEA to make reasonable provision for the child's needs, an application for judicial review may be the best way forward. Delay in making a statement and failure to arrange the provision specified in a statement are outside the remit of the SEN Tribunal. They would usually be within the jurisdiction of both the Ombudsman and the Secretary of State, but both those mechanisms of complaint have proved to be unacceptably time-consuming, taking as they do between one and two years. An application for judicial review would be much faster and therefore more effective. It is possible for parents to make the application in person, but some assistance from a lawyer would be very valuable. That assistance should be available from high street solicitors, Citizens Advice Bureaux and Law Centres. Since the action is brought in the child's name, it is the child's income that will be assessed to determine eligibility for legal aid. Most children have no income and are therefore eligible for legal aid. A solicitor can give initial advice immediately and without charging the parent.

Appendix 1

Sections 68 and 99 (1) of the Education Act 1944 as amended by subsequent legislation

68. If the Secretary of State for Education is satisfied, either on complaint by any person or otherwise, that any local education authority or the governors of any county or voluntary school have acted or are proposing to act unreasonably with respect to any power conferred or the performance of any duty imposed by or under this Act, he may, notwithstanding any enactment rendering the exercise of the power or the performance of the duty contingent upon the opinion of the authority or of the governors, give such directions as to the exercise of the power or performance of the duty as appear to him to be expedient. In this section, references to a local education authority shall be construed as including references to any body of persons authorised in accordance with the First Schedule to this Act to exercise functions of such an authority.

99. (1) If the Secretary of State for Education is satisfied, either on complaint by any person interested or otherwise, that any local education authority or the governors of any county or voluntary school, have failed to discharge any duty imposed upon them by or for the purposes of this Act, the Secretary of State for Education may make an order declaring the authority, or the governors, as the case may be, to be in default in respect of that duty, and giving such directions for the purpose of securing the execution thereof as appear to the Secretary of State for Education to be expedient; and any such directions shall be enforceable, on an application made on behalf of the Secretary of State for Education, by mandamus.

Appendix 2

Sections 156 to 181 of the Education Act 1993 and Schedules 9 and 10 to the Education Act 1993

PART III

CHILDREN WITH SPECIAL EDUCATIONAL NEEDS

Introductory

Meaning of
special
educational
needs and
special
educational
provision etc.

156.–(1) For the purposes of the Education Acts, a child has "special educational needs" if he has a learning difficulty which calls for special educational provision to be made for him.

(2) For the purposes of this Act, subject to subsection (3) below, a child has a "learning difficulty" if—

(a) he has a significantly greater difficulty in learning than the majority of children of his age,

(b) he has a disability which either prevents or hinders him from making use of educational facilities of a kind generally provided for children of his age in schools within the area of the local education authority, or

(c) he is under the age of five years and is, or would be if special educational provision were not made for him, likely to fall within paragraph (a) or (b) when over that age.

(3) A child is not to be taken as having a learning difficulty solely because the language (or form of the language) in which he is, or will be, taught is different from a language (or form of a language) which has at any time been spoken in his home.

(4) In the Education Acts, "special educational provision" means—

(a) in relation to a child who has attained the age of two years, educational provision which is additional to, or otherwise different from, the educational provision made generally for children of his age in schools maintained by the local education authority (other than special schools) or grant-maintained schools in their area, and

(b) in relation to a child under that age, educational provision of any kind.

(5) In this Part of this Act, "child" includes any person who has not attained the age of nineteen years and is a registered pupil at a school.

Code of practice

157.–(1) The Secretary of State shall issue, and may from time to time revise, a code of practice giving practical guidance in respect of the discharge by local education authorities and the governing bodies of maintained or grant-maintained schools, or grant-maintained special schools, of their functions under this Part of this Act.

(2) It shall be the duty of –

    (a) local education authorities, and such governing bodies, exercising functions under this Part of this Act,

    (b) any other person exercising any function for the purpose of the discharge by local education authorities, and such governing bodies, of functions under this Part of this Act,

to have regard to the provisions of the code.

(3) On any appeal, the Tribunal shall have regard to any provision of the code which appears to the Tribunal to be relevant to any question arising on the appeal.

(4) The Secretary of State shall publish the code as for the time being in force.

158.–(1) Where the Secretary of State proposes to issue or revise a code of practice, he shall prepare a draft of the code (or revised code). *Making and approval of code.*

(2) The Secretary of State shall consult such persons about the draft as he thinks fit and shall consider any representations made by them.

(3) If he determines to proceed with the draft (either in its original form or with such modifications as he thinks fit) he shall lay it before both Houses of Parliament.

(4) If the draft is approved by resolution of each House, the Secretary of State shall issue the code in the form of the draft and the code shall come into effect on such day as the Secretary of State may by order appoint.

Special educational provision: general

159. A local education authority shall keep under review the arrangements made by them for special educational provision and, in doing so, shall, to the extent that it appears necessary or desirable for the purpose of co-ordinating provision for children with special educational needs, consult the funding authority and the governing bodies of county, voluntary, maintained special and grant-maintained schools in their area. *Review of arrangements.*

160.–(1) Any person exercising any functions under this Part of this Act in respect of a child with special educational needs who should be educated in a school shall secure that, if the conditions mentioned in subsection (2) below are satisfied, the child is educated in a school which is not a special school unless that is incompatible with the wishes of his parent. *Qualified duty to secure education of children with special educational needs in ordinary schools.*

(2) The conditions are that educating the child in a school which is not a special school is compatible with—

    (a) his receiving the special educational provision which his learning difficulty calls for,

    (b) the provision of efficient education for the children with whom he will be educated, and

    (c) the efficient use of resources.

161.–(1) The governing body, in the case of a county, voluntary or grant-maintained school, and the local education authority, in the case of a maintained nursery school, shall— *Duties of governing body etc. in relation to pupils with special education needs.*

    (a) use their best endeavours, in exercising their functions in relation to the school, to secure that if any registered pupil has special educational needs the special educational provision which his learning difficulty calls for is made,

    (b) secure that, where the responsible person has been informed by the local education authority that a registered pupil has special educational needs, those needs are made known to all who are likely to teach him, and

    (c) secure that the teachers in the school are aware of the importance of identifying, and providing for, those registered pupils who have special educational needs.

(2) In subsection (1)(b) above, "the responsible person" means—

    (a) in the case of a county, voluntary or grant-maintained school, the head teacher or the appropriate governor (that is, the chairman of the governing body or, where the governing body have designated another governor for the purposes of this paragraph, that other governor), and

    (b) in the case of a nursery school, the head teacher.

(3) To the extent that it appears necessary or desirable for the purpose of co-ordinating provision for children with special educational needs—

    (a) the governing bodies of county, voluntary and grant-maintained schools shall, in exercising functions relating to the provision for such children, consult the local education authority, the funding authority and the governing bodies of other such schools, and

    (b) in relation to maintained nursery schools, the local education authority shall, in exercising those functions, consult the funding authority and the governing bodies of county, voluntary and grant-maintained schools.

(4) Where a child who has special educational needs is being educated in a county, voluntary or grant-maintained school or a maintained nursery school, those concerned with making special educational provision for the child shall secure, so far as is reasonably practicable and is compatible with—

    (a) the child receiving the special educational provision which his learning difficulty calls for,

    (b) the provision of efficient education for the children with whom he will be educated, and

    (c) the efficient use of resources,

that the child engages in the activities of the school together with children who do not have special educational needs.

(5) The annual report for each county, voluntary, maintained special or grant-maintained school shall include a report containing such information as may be prescribed about the implementation of the governing body's policy for pupils with special educational needs; and in this subsection "annual report" means the report prepared under the articles of government for the school in accordance with section 30 of the Education (No. 2) Act 1986 or, as the case may be, paragraph 8 of Schedule 6 to this Act.

Provision of goods and services in connection with special educational needs

162.–(1) A local education authority may for the purpose only of assisting—

    (a) the governing bodies of county, voluntary or grant-maintained schools in their or any other area in the performance of the governing bodies' duties under section 161(1)(a) of this Act, or

    (b) the governing bodies of maintained or grant-maintained special schools in their or any other area in the performance of the governing bodies' duties,

supply goods or services to them.

(2) The terms on which goods or services are supplied by local education authorities to the governing bodies of grant-maintained schools or grant-maintained special schools, or to the governing bodies of county, voluntary or maintained special schools in any other area, under this section may, in such circumstances as may be prescribed, include such terms as to payment as may be prescribed.

(3) This section is without prejudice to the generality of any other power of local education authorities to supply goods or services.

Special educational provision otherwise than in schools.

163.–(1) Where a local education authority are satisfied that it would be inappropriate for the special educational provision (or any part of the special educational provision) which a learning difficulty of a child in their area calls for to be made in a school, they may arrange for the provision (or, as the case may be, for that part of it) to be made otherwise than in a school.

(2) Before making an arrangement under this section, a local education authority shall consult the child's parent.

164.–(1) A local education authority may make such arrangements as they think fit to enable a child for whom they maintain a statement under section 168 of this Act to attend an institution outside England and Wales which specialises in providing for children with special needs. Provision outside England and Wales for certain children

(2) In subsection (1) above, "children with special needs" means children who have particular needs which would be special educational needs if those children were in England and Wales.

(3) Where a local education authority make arrangements under this section in respect of a child, those arrangements may in particular include contributing to or paying—
- (a) fees charged by the institution,
- (b) expenses reasonably incurred in maintaining him while he is at the institution or travelling to or from it,
- (c) his travelling expenses, and
- (d) expenses reasonably incurred by any person accompanying him while he is travelling or staying at the institution.

(4) This section is without prejudice to any other powers of a local education authority.

Identification and assessment of children with special educational needs

165.–(1) A local education authority shall exercise their powers with a view to securing that, of the children for whom they are responsible, they identify those to whom subsection (2) below applies. General duty of local education authority towards children for whom they are responsible.

(2) This subsection applies to a child if—
- (a) he has special educational needs, and
- (b) it is necessary for the authority to determine the special educational provision which any learning difficulty he may have calls for.

(3) For the purposes of this Part of this Act, a local education authority are responsible for a child if he is in their area and—
- (a) he is a registered pupil at a maintained, grant-maintained or grant-maintained special school,
- (b) education is provided for him at a school which is not a maintained, grant-maintained or grant-maintained special school at the expense of the authority or the funding authority,
- (c) he does not come within paragraph (a) or (b) above but is a registered pupil at a school and has been brought to the authority's attention as having (or probably having) special educational needs, or
- (d) he is not a registered pupil at a school, is not under the age of two years or over compulsory school age and has been brought to their attention as having (or probably having) special educational needs.

166.–(1) Where it appears to a local education authority that any District Health Authority or local authority could, by taking any specified action, help in the exercise of any of their functions under this Part of this Act, they may request the help of the authority, specifying the action in question. Duty of District Health Authority or local authority to help local education authority.

(2) An authority whose help is so requested shall comply with the request unless—
- (a) they consider that the help requested is not necessary for the purpose of the exercise by the local education authority of those functions, or
- (b) subsection (3) below applies.

(3) This subsection applies—
- (a) in the case of a District Health Authority, if that authority consider that, having regard to the resources available to them for the purpose of the exercise of their functions under the National Health Service Act 1977, it is not reasonable for them to comply with the request, or
- (b) in the case of a local authority, if that authority consider that the request is not compatible with their own statutory or other duties and obligations or unduly prejudices the discharge of any of their functions.

(4) Regulations may provide that, where an authority are under a duty by virtue of subsection (2) above to comply with a request to help a local education authority in the making of an assessment under section 167 of this Act or a statement under section 168 of this Act, they must, subject to prescribed exceptions, comply with the request within the prescribed period.

(5) In this section, "local authority" means a county council, a metropolitan district council, a London borough council or the Common Council of the City of London.

Assessment of educational needs

167.–(1) Where a local education authority are of the opinion that a child for whom they are responsible falls, or probably falls, within subsection (2) below, they shall serve a notice on the child's parent informing him—

(a) that they propose to make an assessment of the child's educational needs,

(b) of the procedure to be followed in making the assessment,

(c) of the name of the officer of the authority from whom further information may be obtained, and

(d) of the parent's right to make representations, and submit written evidence, to the authority within such period (which shall not be less than twenty-nine days beginning with the date on which the notice is served) as may be specified in the notice.

(2) A child falls within this subsection if—

(a) he has special educational needs, and

(b) it is necessary for the authority to determine the special educational provision which any learning difficulty he may have calls for.

(3) Where–

(a) a local education authority have served a notice under subsection (1) above and the period specified in the notice in accordance with subsection (1)(d) above has expired, and

(b) the authority remain of the opinion, after taking into account any representations made and any evidence submitted to them in response to the notice, that the child falls, or probably falls, within subsection (2) above,

they shall make an assessment of his educational needs.

(4) Where a local education authority decide to make an assessment under this section, they shall give notice in writing to the child's parent of that decision and of their reasons for making it.

(5) Schedule 9 to this Act (which makes provision in relation to the making of assessments under this section) shall have effect.

(6) Where, at any time after serving a notice under subsection (1) above, a local education authority decide not to assess the educational needs of the child concerned they shall give notice in writing to the child's parent of their decision.

Statement of special educational needs.

168.–(1) If, in the light of an assessment under section 167 of this Act of any child's educational needs and of any representations made by the child's parent in pursuance of Schedule 10 to this Act, it is necessary for the local education authority to determine the special educational provision which any learning difficulty he may have calls for, the authority shall make and maintain a statement of his special educational needs.

(2) The statement shall be in such form and contain such information as may be prescribed.

(3) In particular, the statement shall—

(a) give details of the authority's assessment of the child's special educational needs, and

(b) specify the special educational provision to be made for the purpose of meeting those needs, including the particulars required by subsection (4) below.

(4) The statement shall—

(a) specify the type of school or other institution which the local education authority consider would be appropriate for the child,

(b) if they are not required under Schedule 10 to this Act to specify the name of any school in the statement, specify the name of any school or institution (whether in the United Kingdom or elsewhere) which they consider would be appropriate for the child and should be speci- . fied in the statement, and

(c) specify any provision for the child for which they make arrangements under section 163 of this Act and which they consider should be specified in the statement.

(5) Where a local education authority maintain a statement under this section—

    (a) unless the child's parent has made suitable arrangements, the authority—

        (i) shall arrange that the special educational provision specified in the statement is made for the child, and

        (ii) may arrange that any non-educational provision specified in the statement is made for him in such manner as they consider appropriate, and

    (b) if the name of a maintained, grant-maintained or grant-maintained special school is specified in the statement, the governing body of the school shall admit the child to the school.

(6) Subsection (5)(b) above does not affect any power to exclude from a school a pupil who is already a registered pupil there.

(7) Schedule 10 to this Act (which makes provision in relation to the making and maintenance of statements under this section) shall have effect.

169.–(1) If, after making an assessment under section 167 of this Act of the educational needs of any child for whom no statement is maintained under section 168 of this Act, the local education authority do not propose to make such a statement, they shall give notice in writing of their decision, and of the effect of subsection (2) below, to the child's parent.   *Appeal against decision not to make statement.*

(2) In such a case, the child's parent may appeal to the Tribunal against the decision.

(3) On an appeal under this section, the Tribunal may—

    (a) dismiss the appeal,

    (b) order the local education authority to make and maintain such a statement, or

    (c) remit the case to the authority for them to reconsider whether, having regard to any observations made by the Tribunal, it is necessary for the authority to determine the special educational provision which any learning difficulty the child may have calls for.

170.–(1) The parent of a child for whom a local education authority maintain a statement under section 168 of this Act may—   *Appeal against contents of statement.*

    (a) when the statement is first made,

    (b) where the description in the statement of the authority's assessment of the child's special educational needs, or the special educational provision specified in the statement, is amended, or

    (c) where, after conducting an assessment of the educational needs of the child under section 167 of this Act, the local education authority determine not to amend the statement,

appeal to the Tribunal against the description in the statement of the authority's assessment of the child's special educational needs, the special educational provision specified in the statement or, if no school is named in the statement, that fact.

(2) Subsection (1)(b) above does not apply where the amendment is made in pursuance of paragraph 8 or 11(3)(b) of Schedule 10 to this Act or directions under section 197 of this Act; and subsection (1)(c) above does not apply to a determination made following the service of notice under paragraph 10 of Schedule 10 to this Act of a proposal to amend the statement.

(3) On an appeal under this section, the Tribunal may—

    (a) dismiss the appeal,

    (b) order the authority to amend the statement, so far as it describes the authority's assessment of the child's special educational needs or specifies the special educational provision, and make such other consequential amendments to the statement as the Tribunal think fit, or

(c) order the authority to cease to maintain the statement.

(4) On an appeal under this section the Tribunal shall not order the local education authority to specify the name of any school in the statement (either in substitution for an existing name or in a case where no school is named) unless—

(a) the parent has expressed a preference for the school in pursuance of arrangements under paragraph 3 of Schedule 10 to this Act, or

(b) in the proceedings the parent, the local education authority or both have proposed the school.

(5) Before determining any appeal under this section the Tribunal may, with the agreement of the parties, correct any deficiency in the statement.

171.–(1) This section applies where–

(a) a local education authority maintain a statement for a child under section 168 of this Act, and

(b) in pursuance of the statement education is provided for the child at—

(i) a school maintained by another local education authority,

(ii) a grant-maintained school, or

(iii) a grant-maintained special school.

(2) Any person authorised by the local education authority shall be entitled to have access at any reasonable time to the premises of any such school for the purpose of monitoring the special educational provision made in pursuance of the statement for the child at the school.

172.–(1) Regulations may prescribe the frequency with which assessments under section 167 of this Act are to be repeated in respect of children for whom statements are maintained under section 168 of this Act.

(2) Where–

(a) the parent of a child for whom a statement is maintained under section 168 of this Act asks the local education authority to arrange for an assessment to be made in respect of the child under section 167 of this Act,

(b) such an assessment has not been made within the period of six months ending with the date on which the request is made, and

(c) it is necessary for the authority to make a further assessment under that section.

the authority shall comply with the request.

(3) If in any case where subsection (2)(a) and (b) above applies the authority determine not to comply with the request—

(a) they shall give notice of that fact and of the effect of paragraph (b) below to the child's parent, and

(b) the parent may appeal to the Tribunal against the determination.

(4) On an appeal under subsection (3) above the Tribunal may—

(a) dismiss the appeal, or

(b) order the authority to arrange for an assessment to be made in respect of the child under section 167 of this Act.

(5) A statement under section 168 of this Act shall be reviewed by the local education authority—

(a) on the making of an assessment in respect of the child concerned under section 167 of this Act, and

(b) in any event, within the period of twelve months beginning with the making of the statement or, as the case may be, with the previous review.

(6) Regulations may make provision—
- (a) as to the manner in which reviews of such statements are to be conducted,
- (b) as to the participation in such reviews of such persons as may be prescribed, and
- (c) in connection with such other matters relating to such reviews as the Secretary of State considers appropriate.

173.–(1) Where— Assessment of educational needs at request of child's parent.
- (a) the parent of a child for whom a local education authority are responsible but for whom no statement is maintained under section 168 of this Act asks the authority to arrange for an assessment to be made in respect of the child under section 167 of this Act.
- (b) such an assessment has not been made within the period of six months ending with the date on which the request is made, and
- (c) it is necessary for the authority to make an assessment under that section,

the authority shall comply with the request.

(2) If in any case where subsection (1)(a) and (b) above applies the authority determine not to comply with the request—
- (a) they shall give notice of that fact and of the effect of paragraph (b) below to the child's parent, and
- (b) the parent may appeal to the Tribunal against the determination.

(3) On an appeal under subsection (2) above the Tribunal may—
- (a) dismiss the appeal, or
- (b) order the authority to arrange for an assessment to be made in respect of the child under section 167 of this Act.

174.–(1) Where in the case of a child for whom a local education authority are responsible but for whom no statement is maintained under section 168 of this Act— Assessment of educational needs at request of governing body of grant-maintained school.
- (a) a grant-maintained school is specified in a direction in respect of the child under section 13 of this Act,
- (b) the governing body of the school ask the authority to arrange for an assessment to be made in respect of the child under section 167 of this Act, and
- (c) such an assessment has not been made within the period of six months ending with the date on which the request is made,

the local education authority shall serve a notice under subsection (2) below on the child's parent.

(2) The notice shall inform the child's parent—
- (a) that the local education authority propose to make an assessment of the child's educational needs,
- (b) of the procedure to be followed in making the assessment,
- (c) of the name of the officer of the authority from whom further information may be obtained, and
- (d) of the parent's right to make representations, and submit written evidence, to the authority within such period (which shall not be less than twenty-nine days beginning with the date on which the notice is served) as may be specified in the notice.

(3) Where—
- (a) a local education authority have served a notice under subsection (2) above and the period specified in the notice in accordance with subsection (2)(d) above has expired, and
- (b) the authority are of the opinion, after taking into account any representations made and any evidence submitted to them in response to the notice, that the child falls, or probably falls, within subsection (4) below,

they shall make an assessment of his educational needs under section 167 of this Act.

(4) A child falls within this subsection if—

    (a) he has special educational needs, and

    (b) it is necessary to determine the special educational provision which any learning difficulty he may have calls for.

(5) Where a local education authority decide in pursuance of this section to make an assessment under that section, they shall give notice in writing to the child's parent, and to the governing body of the grant-maintained school, of that decision and of their reasons for making it.

(6) Where, at any time after serving a notice under subsection (2) above, a local education authority decide not to assess the educational needs of the child concerned, they shall give notice in writing to the child's parent and to the governing body of the grant-maintained school of their decision.

Assessment of educational needs of children under two. 175.–(1) Where a local education authority are of the opinion that a child in their area who is under the age of two years falls, or probably falls, within subsection (2) below—

    (a) they may, with the consent of his parent, make an assessment of the child's educational needs, and

    (b) they shall make such an assessment at the request of his parent.

(2) A child falls within this subsection if—

    (a) he has special educational needs, and

    (b) it is necessary for the authority to determine the special educational provision which any learning difficulty he may have calls for.

(3) An assessment under this section shall be made in such manner as the authority consider appropriate.

(4) After making an assessment under this section, the authority—

    (a) may make a statement of the child's special educational needs, and

    (b) may maintain that statement,

in such manner as they consider appropriate.

Duty of District Health Authority or National Health Service trust to notify parent etc. 176.–(1) This section applies where a District Health Authority or a National Health Service trust, in the course of exercising any of their functions in relation to a child who is under the age of five years, form the opinion that he has (or probably has) special educational needs.

(2) The health authority or trust shall—

    (a) inform the child's parent of their opinion and of their duty under this section, and

    (b) after giving the parent an opportunity to discuss that opinion with an officer of the health authority or trust, bring it to the attention of the appropriate local education authority.

(3) If the health authority or trust are of the opinion that a particular voluntary organisation is likely to be able to give the parent advice or assistance in connection with any special educational needs that the child may have, they shall inform the parent accordingly.

Special Educational Needs Tribunal

Constitution of Tribunal. 177.–(1) There shall be established a tribunal, to be known as the Special Educational Needs Tribunal (referred to in this Part of this Act as "the Tribunal"), to exercise the jurisdiction conferred on it by this Part of this Act.

(2) There shall be appointed—

    (a) a President of the Tribunal (referred to in this Part of this Act as "the President"),

    (b) a panel of persons (referred to in this Part of this Act as "the chairmen's panel") who may serve as chairman of the Tribunal, and

    (c) a panel of persons (referred to in this Part of this Act as "the lay panel") who may serve as the other two members of the Tribunal apart from the chairman.

(3) The President and the members of the chairmen's panel shall each be appointed by the Lord Chancellor.

(4) The members of the lay panel shall each be appointed by the Secretary of State.

(5) Regulations may—
- (a) provide for the jurisdiction of the Tribunal to be exercised by such number of tribunals as may be determined from time to time by the President, and
- (b) make such other provision in connection with the establishment and continuation of the Tribunal as the Secretary of State considers necessary or desirable

(6) The Secretary of State may, with the consent of the Treasury, provide such staff and accommodation as the Tribunal may require.

178.–(1) No person may be appointed President or member of the chairmen's panel unless he has a seven year general qualification (within the meaning of section 71 of the Courts and Legal Services Act 1990). The President and members of the panels 1990 c. 41.

(2) No person may be appointed member of the lay panel unless he satisfies such requirements as may be prescribed.

(3) If, in the opinion of the Lord Chancellor, the President is unfit to continue in office or is incapable of performing his duties, the Lord Chancellor may revoke his appointment.

(4) Each member of the chairmen's panel or lay panel shall hold and vacate office under the terms of the instrument under which he is appointed.

(5) The President or a member of the chairmen's panel or lay panel—
- (a) may resign office by notice in writing to the Lord Chancellor or (as the case may be) the Secretary of State, and
- (b) is eligible for re-appointment if he ceases to hold office.

179.–(1) The Secretary of State may pay to the President, and to any other person in respect of his service as a member of the Tribunal, such remuneration and allowances as he may, with the consent of the Treasury, determine. Remuneration and expenses.

(2) The Secretary of State may defray the expenses of the Tribunal to such amount as he may, with the consent of the Treasury, determine.

180.–(1) Regulations may make provision about the proceedings of the Tribunal on an appeal under this Part of this Act and the initiation of such an appeal. Tribunal procedure.

(2) The regulations may, in particular, include provision—
- (a) as to the period within which, and the manner in which, appeals are to be instituted,
- (b) where the jurisdiction of the Tribunal is being exercised by more than one tribunal—
  - (i) for determining by which tribunal any appeal is to be heard, and
  - (ii) for the transfer of proceedings from one tribunal to another,
- (c) for enabling any functions which relate to matters preliminary or incidental to an appeal to be performed by the President, or by the chairman,
- (d) for the holding of hearings in private in prescribed circumstances,
- (e) for hearings to be conducted in the absence of any member, other than the chairman,
- (f) as to the persons who may appear on behalf of the parties,
- (g) for granting any person such discovery or inspection of documents or right to further particulars as might be granted by a county court,
- (h) requiring persons to attend to give evidence and produce documents,
- (i) for authorising the administration of oaths to witnesses,
- (j) for the determination of appeals without a hearing in prescribed circumstances,
- (k) as to the withdrawal of appeals,

(l) for the award of costs or expenses,

(m) for taxing or otherwise settling any such costs or expenses (and, in particular, for enabling such costs to be taxed in the county court),

(n) for the registration and proof of decisions and orders, and

(o) for enabling the Tribunal to review its decisions, or revoke or vary its orders, in such circumstances as may be determined in accordance with the regulations.

(3) The Secretary of State may pay such allowances for the purpose of or in connection with the attendance of persons at the Tribunal as he may with the consent of the Treasury determine.

1950 c. 27 (4) The Arbitration Act 1950 shall not apply to any proceedings before the Tribunal but regulations may make provision corresponding to any provision of that Act.

(5) Any person who without reasonable excuse fails to comply with—

(a) any requirement in respect of the discovery or inspection of documents imposed by the regulations by virtue of subsection (2)(g) above, or

(b) any requirement imposed by the regulations by virtue of subsection (2)(h) above,

is guilty of an offence.

(6) A person guilty of an offence under subsection (5) above is liable on summary conviction to a fine not exceeding level 3 on the standard scale.

Supervision of and appeals from Tribunal. 1992 c. 53 **181.**–(1) In paragraph 15 of Part I of Schedule I to the Tribunals and Inquiries Act 1992 (tribunals under direct supervision of Council on Tribunals), after sub-paragraph (d) there is inserted—

"(e) the Special Educational Needs Tribunal constituted under section 177 of the Education Act 1993".

(2) In section 11(1) of that Act (appeals from certain tribunals), for "15(a) or (d)" there is substituted "15(a), (d) or (e)".

Section 167.
SCHEDULE 9
MAKING OF ASSESSMENTS UNDER SECTION 167
Introductory

1. In this Schedule, "assessment" means an assessment of a child's educational needs under section 67 of this Act.

Medical and other advice

2.–(1) Regulations shall make provision as to the advice which a local education authority are to seek in making assessments.

(2) Without prejudice to the generality of sub-paragraph (1) above, the regulations shall, except in such circumstances as may be prescribed, require the authority to seek medical, psychological and educational advice and such other advice as may be prescribed.

Manner, and timing, of assessments, etc.

3.–(1) Regulations may make provision—

(a) as to the manner in which assessments are to be conducted,

(b) requiring the local education authority, where, after conducting an assessment under section 167 of this Act of the educational needs of a child for whom a statement is maintained under section 168 of this Act, they determine not to amend the statement, to serve on the parent of the child notice giving the prescribed information, and

(c) in connection with such other matters relating to the making of assessments as the Secretary of State considers appropriate.

(2) Sub-paragraph (1)(b) above does not apply to a determination made following the service of

notice under paragraph 10 of Schedule 10 to this Act of a proposal to amend the statement.

(3) Regulations may provide that, where a local education authority are under a duty to make an assessment, the duty must, subject to prescribed exceptions, be performed within the prescribed period.

(4) Such provision shall not relieve the authority of the duty to make an assessment which has not been performed within that period.

Attendance at examinations

Sch 9.

4.–(1) Where a local education authority propose to make an assessment, they may serve a notice on the parent of the child concerned requiring the child's attendance for examination in accordance with the provisions of the notice.

(2) The parent of a child examined under this paragraph may be present at the examination if he so desires.

(3) A notice under this paragraph shall—
   (a) state the purpose of the examination,
   (b) state the time and place at which the examination will be held,
   (c) name an officer of the authority from whom further information may be obtained,
   (d) inform the parent that he may submit such information to the authority as he may wish, and
   (e) inform the parent of his right to be present at the examination.

Offence

5.–(1) Any parent who fails without reasonable excuse to comply with any requirements of a notice served on him under paragraph 4 above commits an offence if the notice relates to a child who is not over compulsory school age at the time stated in it as the time for holding the examination.

(2) A person guilty of an offence under this paragraph is liable on summary conviction to a fine not exceeding level 2 on the standard scale.

SCHEDULE 10

Sch. 10.

MAKING AND MAINTENANCE OF STATEMENTS UNDER SECTION 168
Introductory

1. In this Schedule, "statement" means a statement of a child's special educational needs under section 168 of this Act.

Copy of proposed statement

2. Before making a statement, a local education authority shall serve on the parent of the child concerned—
   (a) a copy of the proposed statement, and
   (b) a written notice explaining the arrangements under paragraph 3 below, the effect of paragraph 4 below and the right to appeal under section 170 of this Act and containing such other information as may be prescribed,

but the copy of the proposed statement shall not specify any matter in pursuance of section 168(4) of this Act or any prescribed matter.

Choice of school

Section 168.

3.–(1) Every local education authority shall make arrangements for enabling a parent on whom a copy of a proposed statement has been served under paragraph 2 above to express a preference as to the maintained, grant-maintained or grant-maintained special school at which he wishes education to be provided for his child and to give reasons for his preference.

(2) Any such preference must be expressed or made within the period of fifteen days beginning—

    (a) with the date on which the written notice mentioned in paragraph 2(b) above was served on the parent, or

    (b) if a meeting has (or meetings have) been arranged under paragraph 4(1)(b) or (2) below, with the date fixed for that meeting (or the last of those meetings).

(3) Where a local education authority make a statement in a case where the parent of the child concerned has expressed a preference in pursuance of such arrangements as to the school at which he wishes education to be provided for his child, they shall specify the name of that school in the statement unless—

    (a) the school is unsuitable to the child's age, ability or aptitude or to his special educational needs, or

    (b) the attendance of the child at the school would be incompatible with the provision of efficient education for the children with whom he would be educated or the efficient use of resources.

(4) A local education authority shall, before specifying the name of any maintained, grant-maintained or grant-maintained special school in a statement, consult the governing body of the school and, if the school is maintained by another local education authority, that authority.

Representations

4.–(1) A parent on whom a copy of a proposed statement has been served under paragraph 2 above may—

    (a) make representations (or further representations) to the local education authority about the content of the statement, and

    (b) require the authority to arrange a meeting between him and an officer of the authority at which the statement can be discussed.

(2) Where a parent, having attended a meeting arranged by a local education authority under sub-paragraph (1)(b) above, disagrees with any part of the assessment in question, he may require the authority to arrange such meeting or meetings as they consider will enable him to discuss the relevant advice with the appropriate person or persons.

(3) In this paragraph—

"relevant advice" means such of the advice given to the authority in connection with the assessment as they consider to be relevant to that part of the assessment with which the parent disagrees, and

"appropriate person" means the person who gave the relevant advice or any other person who, in the opinion of the authority, is the appropriate person to discuss it with the parent.

(4) Any representations under sub-paragraph (1)(a) above must be made within the period of fifteen days beginning—

    (a) with the date on which the written notice mentioned in paragraph 2(b) above was served on the parent, or

    (b) if a meeting has (or meetings have) been arranged under sub-paragraph (1)(b) or (2) above, with the date fixed for that meeting (or the last of those meetings).

(5) A requirement under sub-paragraph (1)(b) above must be made within the period of fifteen days beginning with the date on which the written notice mentioned in paragraph 2(b) above was served on the parent.

(6) A requirement under sub-paragraph (2) above must be made within the period of fifteen days beginning with the date fixed for the meeting arranged under sub-paragraph (1)(b) above.

Making the statement

5.–(1) Where representations are made to a local education authority under paragraph 4(1)(a) above, the authority shall not make the statement until they have considered the representations and the period or the last of the periods allowed by paragraph 4 above for making requirements or further representations has expired.

(2) The statement may be in the form originally proposed (except as to the matters required to be excluded from the copy of the proposed statement) or in a form modified in the light of the representations.

(3) Regulations may provide that, where a local education authority are under a duty (subject to compliance with the preceding requirements of this Schedule) to make a statement, the duty, or any step required to be taken for performance of the duty, must, subject to prescribed exceptions, be performed within the prescribed period.

(4) Such provision shall not relieve the authority of the duty to make a statement, or take any step, which has not been performed or taken within that period.

Service of statement

6. Where a local education authority make a statement they shall serve a copy of the statement on the parent of the child concerned and shall give notice in writing to him—

(a) of his right under section 170(1) of this Act to appeal against the description in the statement of the authority's assessment of the child's special educational needs, the special educational provision specified in the statement or, if no school is named in the statement, that fact, and

(b) of the name of the person to whom he may apply for information and advice about the child's special educational needs.

Keeping, disclosure and transfer of statements

7–(1) Regulations may make provision as to the keeping and disclosure of statements.

(2) Regulations may make provision, where a local education authority become responsible for a child for whom a statement is maintained by another authority, for the transfer of the statement to them and for Part III of this Act to have effect as if the duty to maintain the transferred statement were their duty.

Change of named school

8.–(1) Sub-paragraph (2) below applies where—

(a) the parent of a child for whom a statement is maintained which specifies the name of a school or institution asks the local education authority to substitute for that name the name of a maintained, grant-maintained or grant-maintained special school specified by the parent, and

(b) the request is not made less than twelve months after—

(i) a request under this paragraph,

(ii) the service of a copy of the statement under paragraph 6 above,

(iii) if the statement has been amended, the date when notice of the amendment is given under paragraph 10(3)(b) below, or

(iv) if the parent has appealed to the Tribunal under section 170 of this Act or this paragraph, the date when the appeal is concluded,

whichever is the later.

(2) The local education authority shall comply with the request unless—   Sch. 10.

(a) the school is unsuitable to the child's age, ability or aptitude or to his special educational needs, or

    (b) the attendance of the child at the school would be incompatible with the provision of efficient education for the children with whom he would be educated or the efficient use of resources.

(3) Where the local education authority determine not to comply with the request—
    (a) they shall give notice of that fact and of the effect of paragraph (b) below to the parent of the child, and
    (b) the parent of the child may appeal to the Tribunal against the determination.

(4) On the appeal the Tribunal may—
    (a) dismiss the appeal, or
    (b) order the local education authority to substitute for the name of the school or other institution specified in the statement the name of the school specified by the parent.

(5) Regulations may provide that, where a local education authority are under a duty to comply with a request under this paragraph, the duty must, subject to prescribed exceptions, be performed within the prescribed period.

(6) Such provision shall not relieve the authority of the duty to comply with such a request which has not been complied with within that period.

Procedure for amending or ceasing to maintain a statement

9.–(1) A local education authority may not amend, or cease to maintain a statement except in accordance with paragraph 10 or 11 below.

(2) Sub-paragraph (1) above does not apply where the local education authority—
    (a) cease to maintain a statement for a child who has ceased to be a child for whom they are responsible,
    (b) amend a statement in pursuance of paragraph 8 above,
    (c) are ordered to cease to maintain a statement under section 170(3)(c) of this Act, or
    (d) amend a statement in pursuance of directions under section 197 of this Act.

10.–(1) Before amending a statement, a local education authority shall serve on the parent of the child concerned a notice informing him—
    (a) of their proposal, and
    (b) of his right to make representations under sub-paragraph (2) below.

(2) A parent on whom a notice has been served under sub-paragraph (1) above may, within the period of fifteen days beginning with the date on which the notice is served, make representations to the local education authority about their proposal.

(3) The local education authority—
    (a) shall consider any representations made to them under sub-paragraph (2) above, and
    (b) on taking a decision on the proposal to which the representations relate shall give notice in writing to the parent of their decision.

(4) Where a local education authority make an amendment under this paragraph to the description in a statement of the authority's assessment of a child's special educational needs or to the special educational provision specified in a statement, they shall give notice in writing to the parent of his right under section 170(1) of this Act to appeal against the description in the statement of the authority's assessment of the child's special educational needs, the special educational provision specified in the statement or, if no school is named in the statement, that fact.

(5) A local education authority may only amend a statement under this paragraph within the prescribed period beginning with the service of the notice under sub-paragraph (1) above.

11.–(1) A local education authority may cease to maintain a statement only if it is no longer necessary to maintain it.

(2) Where the local education authority determine to cease to maintain a statement—
  (a) they shall give notice of that fact and of the effect of paragraph (b) below to the parent of the child, and
  (b) the parent of the child may appeal to the Tribunal against the determination.

(3) On an appeal under this paragraph the Tribunal may—
  (a) dismiss the appeal, or
  (b) order the local education authority to continue to maintain the statement in its existing form or with such amendments of the description in the statement of the authority's assessment of the child's special educational needs or the special educational provision specified in the statement, and such other consequential amendments, as the Tribunal may determine.

(4) Except where the parent of the child appeals to the Tribunal under this paragraph, a local education authority may only cease to maintain a statement under this paragraph within the prescribed period beginning with the service of the notice under sub-paragraph (2) above.

Appendix 3

Regulations 1 to 19 of The Education (Special Educational Needs) Regulations 1994, together with the Schedule

STATUTORY INSTRUMENTS
1994 No. 1047
EDUCATION, ENGLAND AND WALES
The Education (Special Educational Needs) Regulations 1994
Made 7 April 1994
Laid before Parliament 13 April 1994
Coming to into force 1 September 1994
ARRANGEMENT OF REGULATIONS

PART I
General

PART II
Assessments

PART III
Statements

PART IV
Revocation and Transitional Provisions

SCHEDULE

In exercise of the powers conferred on the Secretary of State by sections 166(4), 168(2), 172(6), 301(6) of, and paragraphs 2 and 3 of Schedule 9 and paragraphs 5, 7, and 8 of Schedule 10 to the Education Act 1993 and by section 19 and paragraphs 1 and 3 of Schedule 1 to the Education Act 1981 the Secretary of State for Education, as respects England, and the Secretary of State for Wales, as respects Wales, hereby make the following Regulations:

PART I
GENERAL

Title and commencement

1. These Regulations may be cited as the Education (Special Educational Needs) Regulations 1994 and shall come into force on 1st September 1994.

Interpretation

2. –(1) In these Regulations -

'the Act means the Education Act 1993;

'authority' means a local education authority;

'district health authority' has the same meaning as in the National Health Service Act 1977;

'head teacher' includes any person to whom the duties or functions of a head teacher under these Regulations have been delegated by the head teacher in accordance with regulation 3;

'social services authority' means a local authority for the purposes of the Local Authority Social Services Act 1970 acting in the discharge of such functions as are referred to in section 2 (1) of that Act;

'target' means the knowledge, skills and understanding which a child is expected to have by the end of a particular period;

'transition plan' means a document prepared pursuant to regulation 16(9) or 17 (9) which sets out the arrangements which an authority consider appropriate for a young person during the period when he is aged 14 to 19 years, including arrangements for special educational provision and for any other necessary provision, for suitable employment and accommodation and for leisure activities, and which will facilitate a satisfactory transition from childhood to adulthood;

'working day' means a day other than a Saturday, Sunday, Christmas Day, Good Friday or Bank Holiday within the meaning of the Banking and Financial Dealings Act 1971;

'the 1981 Act' means the Education Act 1981;

the 1983 Regulations means the Education (Special Educational Needs) Regulations 1983.

(2) In these Regulations any reference to the district health authority or the social services authority is, in relation to a particular child, a reference to the district health authority or social services authority in whose area that child lives.

(3) Where a thing is required to be done under these Regulations

    (a) within a period after an action is taken, the day on which that action was taken shall not be counted in the calculation of that period; and

    (b) within a period and the last day of that period is not a working day, the period shall be extended to include the following working day.

(4) References in these Regulations to a section are references to a section of the Act.

(5) References in these Regulations to a regulation are references to a regulation in these Regulations and references to a Schedule are references to the Schedule to these Regulations.

Delegation of functions

3.   Where a head teacher has any functions or duties under these Regulations he may delegate those functions or duties -

    (a) generally to a member of the staff of the school who is a qualified teacher, or

    (b) in a particular case to a member of the staff of the school who teaches the child in question.

Service of documents

4.   –(1) Where any provision in Part III of the Act or in these Regulations authorises or requires any document to be served on or sent to a person or any written notice to be given to a person the document may be served or sent or the notice may be given by properly addressing, pre-paying and posting a letter containing the document or notice.

(2) For the purposes of this regulation, the proper address of a person is -

    (a) in the case of the child's parent, his last known address;

    (b) in the case of a head teacher or other member of the staff of a school, the school's address;

    (c) in the case of any other person, the last known address of the place where he carries on his business, profession or other employment.

(3) Where first class post is used, the document or notice shall he treated as served, sent or given on the second working day after the date of posting, unless that contrary is shown

(4) Where second class post is used, the document or notice shall be treated is served, sent or given on the fourth working day after the date of posting, unless the contrary is shown

(5) The date of posting shall be presumed, unless the contrary is shown, to be the date shown in the post-mark on the envelope in which the document is contained.

PART II

ASSESSMENTS

Notices relating to assessment

5. –(1) Where under section 167(1) or 174(2) an authority give notice to a child's parent that they propose to make an assessment, or under section 167(4) give notice to a child's parent of their decision to make an assessment, they shall send copies of the relevant notice to

(a)   the social services authority,

(b)   the district health authority, and

(c)   if the child is registered at a school, the head teacher of that school

(2)   Where a copy of a notice is sent under paragraph (1) an endorsement on the copy or a notice accompanying that copy shall inform the recipient, what help the authority are likely to request.

(3)   Where under section 172(2) or 173(1) a child's parent asks the authority to arrange for an assessment to be made the authority shall give notice in writing to the persons referred to in paragraph (1) (a) to (c) of the fact that the request has been made and inform them what help they are likely to request.

Advice to be sought

6. –(1) For the purpose of making an assessment under section 167 an authority shall seek -

(a)   advice from the child's parent;

(b)   educational advice as provided for in regulation 7;

(c)   medical advice from the district health authority as provided for in regulation 8;

(d)   psychological advice as provided for in regulation 9;

(e)   advice from the social services authority; and

(f)   any other advice which the authority consider appropriate for the purpose of arriving at a satisfactory assessment.

(2)   The advice referred to in paragraph (1) shall be written advice relating to

(a)   the educational, medical, psychological or other features of the case (according to the nature of the advice sought) which appear to be relevant to the child's educational needs (including his likely future needs);

(b)   how those features could affect the child's educational needs, and

(c)   the provision which is appropriate for the child in light of those features of the child's case, whether by way of special educational provision or non-educational provision, but not relating to any matter which is required to be specified in a statement by virtue of section 168(4)(b).

(3)   A person from whom the advice referred to in paragraph (1) is sought may in connection therewith consult such persons as it appears to him expedient to consult; and he shall

consult such persons, if any, as are specified in the particular case by the authority as persons who have relevant knowledge of, or information relating to, the child.

(4) When seeking the advice referred to in paragraph (1) (b) to (f) an authority shall provide the person from whom it is sought with copies of–

(a) any representations made by the parent, and

(b) any evidence submitted by, or at the request of, the parent under section 167(1)(d).

(5) The authority need not seek the advice referred to in paragraph (1) (b), (c), (d), (e) or (f) if–

(a) the authority have obtained advice under paragraph (1) (b), (c), (d), (e) or (f) respectively within the preceding 12 months, and

(b) the authority, the person from whom the advice was obtained and the child's parent are satisfied that the existing advice is sufficient for the purpose of arriving at a satisfactory assessment.

Educational advice

7. –(1)The educational advice referred to in regulation 6(1)(b) shall, subject to paragraphs (2) to (5), be sought–

(a) from the head teacher of each school which the child is currently attending or which he has attended at any time within the preceding 18 months;

(b) if advice cannot be obtained from a head teacher of a school which the child is currently attending (because the child is not attending a school or otherwise) from a person who the authority are satisfied has experience of teaching children with special educational needs or knowledge of the differing provision which may be called for in different cases to meet those needs;

(c) if the child is not currently attending a school and if advice obtained under subparagraph (b) is not advice from such a person, from a person responsible for educational provision for him; and

(d) if any of the child's parents is a serving member of Her Majesty's armed forces, from the Service Children's Education Authority.

(2) The advice sought as provided in paragraph (1) shall not be sought from any person who is not a qualified teacher within the meaning of section 218 of the Education Reform Act 1988.

(3) The advice sought from a head teacher as provided in paragraph (1) (a) shall, if the head teacher has not himself taught the child within the preceding 18 months, be advice given after consultation with a teacher who has so taught the child.

(4) The advice sought from a head teacher as provided in paragraph (1)(a) shall include advice relating to the steps which have been taken by the school to identify and assess the special educational needs of the child and to make provision for the purpose of meeting those needs.

(5) Where it appears to the authority, in consequence of medical advice or otherwise, that the child in question is–

(a) hearing impaired, or

(b) visually impaired, or

(c) both hearing impaired and visually impaired,

and any person from whom advice is sought as provided in paragraph (1) is not qualified to teach pupils who are so impaired then the advice sought shall be advice given after consultation with a person who is so qualified.

(6) For the purposes of paragraph (5) a person shall be considered to be qualified to teach pupils who are hearing impaired or visually impaired or who are both hearing impaired and visually impaired if he is qualified to be employed at a school as a teacher of a class for pupils who are so impaired otherwise than to give instruction in a craft, trade, or domestic subject.

(7) Paragraphs (3) and (5) are without prejudice to regulation 6(3).

Medical advice

8. The advice referred to in paragraph 6(1)(c) shall be sought from the district health authority, who shall obtain the advice from a fully registered medical practitioner.

Psychological advice

9. –(1) The psychological advice referred to in regulation 6(1)(d) shall be sought from a person–

(a) regularly employed by the authority as an educational psychologist, or

(b) engaged by the authority as an educational psychologist in the case in question.

(2) The advice sought from a person as provided in paragraph (1) shall, if that person has reason to believe that another psychologist has relevant knowledge of, or information relating to, the child, be advice given after consultation with that other psychologist.

(3) Paragraph (2) is without prejudice to regulation 6(3).

Matters to be taken into account in making an assessment

10. When making an assessment an authority shall take into consideration -

(a) any representations made by the child's parents under section 167(1)(d);

(b) any evidence submitted by, or at the request of, the child's parent under section 167 (1)(d); and

(c) the advice obtained under regulation 6.

Time limits

11. –(1) Where under section 167(1) the authority serve a notice on the child's parent informing him that they propose to make an assessment of the child's educational needs under section 167 they shall within 6 weeks of the date of service of the notice give notice to the child's parent –

(a) under section 167(4) of their decision to make an assessment, and of their reasons for making that decision, or

     (b) under section 167(6) of their decision not to assess the educational needs of the child.

(2) Where under section 174(2) the authority serve a notice on the child's parent informing him that they propose to make an assessment of the child's educational needs under section 167 they shall within 6 weeks of the date of service of the notice give notice to the child's parent and to the governing body of the grant-maintained school which asked the authority to make an assessment-

     (a) under section 174(5) of their decision to make an assessment and their reasons for making that decision, or

     (b) under section 174(6) of their decision not to assess the educational needs of the child.

(3) Where under sections 172(2) or 173(1) a parent asks the authority to arrange for an assessment to be made under section 167 they shall with 6 weeks of the date of receipt of the request give notice to the child's parent –

     (a) under section 167(4) of their decision to make an assessment, or

     (b) under section 172(3)(a) or 173(2)(a) respectively of their decision not to comply with the request and of the parent's right to appeal to the Tribunal against the determination.

(4) An authority need not comply with the time limits referred to in paragraphs (1) to (3) if it is impractical to do so because –

     (a) the authority have requested advice from the head teacher of a school during a period beginning one week before any date on which that school was closed for a continuous period of not less that 4 weeks from that date and ending one week before the date on which it re-opens;

     (b) exceptional personal circumstances affect the child or his parent during the 6 week period referred to in paragraphs (1) to (3); or

     (c) the child or his parent are absent from the area of the authority for a continuous period of not less that 4 weeks during the 6 week period referred to in paragraphs (1) to (3)

(5) Subject to paragraph (6), where under section 167(4) an authority have given notice to the child's parent of their decision to make an assessment they shall complete that assessment within 10 weeks of the date on which such notice was given .

(6) An authority need not comply with the time limit referred to in paragraph (5) if it is impractical to do so because –

     (a) in exceptional cases after receiving advice sought under regulation 6 it is necessary for the authority to seek further advice;

     (b) the child's parent has indicated to the authority that he wishes to provide advice to the authority after the expiry of 6 weeks from the date on which a request for such advice under regulation 6(a) was received and that authority have agreed to consider such advice before completing that assessment;

     (c) the authority have requested advice from the head teacher of a school under regulation 6(1)(b) during a period beginning one week before any date on which that school was closed for a continuous period of not less that 4 weeks from that date and ending one week before the date on which it re-opens;

     (d) the authority have requested advice from a district health authority or a social services authority under regulation 6(1)(c) or (e) respectively and the district health authority or the social services authority have not complied with that request within 6 weeks from the date on which it was made;

     (e) exceptional personal circumstances affect the child or his parent during the 10 week period referred to in paragraph (5);

(f) the child or his parent are absent from the area of the authority for a continuous period of not less than 4 weeks during the 10 week period referred to in paragraph (5); or

(g) the child fails to keep an appointment for an examination or a test during the 10 week period referred to in paragraph (5).

(7) Subject to paragraph (8), where an authority have requested advice from a district health authority or a social services authority under regulation 6(1)(c) or (e) respectively they shall comply with that request within 6 weeks of the date on which they receive it.

(8) A district health authority or a social services authority need not comply with the time limit referred to in paragraph (7) if it is impractical to do so because–

(a) exceptional personal circumstances affect the child or his parent during the 6 week period referred to in paragraph (7);

(b) the child or his parent are absent from the area of the authority for a continuous period of not less than 4 weeks during the 6 week period referred to in paragraph (7);

(c) the child fails to keep an appointment for an examination or a test made by the district health authority or the social services authority respectively during the 6 week period referred to in paragraph (7); or

(d) they have not before the date on which a copy of a notice has been served on them in accordance with regulation 5(1) or a notice has been served on them in accordance with regulation 5(3) produced or maintained any information or records relevant to the assessment of the child under section 167.

PART III

STATEMENTS

Notice accompanying a proposed statement

12. The notice which shall accompany a copy of a proposed statement served on the parent pursuant to paragraph 2 of Schedule 10 to the Act shall be in a form substantially corresponding to that set out in Part A of the Schedule and shall contain the information therein specified.

Statement of special educational needs

13. A statement of a child's special educational needs made under section 168(1) shall be in a form substantially corresponding to that set out in Part B of the Schedule, shall contain the information therein specified, and shall be dated and authenticated by the signature of a duly authorised officer of the authority concerned.

Time limits

14. –(1) Where under section 167 an authority have made an assessment of the educational needs of a child for whom no statement is maintained they shall within two weeks of the date on which the assessment was completed either–

(a) serve a copy of a proposed statement and a written notice on the child's parent under paragraph 2 of Schedule 10 to the Act, or

    (b) give notice in writing to the child's parent under section 169(1) that they have decided not to make a statement and that he may appeal against that decision to the Tribunal.

(2) Where under section 167 an authority have made an assessment of the educational needs of a child for whom a statement is maintained they shall within two weeks of the date on which the assessment was completed–

    (a) under paragraph 10(1) of Schedule 10 to the Act serve on the child's parent a notice that they propose to amend the statement and of his right to make representations;

    (b) under paragraph 11(2) of Schedule 10 to the Act give notice to the child's parent that they have determined to cease to maintain the statement and of his right of appeal to the Tribunal; or

    (c) serve on the child's parent a notice which informs him that they have determined not to amend the statement and their reasons for that determination, which is accompanied by copies of the professional advice obtained during the assessment, and which informs the child's parent that under section 170(1)(c) he may appeal to the Tribunal against the description in the statement of the authority's assessment of the child's special educational needs, the special educational provision specified in the statement or, if no school is named in the statement, that fact.

(3) Subject to paragraph (4), where an authority have served a copy of a proposed statement on the child's parent under paragraph 2 of Schedule 10 to the Act they shall within 8 weeks of the date on which the proposed statement was served serve a copy of the completed statement and a written notice on the child's parent under paragraph 6 of that Schedule, or give notice to the child's parent that they have decided not to make a statement.

(4) The authority need not comply with the time limit referred to in paragraph (3) if it is impractical to do so because–

    (a) exceptional personal circumstances affect the child or his parent during the 8 week period referred to in paragraph (3);

    (b) the child or his parent are absent from the area of the authority for a continuous period of not less than 4 weeks during the 8 week period referred to in paragraph (3);

    (c) the child's parent indicates that he wishes to make representations to the authority about the content of the statement under paragraph 4(1)(a) of Schedule 10 to the Act after the expiry of the 15 day period for making such representations provided for in paragraph 4(4) of that Schedule;

    (d) a meeting between the child's parent and an officer of the authority has been held pursuant to paragraph 4(1)(b) of Schedule 10 to the Act and the child's parent has required that another such meeting be arranged or under paragraph (2) of that Schedule has required a meeting with the appropriate person under to be arranged; or

    (e) the authority have sent a written request to the Secretary of State seeking his consent under section 189(5)(b) to the child being educated at an independent school which is not approved by him and such consent has not been received by the authority within two weeks of the date on which the request was sent.

(5) Where under paragraph 8(1) of Schedule 10 to the Act the child's parent asks the authority to substitute for the name of a school or institution specified in a statement the name of another school specified by him and where the condition referred to in paragraph 8(1)(b) of that Schedule has been satisfied the authority shall within 8 weeks of the date on which the request was received either–

    (a) comply with the request; or

    (b) give notice to the child's parent under paragraph 8(3) of that Schedule that they have determined not to comply with the request and that he may appeal against that determination to the Tribunal.

(6) Where under paragraph 10(1) of Schedule 10 to the Act an authority serve a notice on the child's parent informing him of their proposal to amend a statement they shall not amend the statement after the expiry of 8 weeks from the date on which the notice was served.

(7) Where under paragraph 11(2) of Schedule 10 to the Act an authority give notice to the child's parent that they have determined to cease to maintain a statement they shall not cease to maintain the statement–

    (a) before the expiry of the prescribed period during which the parent may appeal to the Tribunal against the determination, or

    (b) after the expiry of 4 weeks from the end of that period.

Review of statement where child not aged 14 attends school

15. –(1) This regulation applies where–

    (a) an authority review a statement under section 172(5) other than on the making of an assessment,

    (b) the child concerned attends a school, and

    (c) regulation 16 does not apply.

(2) The authority shall by notice in writing require the head teacher of the child's school to submit a report to them under this regulation by a specified date not less than two months from the date the notice is given and shall send a copy of the notice to the child's parent.

(3) The head teacher shall for the purpose of preparing the report referred to in paragraph (2) seek advice as to the matters referred to in paragraph (4) from–

    (a) the child's parent;

    (b) any person whose advice the authority consider appropriate for the purpose of arriving at a satisfactory report and whom they specify in the notice referred to in paragraph (2), and

    (c) any person whose advice the head teacher considers appropriate for the purpose of arriving at a satisfactory report.

(4) The advice referred to in paragraph (3) shall be written advice as to–

    (a) the child's progress towards meeting the objectives specified in the statement;

(b) the child's progress towards attaining any targets established in furtherance of the objectives specified in the statement;

(c) where the school is not established in a hospital and is a maintained, grant-maintained or grant-maintained special school, the application of the provisions of the National Curriculum to the child;

(d) where the school is not established in a hospital and is a maintained, grant-maintained or grant-maintained special school, the application of any provisions substituted for the provisions of the National Curriculum in order to maintain a balanced and broadly based curriculum;

(e) where appropriate, and in any case where a transition plan exists, any matters which are the appropriate subject of such a plan;

(f) whether the statement continues to be appropriate;

(g) any amendments to the statement which would be appropriate; and

(h) whether the authority should cease to maintain the statement.

(5) The notice referred to in paragraph (2) shall require the head teacher to invite the following persons to attend a meeting to be held on a date before the report referred to in that paragraph is submitted–

(a) the representative of the authority specified in the notice,

(b) the child's parent,

(c) a member or members of the staff of the school who teach the child or who are otherwise responsible for the provision of education for the child whose attendance the head teacher considers appropriate.

(d) any other person whose attendance the head teacher considers appropriate, and

(e) any person whose attendance the authority consider appropriate and who is specified in the notice.

(6) The head teacher shall not later that two weeks before the date on which a meeting referred to in paragraph (5) is to be held send to all the persons invited to that meeting copies of the advice he has received pursuant to his request under paragraph (3) and by written notice accompanying the copies shall request the recipients to submit to him before or at the meeting written comments on that advice and any other advice which they think appropriate.

(7) The meeting referred to in paragraph (5) shall consider–

(a) the matters referred to in paragraph (4); and

(b) any significant changes in the child's circumstances since the date on which the statement was made or last reviewed.

(8) The meeting shall recommend –

(a) any steps which it concludes ought to be taken, including whether the authority should amend or cease to maintain the statement,

(b) any targets to be established in furtherance of the objectives specified in the statement which it concludes the child ought to meet during the period until the next review, and

(c) where a transition plan exists, the matters which it concludes ought to be included in that plan.

(9) If the meeting cannot agree the recommendations to be made under paragraph (8) the persons who attended the meeting shall make differing recommendations as appears necessary to each of them.

(10) The report to be submitted under paragraph (2) shall be completed after the meeting is held and shall include the head teacher's assessment of the matters referred to in paragraph (7) and his recommendations as to the matters referred to in paragraph (8), and shall refer to any difference between his assessment and recommendations and those of the meeting.

(11) When the head teacher submits his report to the authority under paragraph (2) he shall at the same time send copies to –

(a) the child's parent,

(b) the persons from whom the head teacher sought advice under paragraph (3),

(c) the persons who were invited to attend the meeting in accordance with paragraph (5),

(d) any other person to whom the authority consider it appropriate that a copy be sent and to whom they direct him to send a copy, and

(e) any other person to whom the head teacher considers it appropriate that a copy be sent.

(12) The authority shall review the statement under section 172(5) in light of the report and any other information or advice which they consider relevant, shall make written recommendations as to the matters referred to in paragraph (8) (a) and (b) and, where a transition plan exists, shall amend the plan as they consider appropriate.

(13) The authority shall within one week of completing the review under section 172(5) send copies of the recommendations and any transition plan referred to in paragraph (12) to–

(a) the child's parent;

(b) the head teacher;

(c) the persons from whom the head teacher sought advice under paragraph (3);

(d) the persons who were invited to attend the meeting in accordance with paragraph (5), and

(e) any other person to whom the authority consider it appropriate that a copy be sent.

Review of statement where child aged 14 attends school

16.– (1) This regulation applies where–

(a) an authority review a statement under section 172(5) other than on the making of an assessment,

(b) the child concerned attends a school, and

(c) the review is the first review commenced after the child has attained the age of 14 years.

(2) The authority shall for the purpose of preparing a report under this regulation by notice in writing require the head teacher of the child's school to seek the advice referred to in regulation 15(4), including in all cases advice as to the matters referred to in regulation 15 (4) (e), from –

(a) the child's parent,

(b) any person whose advice the authority consider appropriate for the purpose of arriving at a satisfactory report and whom they specify in the notice referred to above, and

      (c) any person whose advice the head teacher considers appropriate for the purpose of arriving at a satisfactory report.

(3) The authority shall invite the following persons to attend a meeting to be held on a date before the review referred to in paragraph (1) is required to be completed–

      (a) the child's parent;

      (b) a member or members of the staff of the school who teach the child or who are otherwise responsible for the provision of education for the child whose attendance the head teacher considers appropriate and whom he has asked the authority to invite;

      (c) a representative of the social services authority;

      (d) a person providing careers services under sections 8 to 10 of the Employment and Training Act 1973:

      (e) any person whose attendance the head teacher considers appropriate and whom he has asked the authority to invite; and

      (f) any person whose attendance the authority consider appropriate.

(4) The head teacher shall not later than two weeks before the date on which the meeting referred to in paragraph (3) is to be held serve on all the persons invited to attend that meeting copies of the advice he has received pursuant to his request under paragraph (2) and shall by written notice request the recipients to submit to him before or at the meeting written comments on that advice and any other advice which they think appropriate.

(5) A representative of the authority shall attend the meeting.

(6) The meeting shall consider the matters referred to in regulation 15(7), in all cases including the matters referred to in regulation 15(4)(e), and shall make recommendations in accordance with regulation 15(8) and (9), in all cases including recommendations as to the matters referred to in regulation 15(8)(c).

(7) The report to be prepared by the authority under paragraph (2) shall be completed after the meeting, shall contain the authority's assessment of the matters required to be considered by the meeting and their recommendations as to the matters required to be recommended by it and shall refer to any difference between their assessment and recommendations and those of the meeting.

(8) The authority shall within one week of the date on which the meeting was held send copies of the report completed under paragraph (7) to–

      (a) the child's parent;

      (b) the head teacher;

      (c) the persons from whom the head teacher sought advice under paragraph (2);

      (d) the persons who were invited to attend the meeting under paragraph (3); and

      (e) any person to whom they consider it appropriate to send a copy.

(9) The authority shall review the statement under section 172(5) in light of the report and any other information or advice which it considers relevant, shall make written recommendations as to the matters referred to in regulation 15(8)(a) and (b), and shall prepare a transition plan.

(10) The authority shall within one week of completing the review under section 172(5) send copies of the recommendations and the transition plan referred to in paragraph (9) to the persons referred to in paragraph (8).

Review of statement where child does not attend school

17.- (1) This regulation applies where an authority review a statement under section 172(5) other than on the making of an assessment and the child concerned does not attend a school.

(2) The authority shall prepare a report addressing the matters referred to in regulation 15(4), including the matters referred to in regulation 15(4)(e) in any case where the review referred to in paragraph (1) is commenced after the child has attained the age of 14 years or older, and for that purpose shall seek advice on those matters from the child's parent and any other person whose advice they consider appropriate in the case in question for the purpose of arriving at a satisfactory report.

(3) The authority shall invite the following persons to attend a meeting to be held on a date before the review referred to in paragraph (1) is required to be completed–

(a) the child's parent;

(b) where the review referred to in paragraph (1) is the first review commenced after the child has attained the age of 14 years, a representative of the social services authority;

(c) where sub-paragraph (b) applies, a person providing careers services under sections 8 to 10 of the Employment and Training Act 1973; and

(d) any person or persons whose attendance the authority consider appropriate.

(4) The authority shall not later than two weeks before the date on which the meeting referred to in paragraph (3) is to be held send to all the persons invited to that meeting a copy of the report which they propose to make under paragraph (2) and by written notice accompanying the copies shall request the recipients to submit to the authority written comments on the report and any other advice which they think appropriate.

(5) A representative of the authority shall attend the meeting.

(6) The meeting shall consider the matters referred to in regulation 15(7), including in any case where the review is commenced after the child has attained the age of 14 years the matters referred to in regulation 15(4)(e), and shall make recommendations in accordance with regulation 15(8) and (9), including in any case where the child has attained the age of 14 years or older as aforesaid recommendations as to the matters referred to in regulation 15(8)(c).

(7) The report prepared by the authority under paragraph (2) shall be completed after the meeting referred to in paragraph (3) is held, shall contain the authority's assessment of the matters required to be considered by the meeting and their recommendations as to the matters required to be recommended by it, and shall refer to any difference between their assessment and recommendations and those of the meeting.

(8) The authority shall within one week of the date on which the meeting referred to in paragraph (3) was held send copies of the report completed under paragraph (7) to–

(a) the child's parent;

(b) the persons from whom they sought advice under paragraph (2);

(c) the persons who were invited to attend the meeting under paragraph (3); and

(d) any person to whom they consider it appropriate to send a copy.

(9) The authority shall review the statement under section 172(5) in light of the report and any other information or advice which it considers relevant, shall make written recommendations as to the matters referred to in regulation 15(8)(a) and (b), in any case where the review is the first review commenced after the child has attained the age of 14 years prepare a transition plan, and in any case where a transition plan exists amend the plan as they consider appropriate.

(10) The authority shall within one week of completing the review under section 172(5) send copies of the recommendations and any transition plan referred to in paragraph (9) to the persons referred to in paragraph (8).

Transfer of statements

18.– (1) This regulation applies where a child in respect of whom a statement is maintained moves from the area of the authority which maintains the statement ('the old authority') into that of another ('the new authority').

(2) The old authority shall transfer the statement to the new authority, and from the date of the transfer–

(a) the statement shall be treated for the purposes of the new authority's duties and functions under Part III of the Act and these Regulations as if it had been made by the new authority on the date on which it was made by the old authority, and

(b) where the new authority make an assessment under section 167 and the old authority have supplied the new authority with advice obtained in pursuance of a previous assessment regulation 6(5) shall apply as if the new authority had obtained the advice on the date on which the old authority obtained it.

(3) The new authority shall within 6 weeks of the date of the transfer serve a notice on the child's parent informing him -

(a) that the statement has been transferred,

(b) whether they propose to make an assessment under section 167, and

(c) when they propose to review the statement in accordance with paragraph (4).

(4) The new authority shall review the statement under section 172(5) before the expiry of whichever of the following two periods expires later–

(a) the period of twelve months beginning with the making of the statement, or as the case may be, with the previous review, or

(b) the period of three months beginning with the date of the transfer.

(5) Where by virtue of the transfer the new authority come under a duty to arrange the child's attendance at a school specified in the statement but in light of the child's move that attendance is no longer practicable the new authority may arrange for the child's attendance at another school appropriate for the child until such time as it is possible to amend the statement in accordance with paragraph 10 of Schedule 10 to the Act.

Restriction on disclosure of statements

19.– (1) Subject to the provisions of the Act and of these Regulations, a statement in respect of a child shall not be disclosed without the parent's consent except–

(a) to persons to whom, in the opinion of the authority concerned, the statement should be disclosed in the interests of the child;

(b) for the purposes of any appeal under the Act;

(c) for the purposes of educational research which, in the opinion of the authority, may advance the education of children with special educational needs, if, but only if, the person engaged in that research undertakes not to publish anything contained in, or derived from, a statement otherwise than in a form which does not identify any individual concerned including, in particular, the child concerned and his parent;

(d) on the order of any court or for the purposes of any criminal proceedings;

(e) for the purposes of any investigation under Part III of the Local Government Act 1974 (investigation of maladministration);

(f) to the Secretary of State when he requests such disclosure for the purposes of deciding whether to give directions or make an order under section 68 or 99 of the Education Act 1944;

(g) for the purposes of an assessment of the needs of the child with respect to the provision of any statutory services for him being carried out by officers of a social services authority by virtue of arrangements made under section 5(5) of the Disabled Persons (Services, Consultation and Representation) Act 1986;

(h) for the purposes of a local authority in the performance of their duties under sections 22(3)(a), 85(4)(a), 86(3)(a) and 87(3) of the Children Act 1989; or

(i) to one of Her Majesty's Inspectors of Schools, or to a registered inspector or a member of an inspection team, who requests the right to inspect or take copies of a statement in accordance with section 3 (3) of or paragraph 7 of Schedule 2 to the Education (Schools) Act 1992 respectively.

(2) The arrangements for keeping such statements shall be such as to ensure, so far as is reasonably practicable, that unauthorised persons do not have access to them.

(3) In this regulation any reference to a statement includes a reference to any representations, evidence, advice or information which is set out in the appendices to a statement.

SCHEDULE   **Regulations 12 and 13**
PART A
NOTICE TO PARENT

To: **[name and address of parent]**

1. Accompanying this notice is a copy of a statement of the special educational needs of [name of child] which [name of authority] ('the authority') propose to make under the Education Act 1993 .
2. You may express a preference for the maintained, grant-maintained or grant-maintained special school you wish your child to attend and may give reasons for your preference.
3. If you wish to express such a preference you must do so not later than 15 days from the date on which you receive this notice and the copy of the statement or 15 days from the date on which you last attend a meeting in accordance with paragraph 10 or 11 below, whichever is later. If the 15th day falls on a weekend or a bank holiday, you must do so not later than the following working day.
4. If you express a preference in accordance with paragraphs 2 and 3 above the authority are required to specify the name of the school you prefer in the statement, and accordingly to arrange special educational provision at that school, unless–
   (a) the school is unsuitable to your child's age, ability or aptitude or to his/her special educational needs, or
   (b) the attendance of your child at the school would be incompatible with the provision of efficient education for the children with whom he/she would be educated or the efficient use of resources.
5. The authority will normally arrange special educational provision in a maintained, grant-maintained or grant-maintained special school. However, if you believe that the authority should arrange special educational provision for your child at a non-maintained special school or an independent school you may make representations to that effect.
6. The following maintained, grant-maintained and grant-maintained special schools provide **[primary/secondary]** education in the area of the authority:

[Here list all maintained, grant-maintained, and grant-maintained special schools in the authority's area which provide primary education, or list all such schools which provide secondary education, depending, on whether the child requires primary or secondary education. Alternatively, list the required information in a list attached to this notice.]

7. A list of the non-maintained special schools which make special educational provision for pupils with special educational needs in England and Wales and are approved by the Secretary of State for Education or the Secretary of State for Wales is attached to this notice.

8. A list of the independent schools in England and Wales which are approved by the Secretary of State for Education or the Secretary of State for Wales as suitable for the admission of children for whom statements of special educational needs are maintained is attached to this notice.

9. You are entitled to make representations to the authority about the content of the statement. If you wish to make such representations you must do so not later than 15 days from the date on which you receive this notice, or 15 days from the date on which you last attended a meeting in accordance with the next paragraph, whichever is the later date.

10. You are entitled, not later than 15 days from the date on which you receive this notice, to require the authority to arrange a meeting between you and an officer of the authority at which any part of the statement, or all of it, may be discussed. In particular, any advice on which the statement is based may be discussed.

11. If having attended a meeting in accordance with paragraph 10 above you still disagree with any part of the assessment in question, you may within 15 days of the date of the meeting require the authority to arrange a meeting or meetings to discuss the advice which they consider relevant to the part of the assessment you disagree with. They will arrange for the person who gave the advice, or some other person whom they think appropriate, to attend the meeting.

12. If at the conclusion of the procedure referred to above the authority serve on you a statement with which you disagree you may appeal to the Special Educational Needs Tribunal against the description of your child's special educational needs, against the special educational provision specified including the school named, or, if no school is named, against that fact.

13. All correspondence with the authority should be addressed to the officer responsible for this case

    [Here set out name, address and telephone number of case officer, and any reference number which should be quoted.]

_____   _____
[Date]   [Signature of officer responsible]

PART B
STATEMENT OF SPECIAL EDUCATIONAL NEEDS

Part 1: Introduction

1. In accordance with section 168 of the Education Act 1993 ('the Act') and the Education (Special Educational Needs) Regulations 1994 ('the Regulations'), the following statement is made by [here set out name of authority] ('the authority') in respect of the child whose name and other particulars are mentioned below.

Child

Surname   Other names

Home address

                                                  Sex

                                                  Religion

Date of Birth   Home language

Child's parent or person responsible

Surname   Other names

Home address

                                                  Relationship to child

Telephone No.

2. When assessing the child's special educational needs the authority took into consideration in accordance with regulation 10 of the Regulations, the representations, evidence and advice set out in the Appendices to this statement.

PART 2: SPECIAL EDUCATIONAL NEEDS

[Here set out the child's special educational needs, in terms of the child's learning difficulties which call for special educational provision, as assessed by the authority.]

PART 3: SPECIAL EDUCATIONAL PROVISION

Objectives
[Here specify the objectives which the special educational provision for the child should aim to meet.

Educational provision to meet needs and objectives
[Here specify the special educational provision which the authority consider appropriate to meet the needs specified in Part 2 and to meet the objectives specified in this Part, and in particular specify –
  (a) any appropriate facilities and equipment, staffing arrangements and curriculum,
  (b) any appropriate modifications to the application of the National Curriculum,
  (c) any appropriate exclusions from the application of the National Curriculum, in detail, and the provision which it is proposed to substitute for any such exclusions in order to maintain a balanced and broadly based curriculum; and
  (d) where residential accommodation is appropriate, that fact].

Monitoring
[Here specify the arrangements to be made for –
  (a) regularly monitoring progress in meeting the objectives specified in this Part,
  (b) establishing targets in furtherance of those objectives,
  (c) regularly monitoring the targets referred to in (b),
  (d) regularly monitoring the appropriateness of any modifications to the application of the National Curriculum, and
  (e) regularly monitoring the appropriateness of any provision substituted for exclusions from the application of the National Curriculum.
Here also specify any special arrangements for reviewing this statement.]

PART 4: PLACEMENT

[Here specify –
  (a) the type of school which the authority consider appropriate for the child and the name of the school for which the parent has expressed a preference or, where the authority are required to specify the name of a school, the name of the school which they consider would be appropriate for the child and should be specified, or
  (b) the provision for his education otherwise than at a school which the authority consider appropriate.

PART 5: NON-EDUCATIONAL NEEDS

[Here specify the non-educational needs of the child for which the authority consider provision is appropriate if the child is to properly benefit from the special educational provision specified in Part 3.]

PART 6: NON-EDUCATIONAL PROVISION

[Here specify any non-educational provision which the authority propose to make available or which they are satisfied will be made available by a district health authority, a social services authority or some other body, including the arrangements for its provision. Also specify the objectives of the provision, and the arrangements for monitoring progress in meeting those objectives.]

_____   _____
Date   A duly authorised officer of the authority

Appendix A: Parental Representations
[Here set out any written representations made by the parent of the child under section 167(1)(d) of or paragraph 4(1) of Schedule 10 to the Act and a summary which the parent has accepted as acute of any oral representations so made or record that no such representations were made.]

Appendix B: Parental Evidence
[Here set out any written evidence either submitted by the parent of the child under section 167(1)(d) of the Act or record that no such evidence was submitted.]

Appendix C: Advice from the Child's Parent
[Here set out the advice obtained under regulation 6(1)(a).]

Appendix D: Educational Advice
[Here set out the advice obtained under regulation 6(1)(b).]

Appendix E: Medical Advice
[Here set out the advice obtained under regulation 6(1)(c).]

Appendix F: Psychological Advice
[Here set out the advice obtained under regulation 6(1)(d).]

Appendix G: Advice from the Social Services Authority
[Here set out the advice obtained under regulation 6(1)(e).]

Appendix H: Other Advice Obtained by the Authority
[Here set out the advice obtained under regulation 6(1)(f).]

Appendix 4

The Education (Special Needs) (Information) Regulations 1994

STATUTORY INSTRUMENTS

1994 No. 1048

EDUCATION, ENGLAND AND WALES

The Education (Special Educational Needs) (Information) Regulations 1994

Made	*7th April 1994*
Laid before Parliament	*13th April 1994*
Coming into force	*1st September 1994*

In exercise of the powers conferred on the Secretary of State by section 8(5) and (7) of the Education Act 1980 and sections 153(1). 161(5) and 305(1) of, and paragraph 140 of Schedule 11 to, the Education Act 1933, the Secretary of State for Education, as respects England, and the Secretary of State for Wales, as respects Wales, hereby make the following Regulations:

Citation and commencement

1. These Regulations may be cited as the Education (Special Educational Needs) (Information) Regulations 1994 and shall come into force on 1st September 1994.

Publication of information about special educational needs

2.—(1) The governing body of each county, voluntary, or grant-maintained school, shall publish information about the matters set out in Schedule 1.

(2) The governing body of each maintained or grant-maintained special school, other than a special school established in a hospital, shall publish information about the matters set out in Schedule 2.

(3) The governing body of each maintained or grant-maintained special school which is established in a hospital, shall publish information about the matters set out in Schedule 3.

Manner of publication of information

3.—(1) The information referred to in regulation 2 shall be published in a single document by making copies available free of charge –

(a) for distribution -

(i) to parents of pupils or prospective pupils, and

(ii) to the local education authority, District Health Authority or funding authority for the area in which the school is situated,

who or which request a copy at the school or through the post: and

(b) for reference at the school.

(2) The first occasion on which copies of the document referred to in paragraph (1) above are made available in accordance with that paragraph shall be no later than 1st August 1995.

Publication of information – supplementary

4.   Where the information referred to in regulation 2 is to be published by the local education authority with the agreement of the governing body pursuant to section 8(6) of the Education Act 1980 it shall be supplied to them by the governing body and shall be published without material alteration.

Annual reports

5.—(1) The annual report for each county, voluntary, maintained special, grant-maintained or grant-maintained special school shall include a report containing the information about the implementation of the governing body's policy for pupils with special educational needs as specified in Schedule 4.

(2) Paragraph (1) above shall apply in relation to the first annual report prepared after 1st August 1995 and to each annual report prepared thereafter.

Modification of the Education Act 1993 in relation to grant-maintained special schools

6.   The provisions of Part II, Chapter X and Part III of the Education Act 1993 set out in paragraphs (a) and (b) below shall have effect with the modifications as therein stated –

(a) section 153 (provision of information by governing body) shall apply to the governing body of a grant-maintained special school; and

(b) section 161(5) (duties of governing body etc. in relation to pupils with special educational needs) shall apply to each grant-maintained special school and the reference in that subsection to "annual report" shall include a report prepared under the articles of government of a grant-maintained special school.

SCHEDULE I

INFORMATION FROM COUNTY, VOLUNTARY AND GRANT-MAINTAINED SCHOOLS

BASIC INFORMATION ABOUT THE SCHOOL'S SPECIAL EDUCATIONAL PROVISION

1. The objectives of the governing body in making provision for pupils with special educational needs and a description of how the governing body's special educational needs policy will contribute towards meeting those objectives.

2. The name of the person who is responsible for co-ordinating the day to day provision of education for pupils with special educational needs at the school (whether or not the person is known as the SEN co-ordinator).

3. The arrangements which have been made for co-ordinating the provision of education for pupils with special educational needs at the school.

4. The admission arrangements for pupils with special educational needs who do not have a statement in so far as they differ from the arrangements for other pupils.

5. The kinds of provision for special educational needs in which the school specialises and any special units.

6. Facilities for pupils with special educational needs at the school including facilities which increase or assist access to the school by pupils who are disabled.

INFORMATION ABOUT THE SCHOOL'S POLICIES FOR THE, IDENTIFICATION, ASSESSMENT AND PROVISION FOR ALL PUPILS WITH SPECIAL EDUCATIONAL NEEDS

7. How resources are allocated to and amongst pupils with special educational needs.

8. How pupils with special educational needs are identified and their needs determined and reviewed.

9. Arrangements for providing access by pupils with special educational needs to a balanced and broadly based curriculum (including the National Curriculum).

10. How pupils with special educational needs engage in the activities of the school together with pupils who do not have special educational needs.

11. How the governing body evaluate the success of the education which is provided at the school to pupils with special educational needs.

12. Any arrangements made by the governing body relating to the treatment of complaints from parents of pupils with special educational needs concerning the provision made at the school.

INFORMATION ABOUT THE SCHOOL'S STAFFING POLICIES AND PARTNERSHIP WITH BODIES BEYOND THE SCHOOL

13. Any arrangements made by the governing body relating to in-service training for staff in relation to special educational needs.

14. The use made of teachers and facilities from outside the school including links with support services for special educational needs.

15. The role played by the parents of pupils with special educational needs.

16. Any links with other schools, including special schools, and the provision made for the transition of pupils with special educational needs between schools or between the school and the next stage of life or education.

17. Links with child health services, social services and educational welfare services and any voluntary organisations which work on behalf of children with special educational needs.

SCHEDULE 2 Regulation 2(2)

INFORMATION FROM MAINTAINED AND grant-maintained SPECIAL SCHOOLS

BASIC INFORMATION ABOUT THE SCHOOL SPECIAL EDUCATIONAL PROVISIONS

1. The objectives of the governing body in making provision for pupils with special educational needs, and a description of how the governing body's special educational needs policy will contribute towards meeting those objectives.

2. The kinds of special educational needs for which provision is made at the school.

3. Facilities for pupils at the school including facilities which increase or assist access to the school by pupils who are disabled.

INFORMATION ABOUT THE SCHOOL'S POLICIES FOR THE ASSESSMENT AND PROVISION FOR ALL PUPILS S WITH SPECIAL EDUCATIONAL NEEDS

4. How resources are allocated amongst pupils.

5. How the needs of pupils are identified and reviewed.

6. Arrangements for providing access by pupils to a balanced and broadly based curriculum (including the National Curriculum).

7. How the governing body evaluate the success of the education which is provided at the school to pupils.

8. Any arrangements made by the governing body relating to the treatment of complaints from parents of pupils concerning the provision made at the school.

INFORMATION ABOUT THE SCHOOL'S STAFFING POLICIES AND PARTNERSHIP WITH BODIES BEYOND THE SCHOOL

9. Any arrangements made by the governing body relating to in-service training for staff in relation to special educational needs.

10. The use made of teachers and facilities from outside the school including links with support services for special educational needs.

11. The role played by parents of pupils.

12. Any links with other schools, and any arrangements for managing the transition of pupils between schools or between the school and the next stage of life or education.

13. Links with child health services, social services and educational welfare services and any voluntary organisations which work on behalf of children with special educational needs.

SCHEDULE 3

Regulation 2(3)

INFORMATION FROM SPECIAL SCHOOLS IN HOSPITALS

1. The name of the person who is responsible for co-ordinating the day to day provision of education for pupils with special educational needs at the school (whether or not the person is known as the SEN co-ordinator).

2. How pupils with special educational needs are identified and their needs determined and reviewed.

3. How resources are allocated to and amongst pupils with special educational needs.

4. How the educational progress of pupils with special educational needs is monitored.

5. How the contents of a pupil's statement are ascertained and made known to staff.

6. The arrangements for ensuring continuity and the educational provision set out in a pupil's statement differentiating where necessary between long stay and short stay patients.

7. Arrangements for providing access by pupils with special educational needs to a balanced and broadly based curriculum.

8. The use made of teachers and facilities from outside the school including links with support services for special educational needs.

SCHEDULE 4

Regulation 5

INFORMATION IN ANNUAL REPORT

1. The success of the governing body's special educational needs policies in the period since the last annual report.

2. Significant changes in the governing body's policy on pupils with special educational needs since the last annual report.

3. The outcome of any consultation carried out under section 161(3) of the Education Act 1993.

4. How resources have been allocated to and amongst pupils with special educational needs since the last annual report.

Eric Forth
Parliamentary Under Secretary of State
Department for Education

6th April 1994

John Redwood
Secretary of State for Wales

7th April 1994

Appendix 5

The Special Educational Needs Tribunal Regulations 1994

STATUTORY INSTRUMENTS

1994 No. 1910
EDUCATION, ENGLAND AND WALES
The Special Educational Needs Tribunal Regulations 1994

Made	*14th July 1994*
Laid before Parliament	*19th July 1994*
Coming into force	*1st September 1994*

ARRANGEMENT OF REGULATIONS

PART I

GENERAL

PART 2

MAKING AN APPEAL TO THE TRIBUNAL AND REPLY BY THE AUTHORITY

(A) THE PARENT

(B) THE REPLY BY THE AUTHORITY

PART 3

PREPARATION FOR A HEARING

PART 4

THE DETERMINATION OF APPEALS

PART 5

ADDITIONAL POWERS OF AND PROVISIONS RELATING TO THE TRIBUNAL

The Secretary of State for Education, in respect of England, and the Secretary of State for Wales, in respect of Wales, in exercise of the powers conferred by sections 177(5), 178(2), 180(1) and (2), 301(6) and 305(1) of the Education Act 1993, and after consultation with the Council on Tribunals in accordance with section 8 of the Tribunals and Inquiries Act 1992, hereby make the following Regulations:

PART 1

GENERAL

Citation and commencement

1.   These Regulations may be cited as the Special Educational Needs Tribunal Regulations 1994 and shall come into force on 1st September 1994.

Interpretation

2.   In these Regulations, unless the context otherwise requires–
     "the 1993 Act" means the Education Act 1993;
     "authority" means the local education authority which made the disputed decision;
     "child" means the child in respect of whom the appeal is brought;
     "disputed decision" means the decision or determination in respect of which the appeal is brought;
     "the clerk to the tribunal" means the person appointed by the Secretary of the Tribunal to act in that capacity at one or more hearings;
     "hearing" means a sitting of the tribunal duly constituted for the purpose of receiving evidence, hearing addresses and witnesses or doing anything lawfully requisite to enable the tribunal to reach a decision on any question;
     "parent" means a parent who has made an appeal to the Special Educational Needs Tribunal under the 1993 Act;
     "records" means the records of the Special Educational Needs Tribunal;
     "the Secretary of the Tribunal" means the person for the time being acting as the Secretary of the office of the Special Educational Needs Tribunal;
     "the tribunal" means the Special Educational Needs Tribunal but where the President has determined pursuant to regulation 4(1) that the jurisdiction of the Special Educational Needs Tribunal is to be exercised by more than one tribunal, it means, in relation to any proceedings, the tribunal to which the proceedings have been referred by the President;
     "working day" means any day other than–
     (a)   a Saturday, a Sunday, Christmas Day, Good Friday or a day which is a bank holiday within the meaning of the Banking and Financial Dealings Act 1971; or
     (b)   a day in August.

Members of lay panel

3.   No person may be appointed member of the lay panel unless the Secretary of State is satisfied that he has knowledge and experience in respect of–
(a)   children with special educational needs: or
(b)   local government.

Establishment of tribunals

4.— (1)   Such number of tribunals shall be established to exercise the jurisdiction of the Special Educational Needs Tribunal as the President may from time to time determine.
     (2)   The tribunals shall sit at such times and in such places as may from time to time be determined by the President.

Membership of tribunal

5.— (1)   Subject to the provisions of regulation 29(5), the tribunal shall consist of a chairman and two other members.
     (2)   For each hearing–

          (a)   the chairman shall be the President or a person selected from the chairman's panel by the President; and
          (b)   the two other members of the tribunal other than the chairman shall be selected from the lay panel by the President.

Proof of documents and certification of decisions

6.—(1)   A document purporting to be a document issued by the Secretary of the Tribunal on behalf of the Special Educational Needs Tribunal shall, unless the contrary is proved, be deemed to be a document so issued.

(2)   A document purporting to be certified by the Secretary of the Tribunal to be a true copy of a document containing a decision of the tribunal shall, unless the contrary is proved, be sufficient evidence of matters contained therein.

PART 2

MAKING AN APPEAL TO THE TRIBUNAL AND REPLY BY THE AUTHORITY
(A) THE PARENT

Notice of appeal

7.—(1)   An appeal to the Special Educational Needs Tribunal shall be made by notice which–

(a)   shall state–

(i)   the name and address of the parent making the appeal; (ii) the name of the child;

(iii) that the notice is a notice of appeal;

(iv) the name of the authority which made the disputed decision and the date on which the parent was notified of it;

(v)   the grounds of the appeal;

(b)   shall be accompanied (as appropriate) by–

(i)   a copy of the notice of the disputed decision;

(ii)   a copy of the child's statement of special educational needs; and

(c)   may state the name, address and profession of any representative of the parent to whom the tribunal should send replies or notices concerning the appeal instead of to the parent.

(2)   The parent shall sign the notice of appeal.

(3)   The parent must deliver the notice of appeal to the Secretary of the Tribunal so that it is received no later than the first working day after the expiry of 2 months from the date on which the authority gave him notice, pursuant to the 1993 Act, that he had a right of appeal.

Response, amendment of appeal and delivery of supplementary grounds of appeal

8.— (1)   If the authority delivers a reply under regulation 12 the parent may deliver a written response to it.

(2)   A response under paragraph (1) above must be delivered to the Secretary of the Tribunal not later than 15 working days from the date on which the parent receives a copy of the authority's written reply from the Secretary of the Tribunal.

(3)   The parent may in exceptional cases (in addition to delivering a response under paragraph (1) above)–

(a)   with the permission of the President, at any time before the hearing; or

(b)   with the permission of the tribunal at the hearing itself – amend the notice of appeal or any response, deliver a supplementary statement of grounds of appeal or amend a supplementary statement of grounds of appeal.

(4)   The parent shall deliver a copy of every amendment and supplementary statement made under paragraph (3) above before the hearing to the Secretary of the Tribunal.

Withdrawal of appeal

9.   The parent may-

(a)   at any time before the hearing of the appeal withdraw his appeal by sending to the Secretary of the Tribunal a notice signed by him stating that he withdraws his appeal;

(b)   at the hearing of the appeal, withdraw his appeal.

Further action by parent

10.—(1) The parent shall supply the Secretary of the Tribunal with the information requested in the enquiry made under regulation 18.

(2) If the parent does not intend to attend or be represented at the hearing, he may, not less than 5 working days before the hearing, send to the Secretary of the Tribunal additional written representations in support of his appeal.

Representatives of the parent: further provisions

11.—(1) Where a parent has not stated the name of a representative in the notice of appeal pursuant to regulation 7(1)(c) he may at any time before the hearing notify the Secretary of the Tribunal of the name, address and profession of a representative to whom the tribunal should send any subsequent documents or notices concerning the appeal instead of to the parent.

(2) Where a parent has stated the name of a representative, whether in the notice of appeal pursuant to regulation 7(1)(c) or pursuant to paragraph (1) above, he may at any time notify the Secretary of the Tribunal–

(a) of the name, address and profession of a new representative of the parent to whom the tribunal should send documents or notices concerning the appeal instead of to the representative previously notified; or

(b) that no person is acting as a representative of the parent and accordingly any subsequent documents or notices concerning the appeal should be sent to the parent himself.

(3) At a hearing, the parent may conduct his case himself (with assistance from one person if he wishes) or may appear and be represented by one person whether or not legally qualified:

Provided that, if the President gives permission before the hearing or the tribunal gives permission at the hearing, the parent may obtain assistance or be represented by more than one person.

(B) THE REPLY BY THE AUTHORITY

Action by the authority on receipt of a notice of appeal

12.—(1) An authority which receives a copy of a notice of appeal shall deliver to the Secretary of the Tribunal a written reply acknowledging service upon it of the notice of appeal and stating–

(a) whether or not the authority intends to oppose the appeal and, if it does intend to oppose the appeal, the grounds on which it relies; and

(b) the name and profession of the representative of the authority and the address for service of the authority for the purposes of the appeal.

(2) The authority shall include with its reply a statement summarising the facts relating to the disputed decision and, if they are not part of that decision, the reasons for the disputed decision.

(3) Every such reply shall be signed by an officer of the authority who is authorised to sign such documents and shall be delivered to the Secretary of the Tribunal not later than 20 working days after the date on which the copy of the notice of appeal was received by the authority from the Secretary of the Tribunal.

Amendment of reply by the authority

13.—(1) The authority, if it has delivered a reply pursuant to regulation 12, may, in exceptional cases–

(a) with the permission of the President at any time before the hearing: or

(b) with the permission of the tribunal at the hearing itself
  amend its reply, deliver a supplementary reply or amend a supplementary reply.

(2) The President or, as the case may be, the tribunal may give permission under paragraph (1) above on such terms as he or it thinks fit including the payment of costs or expenses.

(3) The authority shall send a copy of every amendment and supplementary statement made before the hearing to the Secretary of the Tribunal.

Notice that an appeal is misconceived

14.– (1) Where the authority is of the opinion that an appeal does not lie to, or cannot be entertained by, the Special Educational Needs Tribunal, it may serve a notice to that effect on the Secretary of the Tribunal stating the grounds for such contention and applying for the appeal to be struck out.

(2) The Secretary of the Tribunal shall send a copy of the notice and of any accompanying documents to the parent.

(3) An application under this regulation may be heard by the tribunal as a preliminary point of law or at the beginning of the hearing of the substantive appeal.

Failure to reply and absence of opposition

15. If no reply is received by the Secretary of the Tribunal within the time appointed by regulation 12(3) or if the authority states in writing that it does not resist the appeal, or withdraws its opposition to the appeal, the tribunal may determine the appeal on the basis of the notice of appeal without a hearing or may (without notifying the authority) hold a hearing at which the authority is not represented.

Representation at hearing and further action by the authority

16.– (1) At a hearing the authority may be represented by one person whether or not legally qualified:

Provided that if the President gives permission before the hearing or the tribunal gives permission at the hearing the authority may be represented by more than one person.

(2) The authority shall supply the Secretary of the Tribunal with the information requested in the enquiry made under regulation 18.

(3) If the authority does not intend to attend or be represented at the hearing it may, not less than 5 working days before the hearing, send to the Secretary of the Tribunal additional written representations in support of its reply.

PART 3

PREPARATION FOR A HEARING

Acknowledgement of appeal and service of documents by the Secretary of the Tribunal

17.– (1) Upon receiving a notice of appeal the Secretary of the Tribunal shall–

(a) enter particulars of it in the records;

(b) send to the parent–

(i) an acknowledgement of its receipt and a note of the case number entered in the records;

(ii) a note of the address to which notices and communications to the Special Educational Needs Tribunal or to the Secretary of the Tribunal should he sent; and

(iii) notification that advice about the appeal procedure may be obtained from the office of the Special Educational Needs Tribunal;

(c) subject to paragraph (5) below, send to the authority–

(i) a copy of the notice of appeal and any accompanying papers;

(ii) a note of the address to which notices and communications to the Special Educational Needs Tribunal or to the Secretary of the Tribunal should be sent, and

(iii) a notice stating the time for replying and the consequences of failure to do so.

(2) Where the Secretary of the Tribunal is of the opinion that, on the basis of the notice of appeal, the parent is asking the Special Educational Needs Tribunal to do something which it cannot, he may give notice to that effect to the parent stating the reasons for his

opinion and informing him that the notice of appeal will not be entered in the records unless the parent notifies the Secretary of the Tribunal that he wishes to proceed with it.

(3) An appeal, as respects which a notice has been given in pursuance of paragraph (2) above, shall only be treated as having been received for the purposes of paragraph (1) when the parent notifies the Secretary of the Tribunal that he wishes to proceed with it.

(4) Subject to paragraph (5) below, the Secretary of the Tribunal shall forthwith send a copy of a reply by the authority under regulation 12 and of a response under regulation 8 together with any amendments or supplementary statements, written representations or other documents received from a party, to the other party to the proceedings.

(5) If a notice of appeal, reply by the authority under regulation 12 or response by the parent under regulation 8 is delivered to the Secretary of the Tribunal after the time prescribed by these Regulations, the Secretary of the Tribunal shall defer the sending of the copies referred to in paragraph (1)(c) or (4) above pending a decision by the President as to an extension of the time limit pursuant to regulation 42.

Enquiries by Secretary of the Tribunal

18. The Secretary of the Tribunal shall, at any time after he has received the notice of appeal-
    (a) enquire of each party-
        (i) whether or not the party intends to attend the hearing;
        (ii) whether the party wishes to be represented at the hearing in accordance with regulation 11(3) or 16(1) and if so the name of the representative;
        (iii) whether the party wishes the hearing to be in public;
        (iv) whether the party intends to call witnesses and if so the names of the proposed witnesses; and
        (v) whether the party or a witness will require the assistance of an interpreter; and
    (b) enquire of the parent whether he wishes any persons (other than a person who will represent him) to attend the hearing if the hearing is to be in private and if so the names of such persons.

Directions in preparation for a hearing

19.- (1) The President may at any time give such directions (including the issue of a witness summons) as are provided in this Part of these Regulations to enable the parties to prepare for the hearing or to assist the tribunal to determine the issues.

(2) Directions given pursuant to regulations 21 and 22 may be given on the application of a party or of the President's own motion.

(3) A witness summons issued pursuant to regulation 23 may only be issued on the application of a party.

(4) An application by a party for directions (other than during a hearing) shall be made in writing to the Secretary of the Tribunal and, unless it is accompanied by the written consent of the other party, shall be served by the Secretary of the Tribunal on that other party. If the other party objects to the directions sought, the President shall consider the objection and, if he considers it necessary for the determination of the application, shall give the parties an opportunity of appearing before him.

(5) Directions containing a requirement under this Part of these Regulations shall, as appropriate-
    (a) include a statement of the possible consequences for the appeal, as provided by regulation 24, of a party's failure to comply with the requirement within the time allowed by the President; and
    (b) contain a reference to the fact that, under section 180(5) of the 1993 Act, any person who without reasonable excuse fails to comply with requirements regarding discovery or inspection of documents, or regarding attendance to give evidence and produce documents, shall be liable on summary conviction to a fine not exceeding level 3 on the standard scale and shall, unless the person to whom the direction is addressed had an opportunity of objecting to the direction, contain a statement to the effect that that

person may apply to the President under regulation 20 to vary or set aside the direction.

Varying or setting aside of directions

20. Where a person to whom a direction (including any summons) given under this Part of these Regulations is addressed had no opportunity to object to the giving of such direction, he may apply to the President, by notice to the Secretary of the Tribunal, to vary it or set it aside, but the President shall not so do without first notifying the person who applied for the direction and considering any representations made by him.

Particulars and supplementary statements

21. The President may give directions requiring any party to provide such particulars or supplementary statements as may be reasonably required for the determination of the appeal.

Disclosure of documents and other material

22.– (1) The President may give directions requiring a party to deliver to the tribunal any document or other material which the tribunal may require and which it is in the power of that party to deliver. The President shall make such provision as he thinks necessary to supply copies of any document obtained under this paragraph to the other party to the proceedings, and it shall be a condition of such supply that that party shall use such a document only for the purposes of the appeal.

(2) The President may grant to a party such discovery or inspection of documents (including the taking of copies) as might be granted by a county court.

Summoning of witnesses

23. The President may by summons require any person in England and Wales to attend as a witness at a hearing of an appeal at such time and place as may be specified in the summons and at the hearing to answer any questions or produce any documents or other material in his custody or under his control which relate to any matter in question in the appeal:
Provided that–

(a) no person shall be compelled to give any evidence or produce any document or other material that he could not be compelled to give or produce at a trial of an action in a Court of law;

(b) in exercising the powers conferred by this regulation, the President shall take into account the need to protect any matter that relates to intimate personal or financial circumstances or consists of information communicated or obtained in confidence;

(c) no person shall be required to attend in obedience to such a summons unless he has been given at least 5 working days' notice of the hearing or, if less than 5 working days, he has informed the President that he accepts such notice as he has been given; and

(d) no person shall be required in obedience to such a summons to attend and give evidence or to produce any document unless the necessary expenses of his attendance are paid or tendered to him.

Failure to comply with directions

24.– (1) If a party has not complied with a direction to it under this Part of these Regulations within the time specified in the direction the tribunal may–

(a) where the party in default is the parent, dismiss the appeal without a hearing;

(b) where the party in default is the authority, determine the appeal without a hearing; or

(c) hold a hearing (without notifying the party in default) at which the party in default is not represented.

(2) In this regulation "the party in default" means the party which has failed to comply with the direction.

Notice of place and time of hearing and adjournments

25.– (1) Subject to the provisions of regulation 26, the Secretary of the Tribunal shall, with due regard to the convenience of the parties, fix the time and place of the hearing and, not less than 10 working days before the date so fixed (or such shorter time as the parties agree), send to each party a notice that the hearing is to be at such time and place.

(2) The Secretary of the Tribunal shall include in or with the notice of hearing–

    (a) information and guidance, in a form approved by the President, as to attendance at the hearing of the parties and witnesses, the bringing of documents, and the right of representation or assistance as provided by regulation 11(3) or 16(1); and

    (b) a statement explaining the possible consequences of non-attendance and of the right of–

        (i) a parent; and

        (ii) the authority, if it has presented a reply, who does not attend and is not represented, to make representations in writing.

(4) The tribunal may alter the time and place of any hearing and the Secretary of the Tribunal shall give the parties not less than 5 working days (or such shorter time as the parties agree) notice of the altered hearing date:

Provided that any altered hearing date shall not (unless the parties agree) be before the date notified under paragraph (1).

(5) The tribunal may from time to time adjourn the hearing and, if the time and place of the adjourned hearing are announced before the adjournment, no further notice shall be required.

PART 4

DETERMINATION OF APPEALS

Power to determine an appeal without a hearing

26– (1) The tribunal may–

    (a) if the parties so agree in writing; or

    (b) in the circumstances described in regulations 15 and 24, determine an appeal or any particular issue without a hearing.

(2) The provisions of regulation 28(2) shall apply in respect of the determination of an appeal, or any particular issue, under this regulation.

Hearings to be in private: exceptions

27.– (1) A hearing by the tribunal shall be in private unless–

    (a) both the parent and the authority request that the hearing be in public; or

    (b) the tribunal orders that the hearing should be in public.

(2) The following persons (as well as the parties and their representatives) shall be entitled to attend the hearing of an appeal, even though it is in private–

    (a) any person named by the parent in response to the enquiry under regulation 18(b) unless the President has determined that any such person shall not be entitled to attend the hearing and notified the parent accordingly;

    (b) a parent of the child who is not a party to the appeal;

    (c) the clerk to the tribunal and the Secretary of the Tribunal;

    (d) the President and any member of the chairmen's or lay panel (when not sitting as members of the tribunal);

    (e) a member of the Council on Tribunals;

    (f) any person undergoing training as a member of the chairmen's or lay panel or as a clerk to the tribunal;

    (g) any person acting on behalf of the President in the training or supervision of clerks to tribunals;

    (h) an interpreter.

(3) The tribunal, with the consent of the parties or their representatives actually present, may permit any other person to attend the hearing of an appeal which is held in private.

(4) Without prejudice to any other powers it may have, the tribunal may exclude from the hearing, or part of it, any person whose conduct has disrupted or is likely, in the opinion of the tribunal, to disrupt the hearing.

(5) For the purposes of arriving at its decision a tribunal shall, and for the purposes of discussing any question of procedure may, notwithstanding anything contained in these Regulations, order all persons to withdraw from the sitting of the tribunal other than the members of the tribunal or any of the persons mentioned in paragraph (2)(c) to (f) above.

(6) Except as provided in paragraph (7) below none of the persons mentioned in paragraph (2) or (3) above shall, save in the case of the clerk to the tribunal or an interpreter as their respective duties require, take any part in the hearing or (where entitled or permitted to remain) in the deliberations of the tribunal.

(7) The tribunal may permit a parent of the child who is not a party to the appeal to address the tribunal on the subject matter of the appeal.

Failure of parties to attend hearing

28.– (1) If a party fails to attend or be represented at a hearing of which he has been duly notified, the tribunal may–

(a) unless it is satisfied that there is sufficient reason for such absence, hear and determine the appeal in the party's absence; or

(b) adjourn the hearing, and may make such order as to costs and expenses as it thinks fit.

(2) Before disposing of an appeal in the absence of a party, the tribunal shall consider any representations in writing submitted by that party in response to the notice of hearing and, for the purpose of this regulation the notice of appeal, any reply by the authority under regulations 12 or 13 and any response by the parent under regulation 8 shall be treated as representations in writing.

Procedure at hearing

29.– (1) At the beginning of the hearing the chairman shall explain the order of proceeding which the tribunal proposes to adopt.

(2) The tribunal shall conduct the hearing in such manner as it considers most suitable to the clarification of the issues and generally to the just handling of the proceedings; it shall, so far as appears to it appropriate, seek to avoid formality in its proceedings.

(3) The tribunal shall determine the order in which the parties are heard and the issues determined.

(4) The tribunal may, if it is satisfied that it is just and reasonable to do so, permit a party to rely on grounds not stated in his notice of appeal or, as the case may be, his reply or response and to adduce any evidence not presented to the authority before or at the time it took the disputed decision.

(5) If after the commencement of any hearing a member of the tribunal other than the chairman is absent, the hearing may, with the consent of the parties, be conducted by the other two members and in that event the tribunal shall be deemed to be properly constituted and the decision of the tribunal shall be taken by those two members.

Evidence at hearing

30.– (1) In the course of the hearing the parties shall be entitled to give evidence, to call witnesses, to question any witnesses and to address the tribunal both on the evidence and generally on the subject matter of the appeal:

Provided that neither party shall be entitled to call more than two witnesses to give evidence orally (in addition to any witnesses whose attendance is required pursuant to paragraph (2) below) unless the President has given permission before the hearing or the tribunal gives permission at the hearing.

(2) Evidence before the tribunal may be given orally or by written statement, but the tribunal may at any stage of the proceedings require the personal attendance of any maker of any written statement.

(3) The tribunal may receive evidence of any fact which appears to the tribunal to be relevant.

(4) The tribunal may require any witness to give evidence on oath or affirmation, and for that purpose there may be administered an oath or affirmation in due form, or may require any evidence given by written statement to be given by affidavit.

Decision of the tribunal

31. (1) A decision of the tribunal may be taken by a majority and where the tribunal is constituted by two members only under regulation 29(5) the chairman shall have a second or casting vote.

(2) The decision of the tribunal may be given orally at the end of the hearing or reserved and, in any event, whether there has been a hearing or not, shall be recorded forthwith in a document which, save in the case of a decision by consent, shall also contain, or have annexed to it, a statement of the reasons (in summary form) for the tribunal's decision, and each such document shall be signed and dated by the chairman.

(3) Neither a decision given orally nor the document referred to in paragraph (2) above shall contain any reference to the decision being by majority (if that be the case) or to any opinion of a minority.

(4) Every decision of the tribunal shall be entered in the records.

(5) As soon as may be the Secretary of the Tribunal shall send a copy of the document referred to in paragraph (2) above to each party, accompanied by guidance, in a form approved by the President, about the circumstances in which there is a right to appeal against a tribunal decision and the procedure to be followed.

(6) Every decision shall be treated as having been made on the date on which a copy of the document recording it is sent to the parent (whether or not the decision has been previously announced at the end of the hearing).

Review of the tribunal's decision

32. (1) If, on the application of a party to the Secretary of the Tribunal or of its own motion, the tribunal is satisfied that—

(a) its decision was wrongly made as a result of an error on the part of the tribunal staff;

(b) a party, who was entitled to be heard at a hearing but failed to appear or be represented, had good and sufficient reason for failing to appear; or

(c) the interests of justice require, the tribunal may review and, by certificate under the chairman's hand set aside or vary the relevant decision.

(2) An application for the purposes of paragraph (1) above may be made immediately following the decision at the hearing. If an application is not made at the hearing, it shall be made not later than 10 working days after the date on which the decision was sent to the parties, and shall be in writing stating the grounds in full. When the tribunal proposes to review its decision of its own motion, it shall serve notice of that proposal on the parties within the same period.

(3) An application for the purposes of paragraph (1) above may be refused by the President, or by the chairman of the tribunal which decided the case, if in his opinion it has no reasonable prospect of success.

(4) If the application is not refused under paragraph (3) above, the parties shall have an opportunity to be heard on any application or proposal for review under this regulation and the review shall be determined by the tribunal which decided the case or, where it is not practicable for it to be heard by that tribunal, by a tribunal appointed by the President; and if, having reviewed the decision, the decision is set aside, the tribunal shall substitute such decision as it thinks fit or order a rehearing before either the same or a differently constituted tribunal.

(5) If any decision is set aside or varied under this regulation or altered in any way by order of a superior court, the Secretary of the Tribunal shall alter the entry in the records to conform with the chairman's certificate or order of a superior court and shall notify the parties accordingly.

Review of the President's decision

33.– (1) If, on the application of a party to the Secretary of the Tribunal or of his own motion the President is satisfied that–

    (a) a decision by him was wrongly made as a result of an error on the part of the tribunal staff; or

    (b) the interests of justice require, the President may review and set aside the relevant decision of his.

(2) An application for the purposes of paragraph (1) shall be made not later than 10 working days after the date on which the party making the application was notified of the decision and shall be in writing stating the grounds in full. Where the President proposes to review his decision of his own motion he shall serve notice of that proposal on the parties within the same period.

(3) The parties shall have an opportunity to be heard on any application or proposal for review under this regulation and the review shall be determined by the President.

(4) If any decision is set aside or varied under this regulation the Secretary of the Tribunal shall alter the entry in the records and shall notify the parties accordingly.

Orders for costs and expenses

34.– (1) The tribunal shall not normally make an order in respect of costs and expenses, but may, subject to paragraph (2) below, make such an order–

    (a) against a party (including any party who has withdrawn his appeal or reply) if it is of the opinion that that party has acted frivolously or vexatiously or that his conduct in making, pursuing or resisting an appeal was wholly unreasonable;

    (b) against an authority which has not delivered a written reply under regulation 12; or

    (c) against the authority, where it considers that the disputed decision was wholly unreasonable.

(2) Any order in respect of costs and expenses may be made–

    (a) as respects any costs or expenses incurred, or any allowances paid; or

    (b) as respects the whole, or any part, of any allowance (other than allowances paid to members of tribunals) paid by the Secretary of State under section 180(3) of the 1993 Act to any person for the purposes of, or in connection with, his attendance at the tribunal.

(3) No order shall be made under paragraph (1) above against a party without first giving that party an opportunity of making representations against the making of the order.

(4) An order under paragraph (1) above may require the party against whom it is made to pay the other party either a specified sum in respect of the costs and expenses incurred by that other party in connection with the proceedings or the whole or part of such costs as taxed (if not otherwise agreed).

(5) Any costs required by an order under this regulation to be taxed may be taxed in the county court according to such of the scales prescribed by the county court rules for proceedings in the county court as shall be directed in the order.

PART 5

ADDITIONAL POWERS OF AND PROVISIONS RELATING TO THE TRIBUNAL

Transfer of proceedings

35. Where it appears to the President that an appeal pending before a tribunal could be determined more conveniently in another tribunal he may at any time, upon the application of a party or

of his own motion, direct that the said proceedings be transferred so as to be determined in that other tribunal:

Provided that no such direction shall be given unless notice has been sent to all parties concerned giving them an opportunity to show cause why such a direction should not be given.

Miscellaneous powers of the tribunal

36.– (1) Subject to the provisions of the 1993 Act and these Regulations, a tribunal may regulate its own procedure.

(2) A tribunal may, if it thinks fit, if both parties agree in writing upon the terms of a decision to be made by the tribunal, decide accordingly.

Power to strike out

37.– (1) The tribunal may, on the application of the President or the authority, at any stage of the proceedings order that an appeal should be struck out–

(a) on the grounds that it is not within the jurisdiction of the Special Educational Needs Tribunal;

(b) on the grounds that the appeal or the notice of appeal is scandalous, frivolous or vexatious; or

(c) for want of prosecution.

(2) Before the tribunal makes an order under paragraph (1) above, the Secretary of the Tribunal shall give to the parent a notice inviting representations and the tribunal shall consider any representations duly made. If the parent does not request an opportunity to make oral representations, the Tribunal need not hold a hearing.

(3) The President may, if he thinks fit, at any stage of the proceedings order that a reply, response or statement should be struck out or amended on the grounds that it is scandalous, frivolous or vexatious.

(4) Before making an order under paragraph (3) above, the President shall give to the party against whom he proposes to make the order a notice inviting representations and shall consider any representations duly made.

(5) For the purposes of paragraphs (2) and (4) above–

(a) a notice inviting representations must inform the recipient that he may, within a period (not being less than 5 working days) specified in the notice, either make written representations or request an opportunity to make oral representations;

(b) representations are duly made if–

(i) in the case of written representations, they are made within the period so specified; and

(ii) in the case of oral representations, the party proposing to make them has requested an opportunity to do so within the period so specified.

Power to exercise powers of the President and Chairman

38.– (1) An act required or authorised by these Regulations to be done by the President may be done by a member of the chairman's panel authorised by the President.

(2) Where, pursuant to paragraph (1) above, a member of the chairman's panel carries out the function under regulation 5(2) of selecting the chairman of a tribunal, he may select himself.

(3) Where, pursuant to paragraph (1) above a member of the chairman's panel makes a decision, regulation 33 shall apply in relation to that decision taking the reference in that regulation to the President as a reference to the member of the chairman's panel by whom the decision was taken.

(4) Subject to regulation 40(5) in the event of the death or incapacity of the chairman following the decision of the tribunal in any matter, the functions of the chairman for the completion of the proceedings, including any review of the decision, may be exercised by the President or any member of the chairman's panel.

The Secretary of the Tribunal

39. A function of the Secretary of the Tribunal may be performed by another member of the staff of the tribunal authorised for the purpose of carrying out that function by the President.

Irregularities

40.– (1) An irregularity resulting from failure to comply with any provisions of these Regulations or of any direction of the tribunal before the tribunal has reached its decision shall not of itself render the proceedings void.

(2) Where any such irregularity comes to the attention of the tribunal, the tribunal may, and shall, if it considers that any person may have been prejudiced by the irregularity, give such directions as it thinks just before reaching its decision to cure or waive the irregularity.

(3) Clerical mistakes in any document recording a decision of the tribunal or a direction or decision of the President produced by or on behalf of the tribunal or errors arising in such documents from accidental slips or omissions may at any time be corrected by the chairman or the President (as the case may be) by certificate under his hand.

(4) The Secretary of the Tribunal shall as soon as may be send a copy of any corrected document containing reasons for the tribunal's decision, to each party.

(5) Where by these Regulations a document is required to be signed by the chairman but by reason of death or incapacity the chairman is unable to sign such a document it shall be signed by the other members of the tribunal, who shall certify that the chairman is unable to sign.

Method of sending, delivering or serving notices and documents

41.– (1) A notice given under these Regulations shall be in writing and where under these Regulations provision is made for a party to notify the Secretary of the Tribunal of any matter he shall do so in writing.

(2) All notices and documents required by these Regulations to be sent or delivered to the Secretary of the Tribunal or the tribunal may be sent by post or by facsimile or delivered to or at the office of the Special Educational Needs Tribunal or such other office as may be notified by the Secretary of the Tribunal to the parties.

(3) All notices and documents required or authorised by these Regulations to be sent or given to any person mentioned in sub-paragraph (a) or (b) below may (subject to paragraph (5) below) either be sent by first class post or by facsimile or delivered to or at–

(a) in the case of a notice or document directed to a party–

    (i) his address for service specified in the notice of appeal or in a written reply or in a notice under paragraph (4) below, or

    (ii) if no address for service has been so specified, his last known address; and

(b) in the case of a notice or document directed to any person other than a party, his address or place of business or if such a person is a corporation, the corporation's registered or principal office and if sent or given to the authorised representative of a party shall be deemed to have been sent or given to that party.

(4) A party may at any time by notice to the Secretary of the Tribunal change his address for service under these Regulations.

(5) The recorded delivery service shall be used instead of the first class post for service of a summons issued under regulation 23 requiring the attendance of a witness.

(6) A notice or document sent by the Secretary of the Tribunal by post in accordance with these Regulations, and not returned, shall be taken to have been delivered to the addressee on the second working day after it was posted.

(7) A notice or document sent by facsimile shall be taken to have been delivered when it is received in legible form.

(8) Where for any sufficient reason service of any document or notice cannot be effected in the manner prescribed under this regulation, the President may dispense with service or make an order for substituted service in such manner as he may deem fit and such service shall have the same effect as service in the manner prescribed under this regulation.

Extension of time

42.– (1) Where, pursuant to any provision of these Regulations anything is required to be done by a party within a period of time the President may, on the application of the party in question, in exceptional circumstances extend any period of time.

(2) Where a period of time has been extended pursuant to paragraph (1) above any reference in these Regulations to that period of time shall be construed as a reference to the period of time as so extended.

Parent's representative

43. Where, pursuant to regulation 7(1)(c) or 11(1) or (2)(a) a parent has stated the name of a representative and has not subsequently notified the Secretary of the Tribunal pursuant to regulation 11(2)(b) that no person is acting as a representative, any reference in Part 3, 4 or 5 of these Regulations (however expressed) to sending documents to, or giving notice to, the parent shall be construed as a reference to sending documents to or giving notice to the representative and any such reference to sending documents to or giving notice to a party or the parties shall in the context of the parent be likewise construed as a reference to sending documents to, or giving notice to the representative.

John Patten
12th July 1994   Secretary of State for Education

John Redwood
14th July 1994   Secretary of State for Wales

Note on Law and Case Citation

In the UK, Parliament makes legislation in the form of Acts of Parliament. These must be passed by both Houses of Parliament and receive royal assent. Acts of Parliament are known as primary or statutory legislation and, with the possible exception of an unintentional contravention of European Law, they cannot be challenged in the courts. The role of the courts is to declare the meaning of legislation. In that role courts are the final arbiter. The consequence is that to be sure of the meaning of the law it may be necessary to refer to both the words of the Statute and the previous decisions of the court.

In this book there are a number of references to decisions of the court. These are cited in the standard form which is explained with reference to the following example of case citation:

R v Essex County Council and the Secretary of State for Education, ex parte Z HC [1994] 1 WLR 301.

A court case is a dispute between two sides. The two sides are separated by *v*. In spoken language the *v* is 'and'. The side whose name is given before the *v* is the side initiating the particular stage in the court procedure. There may be more than one party on each side. In this case one side is R and the other is Essex County Council and the Secretary of State for Education. R is short for Regina or the Crown. In a republic R would be replaced by The People. The court procedure most usually appropriate for SEN cases is judicial review. The citation of the parties in judicial review is exceptional because the Crown is given as the first party but the Crown plays no active part; in practice the party bringing the action is the name following *ex parte*; in this case Z. Because Z is a child, the name is abbreviated to an initial in order to maintain privacy for the child. The case would actually be brought by Z's parents or someone else acting on behalf of Z.

After the names of the parties is an abbreviation of the court where the action was heard, in this case HC, which is the abbreviation for High Court. Other abbreviations used may be found in the list of abbreviations. The date 1994 in [ ] is the year in which the case was reported in one of the law reports and not necessarily the year in which the case was heard. Following the date is the law report reference. The first number is the volume number in which the case is to be found. This is followed by an abbreviation of the relevant series of law reports. In this case WLR which is the abbreviation for Weekly Law Reports. The final number is the page number.

Abbreviations and Acronyms

AEN	Additional Educational Needs
All ER	All England law Reports
ASB	Aggregated Schools' Budget
AWPU	Age weighted pupil unit
BAS	British Ability Scales
CA	Court of Appeal
CFF	Common Funding Formula
DfE	Department for Education. The abbreviation has been used for the Department of State dealing with education even though the name changed from Department of Education and Science (DES) and recently to Department for Education and Employment (DfEE)
EAT	Employment Appeal Tribunal
ELR	Education Law Reports
EP	Educational Psychologist
EPS	Educational Psychology Services
ESN(M)	Educationally Subnormal: Medium or Moderate
ESN(S)	Educationally Subnormal: Severe
FAS	Funding Agency for Schools
FLR	Family Law Reports
FSM	Free School Meals
GCSE	General Certificate of Secondary Education
GM	grant-maintained
GSB	General Schools' Budget
HC	High Court
HL	House of Lords
HMI	Her Majesty's Inspectorate of Schools
IEP	Individual Education Plan
IPSEA	Independent Panel for Special Education Advice
IQ	Intelligence Quotient
J	Judge
KB	King's Bench (Law Reports)
LEA	Local Education Authority
LGR	Local Government Law Reports
LJ	Lord Justice (designation of judges in the Court of Appeal)
LMS	Local Management of Schools
NLJ	New Law Journal

QB	Queen's Bench (Law Reports)
QBD	Queen's Bench Division of the High Court
r	Product moment correlation coefficient
RSG	Revenue Support Grant
SAT	Standard Assessment Tasks or Tests
SEN	Special Educational Needs
SENCO	Special Educational Needs Coordinator
SSA	Standard Spending Assessment
WISC	Wechsler Intelligence Scales
WLR	Weekly Law Reports
WORD	Wechsler Objective Reading Dimensions

References

Ainscow, M. and Florek, A. (1989) *Special Educational Needs: Towards a Whole School Approach,* London: David Fulton.

Ainscow, M. and Muncey (1989) *Meeting Individual Needs in the Primary School,* London: David Fulton.

Audit Commission/HMI (1992) *Getting in on the Act. Provision for Pupils with Special Educational Needs: The National Picture,* London: HMSO.

Audit Commission (1994) *The Act Moves On: Progress in Special Educational Needs,* London: HMSO.

Bibby, P. (1995). *Effective Use of Judicial Review,* London: Tolley.

Bibby, P. and Lunt, I. (1994) 'Special Costs', *Managing Schools Today,* 4, 1, September, p. 7.

Clark, C., Dyson, A., Millward, A. and Skidmore, D. (1995) *Innovatory Practice in Mainstream Schools for Special Educational Needs,* London: HMSO.

Department of Education and Science (1978) *Special Educational Needs: The Warnock Report,* London: HMSO.

Department for Education (1994a) *Code of Practice on the Identification and Assessment of Special Educational Needs,* London: HMSO.

Department for Education (1994b) *Circular 6/94, the Organisation of Special Educational Provision,* London: Department for Education.

Dessent, T. (1987) *Making the Ordinary School Special,* London: Falmer Press.

Frederickson, N. and Reason, R. (1995) 'Discrepancy definitions of specific learning difficulties', *Educational Psychology in Practice,* 10, 4, 195–205.

Goacher, B., Evans, J., Welton, J. and Wedell, K. (1988) *Policy and Provision for Special Educational Needs,* London: Castile.

Lunt, I., Evans, J., Norwich, B. and Wedell, K. (1994) *Working Together, Inter-School Collaboration for Special Needs,* London: David Fulton.

Pumfrey, P. (1995) 'The management of specific learning difficulties (dyslexia): challenges and responses', in Lunt, I., Norwich, B. and Varma, V., *Psychology and Education for Special Needs,* Aldershot: Avebury Press.

Sammons, P., Hallman, J. and Mortimore, P. (1995) *Key Characteristics of Effective Schools: A Review of School Effectiveness Research,* London: OFSTED and University of London Institute of Education.

Stobbs, P., Mackey, T., Norwich, B., Peacey, N. and Stephenson, P. (1995) *Schools' SEN policies pack,* London: National Children's Bureau.

Vevers, P. (1992) 'Getting in on the Act', *British Journal of Special Education,* 19, 3, 88–91.

Wedell, K. (1990) 'Children with special educational needs: past, present and future', in Evans, P. and Varma, V., *Special Education: Past, Present and Future*, London: Falmer Press.

Wedell, K. (1995) *Putting the Code of Practice into Practice: Meeting Special Educational Needs in the School and Classroom*, London: Institute of Education monograph.

Index

www.ingramcontent.com/pod-product-compliance
Ingram Content Group UK Ltd.
Pitfield, Milton Keynes, MK11 3LW, UK
UKHW041840280225
455677UK00010B/267